Fundraising

for the GENIUS™

The only book you'll ever need
to raise more money and support for your
nonprofit organization.

FOR THE GENIUS IN ALL OF US™

Li ‖‖‖‖‖ D1219493 .CFRE

Fundraising for the GENIUS™
One of the For the GENIUS™ books
Published by
For the GENIUS Press, an imprint of CharityChannel LLC
30021 Tomas, Suite 300
Rancho Santa Margarita, CA 92688-2128 USA
www.forthegenius.com

First Edition
Library of Congress Control Number: 2012940491
ISBN: 978-0-9841580-1-0

Printed in the United States of America
10 9 8 7 6 5 4 3 2

This and most For the GENIUS Press books are available at special quantity discounts for bulk purchases for sales promotions, premiums, fundraising, or educational use. For information, contact CharityChannel, 30021 Tomas, Suite 300, Rancho Santa Margarita, CA 92688-2128 USA. +1 949-589-5938

About the Author

Linda Lysakowski is one of fewer than one hundred professionals worldwide to hold the Advanced Certified Fund Raising Executive designation. She has managed capital campaigns, helped dozens of nonprofit organizations achieve their development goals, and trained more than 22,000 professionals in all aspects of development throughout most of the United States, Mexico, Canada, and Egypt.

Linda is a prolific writer. Her books include: *Recruiting and Training Fundraising Volunteers; The Development Plan; Fundraising as a Career: What, Are You Crazy?; Capital Campaigns: Everything You NEED to Know;* and *Raise More Money from Your Business Community: A Practical Guide to Tapping into Corporate Charitable Giving.* Linda is also co-editor of *You and Your Nonprofit: Practical Advice and Tips from the CharityChannel Professional Community;* co-author *of The Essential Nonprofit Fundraising Handbook;* and contributing author to *The Fundraising Feasibility Study— It's Not About the Money.* She also published her first novel, *The Matriarch,* in 2011.

As a graduate of the Association of Fundraising Professionals (AFP) Faculty Training Academy, Linda is a Master Teacher and is a member of AFP's Professional Advancement Division. She serves on the board of the AFP Foundation for Philanthropy. She has received two AFP research grants.

Linda has been a frequent speaker at the international AFP conference, the CharityChannel Summit (which she has chaired), and the CharityChannel Press Authors Symposium which she co-chairs. In addition, she has spoken at numerous international, national and regional conferences.

Author's Acknowledgments

I would like to acknowledge the many authors who came before me, too many to mention by name, writing about the field of philanthropy, development and fundraising. In the early years, fundraising was seen as a volunteer activity or a job, rather than a career or a profession. Without the body of knowledge to which so many talented and wise people have contributed, it would still be viewed that way. I am grateful to all those who provided such a solid foundation from which I could write this book.

I also want to acknowledge my editor, Stephen Nill, for the many hours we spent developing this, the first book of the **For the GENIUS**™ series.

I would also like to thank my husband, Marty, for his patience during the writing, editing, and publishing process that was necessary to get this book into your hands. I hope you will find the book helpful to you as you advance in this profession and that you might be inspired to not only find the genius in yourself, but to share that genius with others. Perhaps this book will even inspire some of you to write a book yourself!

Linda Lysakowski, ACFRE

Contents

Summary of Chapters

PART 1—What is Fundraising and Why is it Important to Nonprofits?

Chapter 1

There are many titles for the activity of raising funds for nonprofits, and for the people involved in the activity of raising these funds. This chapter defines the terminology and explains the difference between fundraising, development and philanthropy.

Chapter 2

Fundraising/development is usually the least understood function in a nonprofit organization. This chapter will explain its role in the nonprofit and why it is important in fulfilling the mission and vision of your organization.

Chapter 3

Fundraising is a team effort that requires participation by your organization's leaders, both staff and board, as well as development staff, volunteers, and consultants. This chapter will lay the groundwork for the in-depth discussion of each of these roles in later chapters.

Chapter 4

There are more than a million nonprofit organizations in the United States, most of which are raising money for a variety of causes. This chapter will discuss the depth of the sector and its impact on our economy.

Chapter 5

In an era where transparency and accountability are becoming more than just buzzwords of the trade, ethical fundraising is of primary importance. This chapter will discuss the various ethical issues that face fundraisers and explain how to address ethical dilemmas.

PART 2—Whose Responsibility is Fundraising?

Chapter 6

The board of directors of your nonprofit has a fiduciary responsibility to assure that your organization is on sound financial footing. Part of this role includes both giving to, and getting money for, your organization. This chapter will discuss the role of the board in fundraising and how to assure that prospective board members understand this role before being recruited to serve on your board.

Chapter 7

Volunteers from your community can serve, and should serve, a key role in raising funds for your nonprofit. This chapter will explain the various roles volunteers can play in fundraising, how to identify and recruit volunteers and how to keep them actively involved in fundraising activities.

Chapter 8

Fundraising is becoming one of the nation's hottest careers. This chapter will talk about the various roles staff members of your organization play in planning and implementing your fundraising efforts.

PART 3—Where Do We Find the Money?

Chapter 9

By far, the largest source of charitable dollars in the United States is individual donors. In this chapter, we will talk about the reasons individuals support charitable organizations and learn how to approach these donors through the various methods that will be explored in detail in **Part 5.**

Chapter 10

Private and corporate foundations typically provide 12 to 14 percent of all charitable donations in the United States. This chapter will talk about how to identify potential foundation funders, and explains the difference between private, family, corporate and community foundations.

Chapter 11

Although businesses and corporations generally account for only from 4 to 6 percent of total philanthropic giving in the United States, there are many opportunities for you to raise money from the corporate sector. This chapter will discuss how to involve corporate leaders in your organization as well as how to raise money from businesses.

Chapter 12

There are numerous professional and service clubs which can be potential donors and a source of volunteers for your nonprofit. This chapter will talk about the ways to approach these organizations for funding and volunteers.

PART 4—What Do We Need in Place Before We Can Effectively Raise Funds?

Chapter 13

Before you can successfully attempt fundraising, your organization must provide programs needed by your community and have a clear vision for your future. In this chapter we will examine the importance of strategic planning for your nonprofit.

Chapter 14

In addition to strategic planning for your organization, it will be critical that you have a well-thought-out development plan that includes strategies and action steps for implementing each objective of your plan.

Chapter 15

Understanding the psychology of philanthropy as well as the importance of a diversity of funding streams is critical. In this chapter we will talk about the importance of an integrated development plan and how to assure that the plan includes strategic goals for moving your donors up the donor pyramid.

Chapter 16

You need to build a strong infrastructure in your development office. Donor software and other essential infrastructure items, such as policies and procedures, will be explained in this chapter.

Chapter 17

Another component of successful fundraising is having a strong community image. It will be difficult for your organization to raise money if no one in the community is aware of your organization and its services. In this chapter I'll discuss the importance of marketing and public relations.

Chapter 18

Building community awareness and credibility for your organization starts with having a compelling case for support. This chapter will explain the difference between the case for support, case statements, and campaign or marketing materials. We will talk about the various ways your case is used and the materials you should develop from the case.

Part 5—What Methods Are Used in Fundraising?

Chapter 19

Direct Mail 189

Direct mail is one method of fundraising that your nonprofit can use as a beginning step. This chapter will explain the difference between acquisition mailing and renewal mailings and talk about the various components of a direct-mail package.

Chapter 20

Telephone Fundraising 201

Many organizations dread the thought of telephone fundraising and stay away from it because they do not understand its benefits and advantages over other fundraising methods. This chapter will talk about effective ways you can use the telephone to build strong donor relationships.

Chapter 21

Internet/Social Media 211

One of the fastest growing forms of fundraising is raising money through social media. We'll talk about the Internet, web-based fundraising and social media fundraising methods, and help you incorporate these methods into your development plan.

Chapter 22

Special events are generally over-used by many nonprofits. It is critical that you understand that events are just one of the many ways to raise funds. This chapter will explain the differences between fundraising events and "friend raising" events and provide tips to help you avoid "special event fever."

Chapter 23

Writing a grant proposal, getting it funded, and managing the grant once you are successful is often a full-time job for development staff. This chapter will talk about the key components of a successful grant and how to assure that you are spending a reasonable amount of time to gain maximum support from foundations and government sources.

Chapter 24

One-on-one personal solicitation is always the most effective way you can raise money. This chapter will talk about working with your staff, board and volunteers to develop an effective annual appeal to approach individual major donors and businesses.

Chapter 25

A capital campaign is a special fundraising effort that you will use when your organization needs to purchase or build a new building, renovate an existing building or fund some other major capital expenditure. There are several key components of a successful capital campaign that will be outlined in this chapter.

Chapter 26

You should develop ways to approach individual donors to make a planned gift. These gifts are often made through bequests. This chapter will outline different planned giving mechanisms and show you how even a small organization can start a planned giving program.

Part 6—Taking it to the Next Level

Chapter 27

The basis for continued growth is being able to realistically evaluate success. This chapter will provide some key assessment tools to help you assure that your fundraising efforts meet acceptable standards and help you plan for improved results. We'll discuss the development audit, and help you determine whether or not your organization would benefit from this kind of internal assessment of your fundraising program, and even to determine if you're organization is ready to embark on new development ventures.

Chapter 28

As in any field, the fundraising arena should always be striving for continuous improvement. As your development department matures, you should be seeing better results each year. In this chapter we will talk about moves management and some other fundraising initiatives you might use to improve results. We will also discuss some of the ways you can provide training and education for board, staff and volunteers to help grow your development program.

Chapter 29

Setting goals for future growth is important. This chapter will help you set goals that are achievable and yet visionary. This chapter will discuss the importance of providing good stewardship of donors' funds and how to make sure your organization is putting the donors' interests above its own.

Appendixes

Appendix A

Appendix B

Appendix C

Appendix D

If you're looking at this book for the first time, by now you've probably realized that it is special. Chances are, you've never seen a **For the GENIUS**™ book. If so, there's a good reason! It is the first book of the **For the GENIUS** line of books!

As with all books envisioned of the **For the GENIUS** line, it is written in a fun, upbeat, easy-to-follow style, but doesn't insult your intelligence. In fact, it assumes you are a genius! By "genius" I don't mean that you're an Einstein (though you might well be, for all I know). Rather, it assumes that you're willing to back up your 1 percent inspiration with 99 percent perspiration (to borrow from the famous definition of "genius" by Thomas Edison). Fundraising, done properly, will make you perspire!

Believe me, I know about perspiration when it comes to fundraising. As someone in his fourth decade as a nonprofit practitioner, I was excited to work with the author, Linda Lysakowski, ACFRE, as her editor to create the first of the **For the GENIUS** books. Linda is widely esteemed to have a near-encyclopedic knowledge of the art and science of fundraising, as well as a knack for lifting the veil on the topic by explaining the "why" of things, often using real-world experiences drawn from her decades of experience. When you've trained more than 22,000 of your peers, as has Linda, you get to be *really* good at explaining things. As you read this book, you'll see what I mean.

If you haven't yet done so, be sure to peruse the Summary of Chapters. There are many good books on fundraising on the market (and plenty of marginal ones, unfortunately). What make this one different is its breadth of coverage—it starts with the basics in **Part 1**, "What is Fundraising and Why is it Important to Nonprofits," and builds from there, step-by-step.

If you are new to the field of fund development, this is the one book you must read to have the proper grounding to become successful. Or, if you are an experienced fund development practitioner, chances are you have experience and expertise in a particular niche of fundraising, but would like to expand your horizons in the fund development arena. If that is the case, you might want to focus on those chapters covering areas in which you haven't spent much (or any) time. It's up to you how you read this book. Most will probably pick and choose what to read, and that's fine. It's written to be able to do that. In case you're skipping around, Linda helpfully reminds you of other chapters where a concept is covered.

If you're like me, you'll especially like the real-world examples Linda sprinkles throughout the book. She makes ample use of sidebars to provide practical tips, define terms, point out important concepts, provide action steps ("Perspiration!" sidebars), point out the best way to do things ("Inspiration!" sidebars), show how NOT to do something ("Uninspired" sidebars), and, my favorite, show how to do something exactly right, usually by showing how an organization did it perfectly ("Pure Genius!" sidebars).

Stephen C. Nill, J.D, GPC
Founder, CharityChannel

Fundraising for the GENIUS! When I was approached to write this book, I wondered what I could possibly say that would be of genius proportions to my colleagues in the field of fundraising. But then I was reminded of Thomas Edison's description of genius—1 percent inspiration and 99 percent perspiration. Well, I've sure had my inspirational insights at moments, but the majority of my career has been spent balancing those moments of pure inspiration with a lot of hard work—the 99 percent perspiration part.

So I approached this book from the standpoint of sharing those moments of inspiration with you, while at the same time recognizing that most of your days are spent on the perspiration part—trying to run a successful development program despite all the obstacles that are put in your way each day. Most people who have spent any time in the profession of fundraising can easily identify some of those obstacles—a board that does not recognize or accept, let alone embrace, its role in fundraising; an executive director who insists on seeing incredible results without making an adequate investment in the development office; a community facing economic crisis; and lack of support from the rest of your organization, most of whom don't understand what purpose the development office serves. The list goes on and, as with me, you've probably faced many of these obstacles. But I hope, as with me, you've also come to know the moments at the top of the mountain when you've landed that major gift, a large grant has come through, the local media has given your organization prime-time exposure, or you've just completed a successful fundraising event.

If you are new to fundraising, it is my hope that this book will help you avoid some of those obstacles and learn how to savor those moments of inspiration, turning them into practical ways to improve your results. If you've been in the field a few years and are trying to hone your skills, I hope you will find both "inspirational" and "perspirational" hints to help you in the day-to-day work of development. If you have been around long enough to be considered one of the true "geniuses" in our field, I hope you will be inspired to take your development program to the next level, and that you will want to share your inspirational moments with others in our field.

You will find numerous sidebars throughout this book with both "inspiration" (ideas that might or might not be new to you, but that provide food for thought) and "perspiration" (the practical tips on how to implement a successful program). Because I know that some of our readers will be new to the profession, you will also find some basic definitions of fundraising terminology. And because often we can learn from mistakes others have made, or by successes they have achieved, I've also included a generous portion of my own and others' "war stories"—things that either worked well, or things that can result in disaster. You will find these in sidebars called, "Pure Genius!" and "Uninspired."

To provide you with some practical tools you can use, and that might save you some "perspiration," I've included a lot of sample forms and tools in the Appendixes. I hope these will make your jobs easier, so perhaps you will have more time for those moments of inspiration.

How you read this book is up to you. If you are new to fundraising, I suggest reading this book from cover to cover. If you do skip around, at least start with **Part 1,** to give you the proper grounding, before jumping to other sections. If you've been in this field for any length of time you might just want to focus on the chapters that offer insights into an area that you find particularly challenging or about which you might be looking for some instant "inspiration."

I encourage you to share the ideas and tools you find here with your board, staff and colleagues. They just might think you are a "genius."

What is Fundraising and Why is it Important to Nonprofits?

There are many words used to describe the process of obtaining charitable contributions—philanthropy, development, advancement, fundraising, fund development, and more. In this section we will look at the whole concept and the process of fundraising and why it is important to nonprofit organizations, most of which could not survive without fundraising! We will talk about the diversity of the nonprofit sector and who is involved in the process of fundraising, and why.

Chapter 1

Fundraising, Development, Philanthropy—What's in a Name?

In This Chapter...

✎ What is the difference between fundraising, development and philanthropy?

✎ Who are the people who do fundraising?

✎ How is the face of fundraising changing?

Before we delve into how to do fundraising or even why nonprofits do fundraising, I thought it would be good to start by defining a few basic terms you will hear bandied about in the nonprofit world and some of the titles given to the staff and volunteers who do fundraising. Let's talk about each of these terms.

Philanthropy has been around since the beginning of recorded history and is mentioned in early Greek and Roman cultures as well as the Egyptian *Book of the Dead*. Every major religion provides a mandate to its followers for taking care of the poor and being generous with one's possessions.

Philanthropy is defined as "the love of humankind." One popular definition of philanthropy is "voluntary action for the good of society."

Development is defined in the Association of Fundraising Professionals (AFP) Fundraising Dictionary as "the total process by which an organization increases public understanding of its mission and acquires financial support for its programs."

Fundraising, on the other hand, is defined by AFP as "the raising of assets and resources from various sources for the support of an organization or a specific project."

important

We most often associate the word "philanthropy" with major donors—those who have impacted society with substantial gifts to endow universities and libraries, and who often have buildings named after them. Some of those that come to mind as philanthropists include Andrew Carnegie, the Rockefellers, Leland Stamford, and more recently people such as Bill Gates and Warren Buffet.

However, most of us at some point in our lives have engaged in philanthropy and many of us are involved in the philanthropic world on a daily basis. Most of us support our churches, synagogues, temples, mosques and other religious institutions. Millions of people respond to massive relief efforts such as Katrina and earthquakes in Haiti and Chile with gifts of goods and services, money or volunteer service. Most of us have bought Girl Scout cookies, responded to a phone call from our college or university, dropped money in a Salvation Army kettle during the holidays, or given blood to the Red Cross. So, in a way, all of us could be thought of as philanthropists. And many of us have been involved in the actual philanthropic process outside of just giving. Perhaps you have stood outside your local K Mart selling Tootsie Rolls for the Knights of Columbus charities for people with disabilities, have served on a stewardship committee for your church, or have been a loaned executive for United Way before becoming involved as a professional fundraiser. My main objection with the accepted definition of philanthropy as "voluntary action" is that it leaves out the thousands upon thousands of us who are engaged in philanthropy as a profession.

Which brings us to the term "development." This term is the best one I've found to explain the process of fundraising, since it is the process of developing relationships with constituents that will enable you to use fundraising methods and techniques to advance the process of philanthropy. Fundraising is used most accurately to describe these methods and techniques used to raise money. It is often said that fundraising is an art and a science. Fundraising, in reality, more correctly applies to the science—the specific techniques that will be discussed in this book. However, the underlying principle of this book is that fundraising is also an art, a process of building long-term relationships (development) with donors that lead to an increase in the spirit of philanthropy. You might think of fundraising as the perspiration, philanthropy as the inspiration behind our work, and development as the process of using that perspiration to cultivate the inspiration.

In most organizations, the term *development* is used most to refer to the department and the people who raise money. We most often speak about the development plan, the chief development officer, the development committee, and the development department. Some organizations might use the terms *fundraising* in a similar way to describe their staff and the process, so they might refer to a fundraising plan or a fundraising committee. Although this book is called *Fundraising for the GENIUS*, I much prefer the word *development* because it better implies the entire process of building relationships than does the word *fundraising*. Organizations that use the word *fundraising* to describe these activities

often tend to focus on events and activities, rather than on the building of long-term relationships.

Although it hasn't quite caught on yet, there is a trend to call the fundraising staff "directors of philanthropy," and to have a philanthropy committee rather than a development

> ### One way to think about terminology
>
> *Overarching vision:* Philanthropy (action for the good of society)
>
> *Strategy:* Development (developing long-term relationships)
>
> *Tactics:* Fundraising (methods and techniques)
>
>
> Inspiration!

committee. I think this is a positive sign, as more and more organizations are recognizing the lofty goal of advancing philanthropy, rather than focusing on the process or the techniques.

Another term often used, especially in higher education, is "advancement," since this process is all about raising funds to advance the mission of the organization. Some people use other terms, but these are the most common.

Whatever terminology you use in your organization, it still comes down to the importance of building relationships that enhance the donor's ability and interest in supporting your organization with philanthropic donations.

Of course, you do need to make some practical decisions for your organization: What are you going to call the department, the staff, and the committees who are engaged in the business of fundraising?

Some options include:

Department	Staff	Volunteers
Philanthropy	Vice President of Philanthropy; Director of Philanthropy; Director of Philanthropic Giving	Philanthropy Committee; Committee for Philanthropy; Philanthropic Advisory Committee
Advancement	Vice President of Institutional Advancement; Director of Advancement	Advancement Committee
Development	Director of Development; Vice President of Development; Development Director, Director of Fund Development	Development Committee
Fundraising	Fundraising Manager; Fundraising Coordinator; Director of Fundraising	Fundraising Committee

The Changing Face of Fundraising

The face of fundraising is changing in many ways. First, there is a trend towards "professionalizing the profession," recognizing that fundraising is an art and a science and that it is a true profession. With the increased body of knowledge, the self-regulation of the profession and the certification of professional fundraisers, the world is beginning to accept fundraising as a viable career choice. In years past, most people "fell into" the profession of fundraising. Now there are undergraduate and graduate courses in philanthropy and development.

Fundraisers themselves are also changing. When I first entered the profession, for example, my local Association of Fundraising Professionals (AFP) meetings were generally attended by a mix of about 60 to 70 percent males and 30 to 40 percent females. Today, when I attend a meeting, it is more like 80 percent women and 20 percent men. Another interesting demographic trend is that the profession is becoming much less "white." It is encouraging to see that there are members representing just about every ethnicity in the profession of fundraising, and that in addition to the gender diversity, there is far more age diversity. Most of the meetings I attend are now populated by some senior members of our profession, or as those of us who fit that description might prefer, "seasoned members," along with "newbies." All this diversity has improved our profession dramatically. We learn much from each other and I encourage you to network with your peers in fundraising, learning from them and teaching them as well.

Donors also are changing. Philanthropists are not all the Carnegies and Rockefellers we might have thought of in the past. We are now learning more about women philanthropists, raising money from Generation X and Generation Y, and the philanthropic profiles of ethnic minorities. Donors are becoming much more sophisticated and more selective in the choices they make about supporting various charities. They are going to the Internet and researching nonprofits before they choose to support them financially. They are reading 990 forms (see the sidebar on the next page) and asking questions of board and staff members of the nonprofits to which they are being asked to contribute. This is an encouraging sign but also a challenging one because it tells us that the fittest will survive—those nonprofits that are doing ethical and professional fundraising and can face up to the scrutiny of donors and the public.

Technology is also dramatically changing the field of fundraising. More organizations are doing Internet fundraising, raising money through Twitter and text messaging, and just about every nonprofit has a website, albeit not always a great one! (More about this later.) Technology has changed the way we communicate with our donors, but has also raised the expectations of donors and colleagues. We are now expected to answer emails from board members within hours or minutes, to submit grant proposals online and to never get lost because we have a GPS system to guide us (so there is no reason to be late for a meeting). And speaking of meetings, if we can't get there in person, we can connect from home and participate through programs such as GoToMeeting and ReadyTalk. In many ways technology has made our jobs much easier, but it also raises the bar on the amount of work we are expected to accomplish in a set amount of time.

990 Form

IRS Form 990—A report annually submitted by almost all nonprofit organizations to the Internal Revenue Service. It includes financial information on income sources, expenditures, and activities.

Governance is also changing. Board members are finally recognizing that they have a fiduciary responsibility to the public and to the donors who support the organizations that they govern. Boards are moving away from "managing" organizations to a true governance model. Board members are asking the tough questions of staff and expecting, and deserving, honest answers. Public scrutiny of nonprofits and more astute boards are becoming more prevalent. While it might seem like these could cause us grief, in reality the fact that staff and board members are more accountable to donors, regulators, and the public only strengthens the nonprofit sector. This can only result in good things for nonprofits. It should lead us to be absolutely certain that our fundraising is done ethically and professionally. And it will enable us to raise more money because donors appreciate the fact that we have strong, capable people governing our nonprofits.

To Summarize

✎ Although this book bears the word "fundraising" in its title, we will actually be talking about fundraising, development and philanthropy throughout. Understanding these subtle differences is important, especially because I want to take you beyond fundraising activities into the world of developing relationships and inspiring philanthropy.

✎ There are many titles for professional fundraisers but no matter what titles you might use in your organization it will be important to understand fundraising as an art and a science.

✎ The face of fundraising, development and philanthropy is changing, and as fundraisers, we must move with the tides of change, or be swept away in the undertow.

Chapter 2

The Role of Fundraising in the Nonprofit Organization

For many persons new to the whole concept of the nonprofit sector, there is a great deal of misunderstanding of what it means to be a nonprofit. Some think that it means the organization can't operate in the black, because it then becomes a "for-profit organization." (Not so.) Many think that nonprofit staff members should be paid less than standard wages because they are working for a "charity." (Also not so.)

For clarification purposes, let's start with what it means to be a nonprofit organization. In the United States, a charitable nonprofit is usually a 501(c)(3) agency, a designation received from the IRS after meeting certain requirements, most importantly that the organization serves a charitable,

> The main characteristic that separates a nonprofit from a profit-making entity is that no individual or group of individuals can benefit financially from the profits of the agency.
>
>
> ! important

educational, scientific, or community service purpose. Individuals may deduct donations to approved nonprofit organizations when filing their income, gift, or estate tax returns. Although government agencies might provide grants for small businesses and sometimes individuals, most foundations will only make grants to nonprofit organizations. Contrary to popular opinion, being a nonprofit does not mean that the organization must operate in the red or that it cannot have a fund surplus.

By receiving nonprofit status, most organizations are exempt from paying federal and state income taxes and often local taxes. However, in some communities, local municipalities are requiring some nonprofits to pay real estate taxes or payments in lieu of taxes (P.I.L.O.T.).

Sometimes the nonprofit community is called the third sector (as opposed to government or the business sector), the independent sector, the public benefit sector, or the voluntary sector. All of these terms are appropriate and accurate. Most nonprofits are thought of as charities, although some are huge operations such as major universities and health care systems; but they still share the commonality of being a nonprofit entity since no individual or group of individuals personally benefit from the surplus revenues of the organization.

Nonprofits are funded in a variety of ways. For many, fees for services are one important source of income. Examples of this would include:

✎ Tuition paid to colleges, universities, private schools or pre-schools.

✎ Admission fees at museums, zoos, aquariums, and art galleries.

✎ Fees for services at health clinics, drug and alcohol abuse treatment centers, counseling centers and other organizations, often based on a sliding scale dependent on the recipients' income.

✎ Ticket sales at concerts, ballet performances, and other performing arts events.

Some organizations are highly dependent on government funding in the form of grants and/or contracts. Government funding can be an important source of funding for many organizations; however, becoming too reliant on these funds can be dangerous.

When administrations change, new priorities often are established and funding sources might pull back substantial amounts of funding or cut funding altogether. You should investigate the sources of funding available through various government sources, including federal, state and local municipalities, but I would urge you to plan a more well-rounded fundraising program so your organization does not fold when government funding dries up.

Many organizations are also investing resources into establishing social enterprises which can be a wonderful source of funding. Organizations such as Goodwill and many others generate money by operating thrift stores, which are not only a great source of revenue but help them advance their mission of putting people with disabilities, low income, or who might be at risk to work in meaningful, competitive employment. Other for-profit subsidiaries or programs include a gift shop in a hospital or museum, a shop at a nonprofit community arts center where people can purchase art made by the artisans in the studio, a book store in a college, or renting space to a pharmacy in a health clinic. There are an unlimited amount of for-profit activities that nonprofits might engage in. If you are considering any of these you need to weigh all your options and be aware of unrelated business income tax (UBIT) laws that might require your organization to pay taxes on some of these activities. As a general rule of thumb, if the activity fits within the scope of your mission, you will not be affected by UBIT liability. Please see your legal counsel or accountant for tax advice in this regard. If you are engaged it taxable activities, it might still be a profitable undertaking even after paying the taxes.

In summary, the basic sources of revenue for many nonprofits include fees for services, government grants and contracts, and income from profit-making activities. However, not all organizations qualify for or choose to be engaged in these income streams. This leaves fundraising activities as the major source of revenue for most nonprofits. Almost all nonprofits need to raise funds, even if they have one or a combination of these other sources of revenue. In most cases, none of the above sources of revenue alone is enough to support a nonprofit. Even private schools and expensive universities usually do not raise sufficient funds through tuition alone.

Nor do insurance and private-pay patients usually cover the true costs of health care in a hospital that provides a lot of charitable service. Hence, the business of fundraising.

However, the role of fundraising in an organization might be perceived differently in the eyes of all the stakeholders of that organization. Some staff members understand the importance of fundraising, but the board might not see the value. Some constituents are very aware of the importance of fundraising, while others are not; perhaps the parents of a student at a private school who are paying substantial tuition fees won't understand why their child's school does so much fundraising.

One of the major roles of a professional fundraiser is to establish a healthy and appropriate climate for fundraising—a culture of philanthropy within the organization. Before you look at how to start a development program or how to increase your fundraising results, assess your organization's philanthropic profile, using the form in **Appendix D**.

Once you've identified weaknesses in your organization's profile, you can start to work on those areas by reading the chapters that relate to those particular areas—such as the chapters on governance and staffing—and putting these theories into practice. In fact, you might want to make this assessment a part of your annual fundraising checkup to see if you are improving your "score."

To Summarize

✎ Nonprofits are different from the for-profit world in that no one in the organization can benefit from the "profits" of the organization. This does not mean that they must operate in the red, or that nonprofit employees should work free or for below standard wages.

✎ Nonprofits can generate revenues from a variety of sources including government grants and contracts, fees for services, and for-profit activities. However, for most organizations, fundraising is a major part of their revenue stream. There might be many people who do not understand the reasons nonprofits, especially those who generate fees for services, need to do fundraising. It is our job, as fundraisers, to raise the level of awareness of the nonprofit sector and develop a philanthropic culture within our organizations.

Chapter 3

Who Raises Funds?

In This Chapter...

- Who should be on the fundraising team?

- What is the role of consultants in fundraising?

- How do I overcome the "tin cup" mentality in my organization?

Who raises funds is a two-part question. First, there is the question of what types of organizations are raising money, and, second, who within the organization is responsible for raising money? The first part of the question will be answered in the next chapter. The second part I will briefly explain here, and in future chapters I will provide more detail on specific roles of the various people involved in fundraising among the board, staff, and volunteers. There are other people involved in fundraising, including consultants and professional solicitors. In this chapter I will explain the differences in and roles of these two groups in your fundraising program.

Fundraising, to be successful, must be a team effort. Many times I've heard boards of directors say after deciding to hire their first director of development or other fundraising staff person, "Whew, boy, are we glad we don't have to worry about that fundraising stuff anymore." Wrong! Once

A colleague accepted a job as the first development officer at a school for the arts. On her first day on the job, there was a gentle knock on her door. When she opened the door, there stood an elderly woman who taught the Suzuki violin method to young students at the school. "I understand you are here to help us raise money for the school," said the woman. "Yes, that's right," the new development director replied. "Well, I've been telling them for years that I know someone who would contribute some money but no one ever listened," came the reply. "Let's go to lunch and you can tell me all about it," was the astute development officer's response. Long story short: This teacher had a student many years ago who was now a program officer at a very large foundation. End result: The school received the largest donation it had received up to that point. All because a program staff member—the teacher—had the right contact and the development officer understood that "fundraising is everybody's business."

Pure Genius!

an organization decides to make a commitment to fundraising, everyone needs to get involved, from the board, the executive director, the development staff, the program staff, to support staff, etc. In other words, "Fundraising is everybody's business."

Other boards feel they can bring in a consultant to handle all the nasty parts of fundraising, such as "making the asks." This approach, as with thinking the staff can do it all, is equally flawed. In fact, more so.

The Role of Consultants

According to a recent survey, more than 40 percent of nonprofits expect to pay more than $50,000 in consulting fees in the coming year. So, how do you decide if you need a consultant and how do you find the right consultant? If your organization is considering hiring a consultant to help with fundraising or development needs, here are few things to think about before you engage a consultant.

Do you need a consultant or a staff person?

The first thing you need to know is whether you are looking for a staff person to fill the role or if you need a consultant. If you need full-time work or someone to be on site on a regular basis, you probably need an employee rather than a consultant. Hiring a consultant is *not* a way to avoid paying benefits to employees. In fact, many states and the IRS have strict regulations about who is an employee and who is an outside contractor. Things such as supplying an office and equipment and supervising the person's work directly usually mean that the person is an employee, and you must pay employment taxes and possibly benefits. For a complete list of IRS guidelines, check the IRS website at http://www.irs.gov.

The IRS specifies guidelines in three areas—behavioral control, financial control and type of relationship—that can help determine the difference between an employee and an independent contractor. Outlined below are some of these guidelines that would pertain to engaging a fundraising consultant, grant writer or professional fundraiser.

Behavioral Control

A worker is an employee when the business has the right to direct and control the worker. The business does not have to actually direct or control the way the work is done—as long as the employer has the right to direct and control the work. The behavioral control factors fall into the categories of type of instructions given, degree of instruction, evaluation systems, training and types of instructions given.

Instructions given

An employee is generally subject to the business's instructions about when, where, and how to work. All of the following are examples of types of instructions about how to do work:

✎ When and where to do the work.

✎ What tools or equipment to use.

✎ What workers to hire or to assist with the work.

✎ Where to purchase supplies and services.

✎ What work must be performed by a specified individual.

✎ What order or sequence to follow when performing the work.

Degree of instruction

Degree of instruction means that the more detailed the instructions, the more control the business exercises over the worker. More detailed instructions indicate that the worker is an employee. Less detailed instructions reflect less control, indicating that the worker is more likely an independent contractor.

Evaluation system

If an evaluation system measures the details of how the work is performed, then these factors would point to an employee. If the evaluation system measures just the end result, then this can point to either an independent contractor or an employee.

Training

If the business provides the worker with training on how to do the job, this indicates that the business wants the job done in a particular way. This is strong evidence that the worker is an employee. Periodic or on-going training about procedures and methods is even stronger evidence of an employer-employee relationship. However, independent contractors ordinarily use their own methods.

Financial Control

Financial control refers to facts that show whether or not the business has the right to control the economic aspects of the worker's job. The financial control factors fall into the categories of significant investment, unreimbursed expenses, opportunity for profit or loss, services available to the market and method of payment.

Significant investment

An independent contractor often has a significant investment in the equipment the person uses in working for someone else. There are no precise dollar limits that must be met in order to have a significant investment. Furthermore, a significant investment is not necessary for independent contractor status as some types of work, such as consulting, simply do not require large expenditures.

Unreimbursed expenses

Independent contractors are more likely to have unreimbursed expenses than are employees. Fixed ongoing costs that are incurred regardless of whether work is currently being performed are especially important. However, employees may also incur unreimbursed expenses in connection with the services that they perform for their business.

Opportunity for profit or loss

The opportunity to make a profit or loss is another important factor. The possibility of incurring a loss indicates that the worker is an independent contractor.

Services available to the market

An independent contractor is generally free to seek out business opportunities. Independent contractors often advertise, maintain a visible business location, and are available to work in the relevant market.

Method of payment

An employee is generally guaranteed a regular wage amount for an hourly, weekly, or other period of time. This usually indicates that a worker is an employee, even when the wage or salary is supplemented by a commission. An independent contractor is usually paid by a flat fee for the job. However, it is common in some professions, such as law, to pay independent contractors hourly.

Type of Relationship

Type of relationship refers to facts that show how the worker and business perceive their relationship to each other. The factors, for the type of relationship between two parties, generally fall into the categories of written contracts, employee benefits, permanency of the relationship, services provided as key activity of the business, and written contracts.

Although a contract might state that the worker is an employee or an independent contractor, this is not sufficient to determine the worker's status. Neither the states nor the IRS are required to follow a contract stating that the worker is an independent contractor, responsible for paying self-employment tax. Rather, how the parties work together determines whether the worker is an employee or an independent contractor.

Employee benefits

Employee benefits include things such as insurance, pension plans, paid vacation, sick days, and disability insurance. Businesses generally do not grant these benefits to independent contractors. However, the lack of these types of benefits does not necessarily mean the worker is an independent contractor.

Permanency of the relationship

If you hire a worker with the expectation that the relationship will continue indefinitely, rather than for a specific project or period, this is generally considered evidence that the intent was to create an employer-employee relationship.

Services provided as key activity of the business

If a worker provides services that are a key aspect of the business, it is more likely that the business will have the right to direct and control the worker's activities. For example, if a law firm hires an attorney, it is likely that it will present the attorney's work as its own and would have the right to control or direct that work. This would indicate an employer-employee relationship.

Know the law and ethics of consulting

While some states in the U.S. do not require nonprofits or consultants to register in order to do fundraising campaigns and activities, most states do; so if your organization is headquartered in one of these states you need to check into state regulations regarding the hiring of a consultant. And of course, the AFP code of ethics prohibits its members, including consultants, from working on a percentage-of-money-raised basis.

Be sure to ask for references of other clients

Ask if the consultant is a member of AFP or another association that requires members to adhere to a standard of ethics. And ask if the person is registered to do business in your state, if registration is required.

Understand what type of consultant you need

Consultants can offer many areas of expertise in different areas of fundraising. There are grant writing consultants, planned giving consultants, event consultants, search firms, capital campaign consultants, board development consultants, and consultants who can help you develop a plan or audit your organization's development office. Some full-service firms will provide a combination or even all of these services. But, you need to know what type of consultant you are looking for. Do not hire a grant writer to run a capital campaign or a capital campaign consultant to plan a special event.

Have you budgeted adequately for consultant fees?

Your organization needs to understand that you are not usually paying consultants for the hours they work, but you are paying for their knowledge, their experience and their expertise. Often, board members who have not worked with consultants before are not prepared to pay the fees involved because they do not understand this concept. Also, be aware of other costs, such as travel expense, if you are hiring a consultant from outside your area. Ask what type of hotel accommodations they expect, what typical airfares will run, and whether they charge for mileage, phone calls, faxes, etc. Is there a charge for materials they provide?

What are the criteria you are looking for in a consultant?

Sometimes organizations feel it is important to have a local consultant. Other times they're looking for someone with a national reputation and experience. Some organizations feel it is important to hire someone who has worked with similar organizations; for example, a YMCA might insist on hiring someone who has worked with other YMCAs. If the consultant is truly knowledgeable about fundraising, these things are often not as important as they seem. Some important criteria to look for are:

✎ Does the consultant understand your needs?

✎ Do you feel the chemistry between the staff and board is good?

✎ Is the consultant willing to learn enough about your organization and your constituents to effectively help you present your case?

Ask about the consultant's work style

Will the consultant be providing actual work products, or only direction so you can produce the products yourself? For example, is the grant writing consultant actually writing the grant proposal, or only reviewing and editing grant proposals you will write? Will the consultant be on site or will the work be performed from the consultant's own office? How accessible is the consultant to you by phone or email? Make sure the consultant's style and services fit your organization's needs.

Does the consultant's personality fit your organization's culture?

Some organizations want a polished, sophisticated person, while another might prefer a more down-to-earth style. You need to be comfortable with your consultant's personality.

Insist on a written contract

A written contract or letter of agreement, signed by your organization and the consultant, should always be in place. This contract should outline fees and other expenses, a schedule of when fees are to be paid, a scope of work to be performed, a starting and ending date for the work, and a provision to extend or cancel the contract.

Welcome the consultant into your organization

Be sure that the staff members of your organization who will be working with this consultant get to meet the consultant early on. Staff should know what they need to provide in order for the consultant arrangement to be mutually satisfactory. Give the consultant a tour of your facility. Introduce the consultant to program staff members and others. And, feel free to tell the consultant if you are unhappy or uncomfortable with anything.

Remember that consultants do not raise money for you, rather they help your staff and volunteers (we'll cover their roles in later chapters) develop the skills and relationships to raise the money.

Ten tips for hiring and working with a consultant

1. List what it is you expect the consultant to do. Have a list of expected outcomes and items to be accomplished, similar to a job description for a staff member.

2. Know whether you need a consultant or a staff member. Refer to the IRS guidelines about the roles of outside contractors and staff members.

3. Determine whether the tasks you need done can be accomplished by someone internally versus an outside expert.

4. Determine the qualities your organization thinks are most important in a consultant: experience with a particular type of organization, geographic location, working style, etc.

5. Research the types of consultants that are available in this specific area of expertise. Some good sources include CharityChannel's Consultants Registry Online or the Consultant Directory Online at AFP International. Or check with your state's association of nonprofits, such as the Pennsylvania Association of Nonprofit Organizations. (For a complete list of state nonprofit associations, check out the National Council of Nonprofit Organizations http://www.ncna.org.)

6. Ask other nonprofits to share their experience with similar projects, i.e. if you are looking for a capital campaign consultant, talk to other nonprofits in your community that have used a consultant for a capital campaign.

7. Call several of the consultants on the list you have developed and determine the ones you think best meet your needs.

8. You might want to develop a simple RFP (Request for Proposal). However, be aware that many consultants do not respond to RFPs, particularly if they are many pages long with a lot of requirements.

9. Schedule in-person interviews only with consultants you are seriously considering. It will save your time and theirs. Make sure you interview the consultant with whom you will actually be working.

10. Remember that the chemistry between your staff and board and the consultant is one of the important ingredients of a successful relationship, if not the key.

Perspiration!

Professional Solicitors

One more category of professionals sometimes involved in fundraising is the solicitor. The professional solicitor, unlike consultants, actually *does* ask for the money, usually through direct mail or telephone programs. Many states require professional solicitors to register and to disclose the percentages they charge to their clients. Professional solicitors are generally allowed by law to work on a percentage basis, although the AFP Code of Ethical Principles and Standards, which I reproduce in **Appendix B,** prohibits percentage-based fundraising. There are, however, reputable professional solicitors that you can hire to do phone programs or direct-mail programs for you that do not work on a percentage basis. In most cases, professional solicitors handle the entire process from the creation of letters and phone scripts to the mailing or actual phone calls, and the follow-up. In some cases they even provide "caging services," which means they collect the money and deposit the proceeds into your account.

> *Fundraising is the magic mingling of a joyful giver, a grateful recipient, and an artful asker.*
>
> —Doug Lawson
>
> **Inspiration!**

You should carefully investigate the fees charged and services provided by professional solicitors. In many cases when you are using solicitors that charge a percentage of money raised, the greatest percentage of the funds donated goes to the professional solicitor to cover costs and profits; your organization could end up with 5 percent or less of the proceeds. You should, if you are planning to hire a professional solicitor, work with a company that works on a flat fee basis, not a percentage. You can also find these firms in the AFP consultant directory , the CharityChannel Consultant's Registry, and some of the other sources listed under the "finding a consultant" section.

Creating a Philanthropic Culture

So how do you approach fundraising to make sure everyone is involved and embraces their role? Creating a philanthropic environment is critical. Boards and staff cannot view fundraising as a necessary evil, or with the "tin cup" mentality. Philanthropy, as you have seen in previous chapters, is a huge part of most nonprofits' ability to fulfill their mission. Philanthropy is always done with the interests of the donor given top priority. Being involved in the noble profession of fundraising is rewarding because as a fundraiser you will see first-hand the impact donations have on the people served by your organization. And a good fundraiser always makes sure donors have the ability to see their money at work. Fundraising is a process of building relationships and those relationships will draw donors closer to the organization and the people it serves. We will discuss more about this throughout this book.

To Summarize

✎ Fundraising is a team effort. Everyone in your nonprofit organization must be aware of the importance of fundraising and be involved in assisting the philanthropic process. Boards, staff and volunteers must work together to enhance the fundraising process. Each of these roles will be discussed in more detail in future chapters.

✎ You might at some point decide that you need a consultant to help with your fundraising. You need to know what kind of help you need before engaging a consultant or a professional solicitor. You also must be aware of the legal and ethical issues involved when you engage outside help. Remember that consultants do not raise the money for you, but are part of your development team and usually serve more in the role of coach and guide.

✎ You also need to develop a culture of philanthropy in your organization in order to be successful. It is your job as a fundraising professional to eliminate the "tin cup" mentality that is often present in nonprofits.

Chapter 4

The Competition: Diversity of the Nonprofit Sector

The other side of the question of "who raises funds" is the number and types of nonprofit organizations that are out there raising funds. Although not all of the million plus nonprofits are charitable organizations, many of these are your competition for dollars.

Even nonprofits such as chambers of commerce and professional associations are sometimes raising sponsorship dollars from businesses or might have a separate foundation to raise charitable dollars. And sometimes private foundations receive money from other foundations. In other words, you have a lot of competition, so the more professional and strategic you can be in your approach, the more you will raise your organization above the crowd of nonprofits that proliferate in the marketplace.

The types of charitable organizations include:

✎ Religious institutions, which receive the bulk of the charitable dollars, about 33 percent

✎ Educational institutions, which typically receive the next highest amount of the charitable donations, generally around 13 percent

✎ Human service organizations, receiving approximately 9 to 10 percent of charitable donations

✎ Health care institutions and agencies, receiving about 7 percent of charitable donations

✎ Arts and cultural institutions, typically receiving about 4 percent of charitable donations

✎ Public or society benefit organizations, receiving about 8 percent of donations

✎ Environmental and animal-related organizations, receiving about 2 percent of donations

✎ International relief organizations, which usually receive around 3 percent of donations

✎ Other organizations which typically receive about 20 percent of all giving

In addition to the traditional 501(c)(3) organizations raising money, the trend is for more competition from public schools and other public entities that need to raise money beyond what tax dollars can provide. So, you face competition not only from traditional nonprofits, but from these public and quasi-public entities as well.

It is also clear that organizations that do not have strong programs, and ones that are perceived to be needed in their communities, will not survive.

It is estimated that 10 percent of the 1.8 million nonprofits that exist as I write this book will not be around five years from now. Why?

Where Nonprofits Go to Die

The I.R.S. removed the tax-exempt status of approximately 300,000 nonprofits during 2011 for failure to comply with reporting requirements.

! important

- ✎ Their mission is no longer relevant.

- ✎ They do not have a vision for the future.

- ✎ They have not listened to their stakeholders.

- ✎ There is no strategic plan for growth.

- ✎ They have not learned to collaborate effectively.

- ✎ They are duplicating services, often perceived to be provided better by other organizations.

- ✎ They have not learned the importance of effective governance and staff leadership.

- ✎ They do not have the financial wherewithal to maintain or expand their programs and services.

- ✎ There is not a strong culture of philanthropy in the organization.

Relevant Mission

Your organization must have a viable and relevant mission in order to survive. And you must translate that mission to your constituents as clearly and as often as possible. In the chapter on creating awareness, we will discuss in more detail how to advance your mission. But first you must have a mission statement that all your staff and board members understand and agree on. Your mission statement should be revisited on a regular basis, usually at an annual retreat. It is also critical that all your programs are designed to fulfill your mission and that you are not just fundraising to chase dollars that might be available. There is always the danger of

Answer these Planning Questions

✎ Is your mission statement brief (no more than one paragraph)? If not, rewrite it.

✎ Are your goals realistic?

✎ Do you have specific objectives?

✎ How do you measure whether or not you are meeting your goals and objectives?

Perspiration!

"mission drift" when organizations go after grants or funding for services that really do not fit in with their mission. This is a sure kiss of death for organizations that do not keep their mission at the forefront of all they do.

Clear Vision for the Future

In addition to your mission, you also must have a vision for the future. Organizations that have neither a clear vision nor visionary leadership will not be around to face the future. The vision is not just centered on your organization but on what your community needs. We will talk more about mission and vision in the chapter on strategic planning, but remember that you should have a vision that focuses on where your organization expects to be in ten or more years and how it will meet the needs of your community.

Listening to Stakeholders

A for-profit business, if publicly held, is accountable to its stockholders. Although nonprofits do not have stockholders who own them, every nonprofit organization has stakeholders. Among your stakeholders might be your staff, board, donors, people who use your services, friends and relatives of the users of your services, volunteers, government agencies, the media, foundations, businesses, and the community at large. You need to identify these stakeholders and listen to their needs, desires, and dreams for the future in order to remain a viable, needed part of your community.

A Strategic Plan for Growth

Even if you think your organization does not need to grow, or if it sometimes seems as if you are growing too fast, you still need to think strategically about growth. Does your community have emerging needs that must be addressed? For example, are demographics radically shifting in your community? Perhaps the ethnicity of your community has changed; are you meeting the needs of the diverse populations in your community? Perhaps there is a geographic shift in population; are you located in the areas where the users of your service are living? Perhaps your community is aging or growing younger; do you serve these populations adequately? Growth might also include your facility needs. Are your facilities large enough, environmentally sensitive, safe, and accessible?

> ### Four Key Steps to Stakeholder Management
>
> **Step 1:** During a planning session, determine who your stakeholders are.
>
> **Step 2:** Determine how each stakeholder group perceives your organization.
>
> **Step 3:** Determine what each stakeholder group is looking for from your organization.
>
> **Step 4:** Plan program and services that address each stakeholder group's needs.

Perspiration!

Collaboration

Organizations that have not learned to collaborate will not survive. Funders usually want to see that you cooperate and collaborate with other groups in your community, both nonprofits and profit-making entities. You need to look at those groups that in the past you might have considered competition, and see if there are ways you can work together. You should evaluate on a regular basis whether you "play well with others." If you can show funders that you are willing and able to collaborate, you will increase your funding possibilities and assure a strong future for your organizations. You can collaborate both on programs and on fundraising events and activities.

Collaboration at Work

Two organizations that served young people pooled their resources to hold a successful fundraising event. One was a human services organization that served people with disabilities and, while many of its program participants were adults, it ran a summer camp program for children that needed funding. The other organization was a local tennis club that offered scholarships for young people to learn tennis. This club was an all-volunteer group that had no staff resources to help pull off a special event, but that had a lot of expertise in the sport of tennis. The human services organization had staff resources and seed money it could contribute to the event, but its donor base did not include people who would attend the type of elegant event it wanted to hold.

The two groups got together and planned a tennis tournament and black tie "tennis ball" dinner dance. The nonprofit with the development staff handled all the invitation mailing, gathering and storing door prizes, and made the arrangements for the dinner dance, including covering payments necessary to reserve the venue and entertainment. The tennis club supplied the invitation list, handled tournament logistics, and obtained prizes and awards.

The event was successful because each group had something to offer, and each had a need it couldn't fill on its own.

Pure Genius!

Avoiding Duplication and Emphasizing Uniqueness

The general public often does not understand why there are so many nonprofits, many of which appear to be doing the same thing. Some of the things you need to ask yourself (and these are tough questions) are: What would happen if our organization no longer existed? Who would step in and do the work we are doing? Would we be missed? Is there another organization that does a better job of what we do? What is unique about us? Are we doing a better job than anyone else? Answering these questions can help you discover what is unique and special about your organization and how you can describe your uniqueness to your constituents.

Visionary Governance and Staff Leadership

The leaders of your organization must not only supply good management skills but must be visionary leaders as well. We will be talking a lot more about the role of staff and board in creating a strong philanthropic culture, but for now ask yourself if your leaders are the kind of people who inspire greatness in your staff, who are well known in the community, have the respect of their peers, and are not afraid of a challenge. If they are, your organization has a good chance of survival in an uncertain and sometimes rapidly changing future.

Maintaining a Strong Financial Position

Your organization must have a strong financial position in order to inspire confidence in donors and members of the public. Today it is quite a simple task for anyone who is interested to obtain your 990 forms and look at things such as your major sources of funding, your top gifts, and the salaries of your key staff members.

One of the things that remain constant throughout fluctuating economic cycles is that nonprofits consistently anticipate increased demands for their services even in times of economic uncertainty. In fact, for many organizations such as those that feed the hungry, house the homeless, and provide other critical social services, the demand is greatly increased as resources continue to dry up.

Studies show the majority of nonprofits have fewer than three months' operating cash in their reserves at any given time. This can be a scary position for any nonprofit. But there are some steps you can take to become more fiscally sound. Some questions you should be able to answer include:

✎ Are you meeting your fundraising goals (revenue) as well as holding the line on expenses?

✎ If there are extreme fluctuations in revenue or expenses, have you analyzed why and taken steps to address these issues?

✎ Do you have a good way to track outstanding pledges and a system in place to collect those pledges?

✎ Do you have a line of credit available to you to cover unexpected increases in expenses or decreases in revenue?

✎ Do you have a reserve fund or endowment fund to cover fluctuations in expenses and revenue?

✎ Are there ways you can reduce expenses, such as reviewing vendor contracts and shopping for the "best deal?"

✎ Are you aware of the true costs of operating your programs and have you evaluated each program to make sure it is still viable?

✎ Is your board fully aware of and comfortable with your financial position?

If the answers to these questions are not positive, it might be time to take a serious look at your financial position and possibly to seek outside help.

Building a Culture of Philanthropy

We will be talking more about building a strong culture of philanthropy in your organization but, for now, return to the form in **Appendix D,** and consider having all the members of your administrative management team complete this questionnaire to help assess your organization's philanthropic culture. Using the tools in the chapters ahead in this book, I hope you will be able to build a stronger culture of philanthropy to help ensure that your organization will be among those that not only survive, but thrive, in the future.

To Summarize

✎ There is a lot of competition out there for charitable dollars. To survive among your competitors you need to assure that you have a relevant mission, a clear vision for the future, and that you listen to your stakeholders. You also need to plan strategically for growth, often by collaborating with other nonprofits and with your community. Your staff and board must be comprised of visionary leaders who monitor the financial health of your organization on a regular basis and who build a culture of philanthropy within the organization.

Chapter **5**

What Happens if Our Fundraising is not Effective and Ethical?

Fundraising is not a necessary evil. It is not something you can do "when you have time." It is not something that "anyone can do." It is a profession and must be viewed as such. If your organization thinks it can just find a volunteer to handle the fundraising or hire someone without the skills and experience needed to be effective at fundraising, it is doomed to failure.

It is true that a person can enter this field with no experience and learn on the job, but only if the organization is willing to invest in the development program and the staff.

If you think that your nonprofit "deserves" funding and that people who are wealthy "owe it to us," you will not be successful in fundraising. As we've seen in **Chapter 3,** donors have many options to contribute their money, and they have no obligation to make any charitable contributions. Understanding the donor's intentions and motivation is critical. Providing good stewardship to donors is critical. We will discuss these areas more in future chapters.

You might need to shift your own perception of fundraising and/or that of people within your organization before you can succeed at fundraising. I once worked with a board whose chair stated at a meeting, "I don't understand why we need to do fundraising; we have government contracts that pay for the services we provide." How she got to be chair of the board was lost on me. She had no idea that the money received from government sources only covered about 65 percent of the cost of the organization's services. And the organization had no endowment fund to fall back on if government funding was cut. Other board members I've worked with have made comments such as, "I'll do anything for this organization except ask my friends, or anyone else, for money." Or, "I can't understand why foundations won't fund us, we do great work." If any of these scenarios sound familiar, these perceptions need to change in order for your organization to be successful

> ### Donor Attrition
>
> Judith Nichols, CFRE, cites that out of every one-hundred persons who stop supporting your organization,
>
> ✎ Four have died or moved.
>
> ✎ Fifteen are angry with your organization.
>
> ✎ Fifteen think another organization does a better job serving the cause they care about.
>
> ✎ Sixty-six think your organization does not care about them!
>
>
> **Did You Know?**

in its fundraising. Board members must first understand your funding streams and expenses, and they need to understand and monitor the budget on a regular basis. They also need to understand the competition for dollars and the reasons foundations, businesses, and individuals support

A Good Rule of Thumb for Effective Fundraising

The rule of thumb in fundraising, previously known as the 80/20 rule (80 percent of your donations will come from 20 percent of your donors), has become more like 90/10 or even, as some studies have shown, 95/5 (95 percent of donations coming from just 5 percent of your donors).

Inspiration!

the organizations they do support (and why they do not support others). You need to build awareness of your organization in the community, and you need to make a strong case for support. And, your board members must be enthused enough about their service on your board to want to share that enthusiasm with others, to accept their responsibility for fundraising, and to be willing to always have your organization "in their minds, on their lips and in their hearts." Board members need that "fire in the belly," that passion that drives them to want your organization to succeed.

It will be critical as you read through this book to remember that 66 percent of lapsed donors simply think your organization does not care about them. You need to be always thinking from the donor's perspective. How would I feel if I attended this event and had a bad experience? How would I feel if I gave a gift, and my name was spelled wrong in the annual report? What if I hate direct mail, and they keep mailing to me every month? Or I've told them that I don't make pledges by phone, and they repeatedly call me for a gift? Or they mail me three newsletters every month? Or I served on the board and, when my service ended, they never contacted me again? Or I volunteered to help, but when I showed up at the organization they had nothing for me to do?

Most organizations don't follow the 95/5 Rule. In fact they do the exact opposite. They spend 95 percent of their time worrying about the 95 percent of their donors who collectively supply about 5 percent of their funding. They spend countless hours working on special events that often have fewer than one-hundred people in attendance and do nothing to build long-term relationships with donors. They plan months in advance for a mail appeal that yields less than a dollar for every dollar spent and has a response rate of less than 1 percent. And they do hours and hours of research and writing for a $5,000 grant. As we will see in future chapters, grants, events and direct mail all have their place in an integrated development program, but none of these should alone consume all of your time. Through this book, I want to teach you to work smarter, not harder, and focus your energy on the donors who have the most potential.

Putting the 95/5 Rule into Practice

An analysis of your donor database dictates how much time you should spend in face-to-face solicitations with major donors. I suggest running a list of your donors in descending order of size of gifts. Then calculate the top 5 or 10 percent of your donors, and see what percentage of your donations is coming from this segment of your donors.

As a general rule, you should be spending 90-95 percent of your time identifying, cultivating, and soliciting those major donors who will provide 90-95 percent of your donations. In other words, face-to-face solicitations are the best way to land major gifts. The rest of your time should be spent in efforts to acquire new donors and renew and upgrade smaller donors. This can be done through phone and mail appeals.

Perspiration!

To Summarize

✎ If your organization does not have a strong culture of philanthropy, you need to start the process of changing that. Build a board and a staff that understand the importance of fundraising, the psychology of philanthropy and the importance of investing in the development program.

✎ The 95/5 rule states that 95 percent of your donations will generally come from about 5 percent of your donors. Learn how to avoid losing those high-end donors, and how to build relationships that will result in low-end donors becoming major supporters of your organization. Spend 95 percent of your time focusing on the top 5 percent of your donors.

Whose Responsibility is Fundraising?

So, who is responsible for fundraising in your nonprofit organization? As I mentioned previously, many boards and executive directors breathe a collective sigh of relief once they hire a development staff person. "Whew, we're so glad we don't have to worry about all that fundraising stuff anymore." Wrong! Once your organization sees philanthropy as a priority and decides to establish a development office, the board and leadership of your organization will be more involved in fundraising than ever before.

Fundraising is a team effort. In fact, when you hold any position in a nonprofit organization, from executive director to receptionist, security guard, maintenance staff, or clerical support, you need to know that to be successful the organization must take the approach that, "Fundraising is everybody's business." Fundraising cannot be viewed as a distraction from providing services, but as the foundation that allows your organization to provide needed programs to the community. The following chapters will outline in detail the roles of the board, staff, and volunteers of your organization and the importance of their role in the development program.

Chapter 6

The Role of the Board

In This Chapter...

✎ How do you find and recruit effective board members?

✎ How important is board giving?

✎ How do you get your board involved in fundraising?

The key to getting your board members to embrace fundraising lies in three simple steps—the recruitment process, assuring that board members are committed to your organization, and removing the fear of fundraising that is inherent in most people. First, let's talk about the recruitment process.

For most nonprofit organizations, building an effective board is one of the greatest challenges. How do you find good board members? How do you get them to join the board and become active in fundraising? And how do you keep them involved once they are on the board?

Often, good board members are hard to find and, sometimes, it's difficult to assess their commitment to the organization until they are on the board, when it is then too late! Some board members flounder because there is no clear direction for them, and they haven't bought into the vision of the organization. Finding committed, dedicated board leadership is often a challenge. Board members are often reluctant to fundraise because they have not been recruited with that purpose in mind. Even if you originally intended for your board to be involved in fundraising, many times board recruiters are reluctant to use the "F" word for fear of scaring off potential members. Many well-intentioned organizations operate under the noble idea that, "once they get on our board and see the great work we are doing, they will want to go out and ask for money." Wrong! If they have not been told up front that fundraising is a part of their role, they will not embrace it later when you decide to "slip it into" their job description.

Take a New Look at How You Recruit Board Members

You might need to rethink *who* does the recruiting of your board members. Instead of a nominating committee that meets once a year to fill vacant seats, you should appoint a year-round governance committee. This committee can also be called the board resource committee or the committee on directorship or any name with which you feel comfortable. Whatever the title, the key functions to remember about this committee are that it:

- ✎ Needs to meet year round.

- ✎ Should be chaired by the one of the strongest members of your board.

- ✎ Should assess board performance as a whole and as individual board members.

- ✎ Is responsible for developing or refining board position descriptions.

- ✎ Evaluates the needs of your board and develops a profile of the kinds of people needed to fill vacancies on the board.

- ✎ Works with your whole board to help find the right people to fill vacant positions.

- ✎ Assures diversity on the board. Remember that diversity includes more than just ethnic diversity—it should include age, gender, and geographic diversity as well as a diversity of skills and talents your organization needs.

✎ Works with staff to plan and implement board orientation.

✎ Is responsible for planning and implementing ongoing education for the board.

Your governance committee, working thoughtfully, diligently, and on an ongoing basis, can make all the difference in the world between an effective, enthused, and inspired board and a lackadaisical board that does not understand its role in advancing your organization's mission and is reluctant to involve itself in the fundraising process. One of the key roles of this important committee is to develop a board position description that includes a required financial contribution from each board member as well as the expectation that each board member be involved in your fundraising efforts through attendance at events, planning development activities, and helping to identify, cultivate, and solicit potential donors. A sample board position description can be found in **Appendix E.**

> ## Board position descriptions need to include:
>
> ✎ An overall description of the board's duties
>
> ✎ Expectations for individual board members (financial commitment, time commitment, skills required)
>
> ✎ Term limits
>
> ✎ Conflict-of-interest and confidentiality policies
>
>  practical tip

This committee is also responsible for assuring that the position descriptions are not glossed over during the recruitment process and to make sure that each potential board member understands the roles and responsibilities of board service. Members of this committee must be expected to deal with potential board members who are obviously reluctant to accept these responsibilities. It is better to turn away prospective board members who are not willing to accept their full responsibilities, including that of fundraising, than to "fill a seat with a warm body" just so the committee can say it has met its expectation to bring on a certain number of new board members each year. The reluctant prospective board member might instead be invited to serve on a committee or in some other volunteer position, other than being invited to serve on the board.

Uninspired, to say the least!

I once experienced a board meeting that was the worst example I have ever witnessed of how some organizations recruit board members. It was December. The executive director said toward the end of the meeting, "Well a few of you are coming to the end of your terms on the board, so we need about three new board members, does anyone have any ideas?" Eeeek, I wanted to scream! What was wrong with this picture? Several things: It was December and the new board members were to be in place in January! The executive director was the one to raise the issue, not a board member! And, there was no thought given to what skills were needed on the board and who the people might be who possess those skills! Please, please, please don't *ever* recruit board members this way!

Uninspired

So, where do you find the right board members and convince them to get involved on your board, and even to accept a leadership role? The best place to find good board members is to have active committees of your board. Serving on a committee gives both the volunteer and the organization time and place to "get to know each other." If the committee members are faithful in attending meetings, accepting responsibility, and delivering on promises, they will be likely to do the same when serving as board members. The committee process, in addition to helping you get things done, can often be a sort of refining process to sort out the wheat from the chaff and identify the volunteers who will be good board members.

The governance committee should help to assure board diversity including:

- ✎ Profession
- ✎ Income level
- ✎ Religion
- ✎ Age
- ✎ Gender
- ✎ Geographical location
- ✎ Ethnic groups
- ✎ Length of time living in community
- ✎ Skills and talents

If your board has a diverse membership, it will be easier for you to identify potential donors from a variety of constituencies. Make sure your board is representative of the community you serve. Fundraising is much more difficult if your board members do not know people who live in a particular geographic community, members of a particular religious group or ethnic community, all your constituent groups, or potential major donors.

The Nominating Committee

Nominating committees tend to meet at the end of the board meeting year, are often chaired by one of the weaker members of the board, and operate under the belief that their job is simply to find new board members and nominate board officers.

Uninspired

Get rid of Your Nominating Committee!

Instead of a nominating committee that meets once a year to fill vacant seats, try a year-round governance committee. This committee can also be called the board resource committee or the committee on directorship or any name with which your organizations feels comfortable.

Inspiration!

Getting Your Board Involved in Fundraising

Once you have a board in place with the diverse skills, talents and connections needed to expand your resource development program, where do you start?

Once you have the board convinced that giving and getting is important, how do you make it happen? First, let's talk about board giving.

How much should board members give?

Requiring your board members to give a set dollar amount each year is discouraged for several reasons—it limits you

Suggesting a Giving Level to Your Board Members

Re-word your board position description, under the area of board giving, to state that board members are expected to make your organization one of the top three priorities for their charitable giving! This makes it clear that you expect them to give at what they would consider to be a meaningful level.

Pure Genius!

The Importance of Board Giving

There are several reasons board giving is critical to your organization:

✎ It increases the level of "ownership" the board members feel towards your organization.

✎ It shows donors and prospective donors that your board members are good stewards.

✎ It enables your organization to raise funds from foundations and other entities that ask, "How much has the board given?"

✎ It makes them feel good about their involvement with your organization and enables them to ask others for money!

Inspiration!

in recruiting board members who might have a lot of talent and skills but are not able to give at the required level. On the other hand, board members who could easily give more tend to give at the stated minimum level. Therefore, it is better to stress in the board's position description that all board members are required to give at a meaningful level. The two key words are *all* (100 percent of the board should be giving annually) and *meaningful*. Board members should be rated individually for an appropriate ask amount.

When should you ask board members for their gift?

You should ask board members to make their contributions before asking others to give. For the annual appeal, the best time to do your board appeal is at the very beginning of your fiscal year. If your organization is on a July-June fiscal year, summer is a good time to "gear up" for your fall campaign and having the board appeal out of the way during July and August puts you in a good position for your annual appeal. If you are on a calendar year, you should approach your board in January. If you are engaged in a capital campaign, you will want to make sure 100 percent of your board members have made campaign pledges before you begin soliciting any major donors or the general public. Likewise, with your planned giving program, the first people you should approach to make a bequest or other type of planned gift are your board members.

> ### Make Your Pledge Now!
>
> A colleague called me shortly after accepting a new development position. He sought advice about how to handle his organization's approach to board giving. He had just come from his first board meeting in his new position and he said the board chair started the meeting by saying that board members were expected to contribute to the organization, handed out pledge cards, and said, "fill out your pledge card and hand it to me before you leave the meeting tonight." Not exactly a well-planned, thoughtful approach to board giving!
>
>
>
> Uninspired

A Helpful Tool for the Board Appeal

A tool that can help with your board appeal is a list showing board members various ways you need their support throughout the year. Most board members get annoyed at being "nickled and dimed" to death for every special event that comes along. A menu of options as to how they can direct their support will be helpful, but should always include unrestricted board giving.

Perspiration!

How Do You Approach Board Members for Their Contributions?

Begin by appointing a board appeal committee. Members of this committee should include the chair of your board, the chair of the development committee and as many other board members as are needed to personally solicit the board, keeping in mind that one solicitor should be responsible for no more than five calls. You should select committee members from those board members who are themselves regular generous givers. Your chief development officer should be on the committee but should not solicit board members. A staff member will need to solicit the board chair before the board chair can ask others to join in giving.

Motivating Board Members

One of my clients posts a board tracking report in the form of a huge poster on the wall of its board room, listing every board member's name and the various areas in which each board member is expected to contribute throughout the year. Some categories included the annual board appeal, sponsoring various events, selling tables/foursomes to events, gifts in kind, and gifts solicited from their employer or others. Each board gift is tracked on a monthly basis, and board members not only see their results compared to other board members on the wall, but receive a printout of these results in their board packet. It works because board members want to outshine others and do not want to be embarrassed in front of the other board members.

Pure Genius!

This committee then does a screening and rating session of the entire board (this concept will be explained in the chapter on soliciting individual donors). Treat the board appeal just as you would any major fundraising appeal; make it personal, challenging and exciting. You won't need glitzy campaign material for your board, after all they should know the "case," but you might want to put together a one page summary of the case and a graphic showing the importance of the board appeal (a pie chart with the annual fund broken down by categories is helpful to do this, i.e. how much comes from grants, events, mail, board appeal, corporate appeal, etc.).

Your board appeal committee might need training in how to schedule the appointment and how to make an ask, but remember that the board appeal should be a serious effort that involves personal visits to your board members, not just having the board chair hand out pledge cards at a meeting and saying, "Okay everyone, make your commitment now." This method usually offends board members and results in a much lower gift. The board members should be made to feel special enough for a personal visit and a face-to-face opportunity for them to be thanked for their past support, to ask questions, and to share their interests.

The "Give Us Fifteen Names" Fallacy

Many organizations ask their board members to each hand in fifteen names of people they will solicit for a gift to the organization.

This never works! Why? Board members usually feel they don't want to "hit up" their friends and relatives for money, and they can't think of anyone else to put on the list.

Every organization I have talked to that has tried this has received one or two lists at the most and, most often, none of the board members return a list.

Please, try something different!

Uninspired

Uncovering Your Board's Sphere of Influence

Once you've recruited an effective board and all board members have made their personal financial commitment, the next step is getting them involved in the process of identifying, cultivating and soliciting donors. Remember, *every board member* has a sphere of influence that can be used to help your organization. They just need to be made aware of the value of their connections and how they can use those connections to help your organization.

First, your board members need to understand the reason fundraising is important to you, and they need to understand their own role in the development process. You can start by holding an educational session at a board meeting. Explain how important development is to your organization and what unfunded programs need support from private

Basic Principles for Board Participation in Fundraising

✎ Board members are (or should be) selected because they believe in the mission of your organization, so they should also have the desire to support the agency financially.

✎ It will be difficult to ask the public to support your special events if your board members do not attend these events.

✎ Members of your community will contribute more to your organization when they are asked by a volunteer who they know than if they are asked by a paid staff member.

✎ Ultimately, board members have assumed the responsibility for implementing the mission of your agency, and raising funds is a critical component of this responsibility.

✎ Many foundations and other donors will not contribute if they do not see 100 percent board participation.

Inspiration!

donors. You should explain the function of the development office and how the board and staff work together as a team to raise money. This is a good time to introduce board members to the fact that most giving comes from individuals. Remember that if you've recruited in the right way, board members will want to get involved in fundraising.

You should schedule a brainstorming session in which your board members (this works well with the development committee and staff, too) develop a list of people they know who could be potential donors. Don't, however, start them out with a "blank slate." The "Give us fifteen names"

Getting Your Board Enthused About Fundraising

✎ Help board members understand their role in fundraising by including it in their job description and by holding an educational session led by an outside "expert."

✎ Assess your organization's fundraising activities, and make sure board members aren't "nickeled-and-dimed" throughout the year.

✎ Stress the importance of having a development plan that clearly spells out the fundraising role of the board, staff, and volunteers.

✎ Establish a development committee that includes both board and non-board members.

✎ Select a board member who "gets it" about fundraising, and have this individual chair your development committee.

✎ Provide fundraising training for the board in specific areas they feel they need help understanding, i.e. planned giving, capital campaigns, or telephone fundraising.

✎ Ask the board chair and CEO to allow your input into the board recruitment process, so the board will include more people who are willing to be involved in your fundraising program.

Inspiration!

method will almost always result in having board members return a bunch of blank pieces of paper. You need to give them a starting point to spark their ideas. Included in **Appendix F** is a form that can serve as a tool to start ideas rolling. Or, you can provide a list of people who already contribute to or are connected to your organization, and ask board members to discuss each name to determine who knows these people and who is willing to talk to them about making a gift or increasing their current level of giving.

The next step is refining the list into potential major donors, other potential donors and those who need further research to determine their giving ability. You can do this, based on your knowledge of the person's ability, interest and the strength of the linkage with this prospect. The prospects that you think are not major donors can be added to your mailing list to receive newsletters and direct mail, and the ones you are not sure about should be set aside until you do further research to determine their ability, linkage and interest. This research can be done through a number of ways, including electronic searches, further screening meetings, a review of community donor lists, or a combination of all of these methods.

After this process is completed, those prospects that you believe could be major donors should be turned over to the major gift committee, or staff person responsible for major gifts, to plan the next phase in the solicitation strategy. This process will almost always uncover connections that most board members haven't thought about as potential donors. A good facilitator will help the board work through this process. A consultant, a board member, or staff member who has gone through this process is essential. An experienced facilitator will be aware of ethical issues and organizational policies about what can be discussed within this group. Once the calls are assigned, the next step is the solicitation

The Dreaded Board "Training"

Building an effective and enthusiastic board is one of the most critical elements in fundraising. But of course, your board members don't think they need training, they don't have time for it, and they won't listen to what you have to say, anyway.

Uninspired

process, which is discussed in **Chapter 24,** personal solicitation.

If your board members are reluctant to assume their fundraising role, you might start by getting them involved in some "painless" ways of fundraising:

✎ Serve on the development committee to help plan fundraising activities.

✎ Develop and review mailing lists.

✎ Sell tickets for an event.

✎ Serve on an event committee.

✎ Ask their friends and family to contribute to your organization in lieu of birthday, anniversary, or other special occasion gifts.

✎ Ask companies with whom they do business to sponsor an event or take out an ad in a program book for an event.

✎ Sign appeal letters to individuals they personally know.

✎ Participate in a "thank-a-thon" in which they call current donors just to thank them for their gifts, not to ask for money.

Once you've built the board you want, how do you keep the board members? A few hints:

✎ Have a sufficient number of committee members to share the work load. I provide a sample board organization chart is provided in **Appendix G.**

✎ Make sure board and committee meetings are productive.

"Training" is a Four-Letter Word

Avoiding the word "training" is the first essential ingredient. One of my clients used the title *Executive Leadership Institute* for a board "training session." You might try this or a similar title for your "board training." After all, your board members *are* the organization's leaders.

Inspiration!

✎ Assure that meetings start and end on time.

✎ Send agendas and committee reports in advance of the meeting or post them on a "board portal" site.

✎ Have term limits and enforce them to avoid "perpetual" board members and founder's syndrome.

✎ Provide education and training for the board in areas in which they need to be knowledgeable.

Keeping Your Board Enthused

If your organization is overly involved in special events, board members can easily get burned out. Your board members will not be happy if they are expected to sell tickets to their friends and family members for too many special events. Many of them will not be interested in golf, running, dancing, or whatever these events involve. You need to focus on one or two successful events and stress the board members' attendance to show the community that the board supports your organization. You will be more successful in enlisting their participation if you involve board members in planning these events.

Make sure your board members understand the importance of having a development plan that covers all areas of fundraising, from events to major gifts and planned gifts. Your development committee should be deeply involved in formulating this plan and presenting it to your board. It is better to have your board members ask other board members to get involved in fundraising than for staff to be the ones who insist on board involvement.

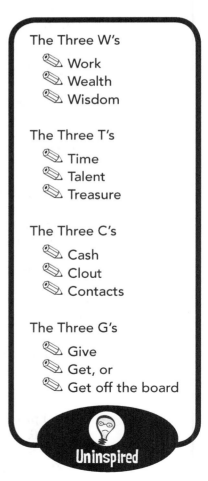

The Three W's

✎ Work
✎ Wealth
✎ Wisdom

The Three T's

✎ Time
✎ Talent
✎ Treasure

The Three C's

✎ Cash
✎ Clout
✎ Contacts

The Three G's

✎ Give
✎ Get, or
✎ Get off the board

Uninspired

You can get your board members excited about fundraising by selecting the one individual on your board who most "gets it" about fundraising and have this individual chair your development committee. This board member's enthusiasm will be contagious and might even spur fundraising competition among board members. You can also try bringing in a consultant to help motivate the board. If your organization cannot afford a consultant, try inviting a board member from a nonprofit whose board has been successful at fundraising to talk to your board about this guest's role in fundraising. Be sure to select this person carefully. You don't want someone who will just brag about this guest's own success, try to shame your board members into fundraising, or get dragged into the morass of a stagnant board. You want someone who will inspire and motivate your board!

The New Three G's

- Gather
- Get Ready
- Grow

Inspiration!

Board education is essential. Timing of this education, however, is a critical element. You should plan some type of board education at every board meeting; even if it is a ten minute presentation on the role of boards in nonprofits, ethical issues for boards, making the case for your organization—you get the idea. For more intense sessions, schedule at a time convenient for most board members—often a Saturday morning or a two-hour session in place of, or before or after, a regular board meeting works well. Once a year, take your board away from the organization for a day-long retreat that includes some educational opportunities, as well as time to plan.

Board educational sessions can be led by staff, but are usually more effective when brought from an outside perspective. Education needs to be ongoing, but should be taken in "chunks" of time and information given. Board members who have never before raised funds can't grasp it all in one sitting. A consultant, a board member from another organization, a video from BoardSource or CharityChannel, or some other resource can often tell your board the things they need to hear in a new light.

Restructuring Your Board

When all else fails, you might need to look seriously at your board and restructure it with people who are willing and able to be involved in fundraising. Some ways to help you restructure your board include:

- ✎ Make certain to include a provision in your board position description that outlines the board member's expected involvement in your fundraising program.

- ✎ Be sure that the governance committee reviews this provision with all prospective new board members and that the prospective board members agree to it *before* being invited to serve on the board.

- ✎ Make sure there are term limits on your board and that they are enforced.

The Most Important Qualification of a Board Member

All board and committee members *must* have a passion for the mission of the organization. If they have that passion, it will be easy for them to help in fundraising. In fact, they will be eager to do it!

Inspiration!

- ✎ If some of your board members refuse to participate in fundraising, do not nominate them for another term when their first term on the board expires.

- ✎ Ask your board chair or the chair of your development committee to speak privately to board members who are not participating in fundraising, and encourage them to become involved.

- ✎ Plan educational sessions on various aspects of fundraising so board members will understand fundraising strategies and feel more comfortable with the process.

Board governance has long been associated with the three W's, the two T's, the three C's and the three G's. I would like to offer something more positive.

The problem with all of these philosophies is, do you look for someone who has (and is willing to give you) all three, or do you look for one or two of these traits in each prospective board member? Ideally, of course, board members would contribute their work, wealth, *and* their wisdom; would happily give you their time, talent, *and* their treasure; would be able to supply cash, clout, *and* be willing to open the doors to their contacts; and would both give *and* get so you don't have to ask them to get off the board. I would like to offer a new way to think about the three G's.

Try looking at this new way of recruiting and retaining enthused, knowledgeable, and active board members who will embrace their fundraising role.

The First G—Gather

Gather your board members together to determine what the board needs in the way of skills, talents, and diversity, and how these attributes can help the organization.

Often bringing in an outside person to do this assessment is useful. Either a paid consultant or perhaps a volunteer from another nonprofit (one with a dynamic, effective board) can help objectively assess your board's performance.

Have board members do a self-assessment of their performance as a whole and as individuals. This assessment should be done on an annual basis.

The Second G—Get Ready

Once the board has assessed its makeup and performance, it will need to develop a plan for filling any gaps.

Your governance committee must be in place year-round to coordinate all the activities involved in board development. The best board member you have should chair this committee.

Educate the entire board on the role and responsibilities of board members and the importance of the board recruitment process. It is in the recruitment process that good boards are created or that terrible boards result!

The Third G—Grow

Once a board profile is complete, a list of potential board members who fill the needs required by the board must be developed. It is critical that every board member understand that board recruitment is never accomplished by just one person on the board, and that all names must be submitted for approval to the full board before they are invited to join the board.

It is also essential that the board position description outlining roles and responsibilities of individual board members are reviewed with each candidate before they are invited to serve on the board.

Provide an exciting, compelling board orientation for new board members as well as an ongoing education program for all board members.

To Summarize

✎ The role of the board in fundraising is critical. However, board members who have not been told that fundraising is part of their responsibility often will not be willing to become involved. You need to have a thoughtful board recruitment process that includes a job description outlining the board's role and responsibility in fundraising. Board nominations should be done through a year-round process involving a board resource committee.

✎ Board giving is important to show your funders that the "family" of your organization has accepted its responsibility for supporting it. An annual board appeal should be given as much thought and preparation as any major gift appeal.

✎ Board members need to have their fear of fundraising removed before they can be effective. There are various ways by which you can train and educate your board members so they will embrace their fundraising role once they understand how easy it is and how much fun it can be.

Chapter 7

Involving Volunteers in Your Fundraising Program

In This Chapter...

✎ What roles can volunteers play in your fundraising?

✎ Where can you find good volunteers?

✎ How do you keep volunteers motivated and involved?

Your organization might already use volunteers in your program activities and/or to help with clerical work, but you should also involve volunteers in your fundraising program. Volunteers can play a critical role in fundraising, working along with board and staff. The key is learning how to recruit the right volunteers for the right job and to provide these volunteers with the tools they need in order to be effective fundraisers.

Volunteers can be some of the best advocates for your organization. Your ability to recruit volunteer fundraisers can help lend credibility among your constituents by showing that community members are enthused about and committed to your organization.

As with donors, volunteers will become involved in your organization for many reasons, including their own family history, religious influence, altruism, wanting to give back, community spirit, investing in their own or someone else's future, or because it is fun. If they do not believe in your mission, however, they will not be effective fundraising volunteers.

Key Concepts for Involving Volunteers as Fundraisers

- Volunteers will only be effective if they truly believe in the mission of your organization.

- Volunteers should be invited to give of their time, talent, and treasure.

- Volunteers must be given meaningful work, not just "busy work."

- Volunteers require staff support in order to be effective.

Inspiration!

What Qualities Should a Volunteer Fundraiser Possess?

- Volunteer fundraisers must have integrity in order to gain the trust of potential donors.

- Volunteer fundraisers should be good listeners.

- Volunteer fundraisers must care about people and be able to relate to your constituents.

- Volunteers who serve in leadership roles must be able to inspire and motivate others to action.

Fundraising Roles for Volunteers

There are lots of ways you can involve volunteers in your fundraising activities. Each of these fundraising methods will be discussed in more detail in future chapters. However, let's start thinking about how volunteers can be effective in each of these areas. Among the activities volunteers can help with are:

- ✎ Special events
- ✎ Direct mail
- ✎ Telephone fundraising
- ✎ Corporate appeals
- ✎ Grant proposals
- ✎ Major gifts appeals
- ✎ Capital and endowment campaigns
- ✎ Planned giving efforts

Keeping Volunteers Involved

- ✎ Clearly communicate your expectations to volunteers.
- ✎ Provide the tools that will enable your volunteers to succeed.
- ✎ Acknowledge that the volunteer role is important to your organization.

Perspiration!

You should involve volunteers in every aspect of your fundraising effort, starting with your annual fund. Having a volunteer chair or co-chair for your annual fund can lend special credibility when approaching donors. The chair of the annual fund will create a special importance for your overall appeal, which might include a corporate appeal, a major gift effort, a phonathon, a direct-mail campaign and/or special events. All of these segments of your annual fund can effectively use volunteers, and each should have its own chair and committee of volunteers.

Development Planning

Volunteers can be helpful with your development planning. The development committee should be intimately involved with setting goals and objectives for the plan as well as exploring strategies to implement the plan. In addition to the development plan, volunteers can help research potential donors. Screening meetings, as described in a later chapter, should involve volunteers who have broad community connections and move in circles that include major philanthropists in your community. You might also find a volunteer who can help with researching foundations and corporations that could be good prospects for grants and contributions.

Developing your case for support can also include volunteers. However, you should not expect a volunteer to write your case for support unless you have a retired development professional as a volunteer or one who works for another nonprofit but can devote the time to write your case, since they might not be able to help with donor solicitation.

Another effective way to involve volunteers is to test your case for support before you translate it into fundraising materials. One of my clients did this very effectively.

The Development Committee

The development committee, along with staff, leads the organization's fundraising program. This committee, however, should not consist solely of board members. Involving volunteers on the committee not only helps you meet your fundraising goals but also provides a great training ground for prospective board members.

Finding members of committees is often easier than finding board members. Many people who are not ready to accept the fiduciary responsibilities of serving on your board might want to become involved with your organization in other capacities. You should try to recruit development committee members who are bankers, financial planners, attorneys, media representatives, and entrepreneurs. It will also be helpful to look for people who have served on boards or development committees of other organizations, because they will be experienced in fundraising.

Recruiting a development professional from another institution, provided that the organization is not a direct competitor of yours, might prove helpful. Development professionals serving as volunteers will often choose not to help actively solicit donors because it could be a real or perceived conflict of interest. However, they are often willing to assist in planning, writing, or identifying donors. For example, a development officer from a university could be a good individual to add to the fundraising committee of a human service agency whose programs and donors will not be in competition with the university.

So, who should you recruit to serve on *your* development committee? The chart provided in **Appendix H** gives you one typical structure for a development committee, but each organization will have different needs.

A Case Study

A human service organization that provided several needed community programs had just written its very first case for support and was not sure if it had done an effective job of explaining its programs and its need for support. The chair of the development committee suggested it hold a focus group and helped develop a list of people to invite to the focus group. Some were donors to the organization but most were not. Invitations made it clear that they would not be asked for a contribution. The case was then translated into a PowerPoint presentation.

Volunteers were invited to the organization for a catered lunch buffet. After everyone had been greeted, introduced, and invited to start their lunch, the executive director thanked them for coming, explained why they were holding the focus group, and assured the volunteers that they were not going to be solicited for a donation. The chair of the development committee then went through the PowerPoint presentation of the case and then asked for input from the group. He asked questions such as:

✎ What programs of ours were you aware of before coming to this meeting?

✎ Have you learned more about the organization after participating in this presentation?

✎ What programs that we provide do you think are especially vital to our community?

✎ Are there areas we should emphasize more, or less, in our case statement?

✎ Are there questions you have about our organization that were not answered in the case as presented?

✎ After hearing this case would you, if asked, contribute to our organization?

The organization received some great input and was able to strengthen its case before spending the time and money to translate it into printed materials.

Pure Genius!

Where do you find volunteers for your development committee?

Try the following steps to build your development committee:

✎ Determine how large you want your committee to be and what types of people you need on the committee (event planners, planned giving experts, philanthropists, etc.).

✎ Always develop a position description before talking to volunteers about serving. A sample development committee position description is provided in **Appendix I.**

✎ Decide who is going to ask these people to serve on the committee.

✎ Develop a volunteer recruitment packet that contains your case for support, your development plan (if you have one), a list of board members, the development committee position description, a list of meeting dates, and any other pertinent information about your organization. I provide a list of what should be in the packet in **Appendix J.**

✎ Start the recruitment process by determining who is the person on your board who most "gets it" about fundraising and ask that board member to chair the development committee.

✎ Ask you board members for suggestions, particularly members of the nominating or governance committee who might have some names of people who were suggested as board members but for one reason or another were not invited onto the board. Be sure the reason they were not invited is not that they were deemed "unworthy" of a board position. If they are not good potential board members they are probably not good potential development committee members, either. However, many of the names your committee will provide might not have been invited onto the board for other reasons and would possibly be good candidates for the development committee.

✎ Ask your staff for suggestions. Often they know people who are interested in your program and meet the requirements you've outlined in the position description for development committee members.

✎ Review your donor list and make sure you have donors on the development committee, preferably major donors.

✎ Talk to those who already volunteer for your organization in other ways, perhaps at special events or other fundraising activities. Pick the best volunteers to serve on your development committee.

✎ Use your networks through groups such as the Chamber of Commerce, leadership programs, and service and professional clubs to which you belong.

Involving Volunteers in Your Special Events

Special events are especially volunteer intensive. Most successful events have a committee of a dozen or more volunteer leaders who are responsible for planning and implementing the event along with additional volunteers who work on specific tasks for the event. Volunteers usually serve in a variety of capacities on special event committees, such as handling publicity for the event, making physical arrangements such as booking locations, arranging for entertainment if that will be part of the event, and securing sponsors. As with any type of fundraising effort, leadership is critical to success. A special event committee chair can make or break the event.

Involving Volunteers in the Grants Process

Staff members usually prepare grant proposals, except in very small organizations that have no staff. Volunteers might then step in to fill this role. However, proposals to foundations and corporations still need that personal touch. One way to give volunteers a meaningful part in your grant fundraising is to review the list of potential grant funders with your development committee and/or your board members to determine if they have any personal contacts with foundation trustees. You should develop a list of the foundations you plan to approach with the trustees of the foundations and other information about the foundation (a form to help with this process is included in **Appendix M**). Asking volunteers to review this list and identify any trustees with whom they have a personal contact will help you develop a personalized appeal. Volunteers can also be invited to attend meetings with potential funders to help add credibility to your organization and speak to the funders from the point of view of a volunteer

Getting it Wrong is Costly!

One of the organizations I supported as a member has always approached me by direct mail. When I achieved ACFRE status, I sent the organization a change of name to read, "Linda Lysakowski, ACFRE." However, when adding the ACFRE designation it apparently thought "ACFRE" was part of my last name and changed my last name to "Lysakowskiacfre." This took up so much space my first name became "Da." So I am now "Da Lysakowskiacfre" to this agency. Guess what? I haven't sent it any money since it started addressing me incorrectly! If the agency had a volunteer committee reviewing its mailing list, perhaps someone would have spotted this error and corrected it, thus retaining me as a donor.

Uninspired

who has committed time and money to the organization.

Involving Volunteers in Your Direct-Mail Appeal

You might currently utilize volunteers to stuff mailings. You will often find that groups such as senior or youth groups are happy for an activity that helps them meet their service requirements or fill time. But volunteers can also be used in other, more meaningful, ways in your direct-mail appeal. Your donors will respond much better to a letter "written" by the parent of a child killed by a drunk driver, a student on a scholarship, or a recovering addict than they are likely to respond to a letter from the staff or board chair of your organization. Staff members, however, should write the letter for the volunteer, inviting the signer's input to personalize it.

Another way you can involve volunteers effectively is to hold a focus group with potential donors and have attendees provide input into your direct-mail package as it is being developed. Ask volunteers how they would respond to the carrier (outside) envelope, the letter and any enclosures that will be included in the package. Volunteers also can be extremely helpful in expanding and correcting your mailing list. Many times direct-mail appeals are not successful because the mailing list is not "clean." A misspelled name, an envelope addressed to a deceased or divorced spouse, or addressing someone as Mr. and Mrs. John Jones when the wife might use her own name can be very offensive for some people. Assembling a group of volunteers who have good insight on your community and having them review your list is an effective way to clean up your list.

Involving Volunteers in Your Telephone Fundraising

Volunteers can be very effective in your phonathon. It is important to remember, however, that you need to provide training for these volunteers. Before the training you will need to prepare talking points and other materials they will need to be successful. Your volunteers should identify themselves right away as volunteers, since many people will respond well to volunteers they know are giving of their own time, talent, and treasure. Volunteers can also be invited to participate in thank-a-thons in which they call donors to thank them for their gift, not to ask for money. You might want to introduce this concept to your board members as an introduction to fundraising. You might even try asking recipients of your organization's services to volunteer for your phonathon or thank-a-thon. Who better to tell the story of why your organization is so vital to the community?

Involving Volunteers in Your Corporate/Business Appeal

Your corporate/business appeals will be far more effective if you involve a team of volunteers to make visits to business owners or managers. An annual corporate appeal, done through face-to-face, personal solicitations is an area that many nonprofits have tried and found to be the most successful way to approach businesses. Volunteers enable your organization to reach many business leaders that you might have found it impossible to meet in person. These volunteers will be calling on someone with whom they have a personal and/or a business relationship. We talk more about this in the Chapter 11, Raising Money from Businesses.

Involving Volunteers in Soliciting Major Gifts

While there are numerous roles volunteers can play in the annual fundraising program, perhaps none is more critical than the role of identifying, cultivating, and soliciting major donors. For many donors, the person who asks them to contribute is one of the most important factors in determining the financial commitment they will make. Most people like to be asked by someone they know. A colleague or friend, sometimes even a relative, usually has much more success than a staff member.

Why Volunteers Make Good Fundraisers

✎ They are not getting paid to do it, so they are not under pressure to perform.

✎ They have a real commitment to the mission of your organization.

✎ They have already made a contribution themselves, ideally at the level at which they are asking the prospective donor to contribute.

✎ They care enough that they are taking time to participate in your fundraising program.

✎ They generally have strong relationships with potential donors.

Inspiration!

Involving Volunteers in Planned Giving Efforts

While planned giving is often thought of as a staff or consultant's role because of the specialized knowledge involved, volunteers can be instrumental in a variety of ways with your planned giving efforts. A committee of volunteer professional advisors can be effective in teaching your staff about various planned giving instruments, developing effective promotional materials for planned giving, making connections for your organization with potential donors, and conducting planned giving seminars.

Volunteers who have already made a planned gift themselves are the best spokespersons for your organization's planned giving program. Once a person has made a planned gift to your organization, you should invite the donor to help identify other potential donors and to introduce these donors to your organization. Volunteers can also be asked to give testimonials or write an article for your newsletter about why they made planned gifts to your organization.

Why Volunteers Are Effective at Making the Ask

One of the reasons volunteers are so good at asking for money is simply that they *are* volunteers. They are not viewed as a professional solicitor whose job depends on raising money or as a "hired gun" that might not have the best interest of the donor in mind. They will come across as persons with a genuine interest in the mission of the organization, because they have already supported this mission with contributions. The main reason volunteers can be more effective than staff is that they are usually soliciting their peers and approaching people to give at a level at which they themselves have already given.

Volunteers play a critical role in fundraising. They bring sincerity and commitment to the table. They usually have connections that often would not be available to you as a staff member. Their special expertise and leadership qualities lend credibility to your organization.

Finding Volunteer Fundraisers

If you are already involving volunteers in areas such as program or administration, you might want to begin with those volunteers who already have demonstrated a commitment to your organization. You can bring these volunteers together for a meeting to invite them to consider taking on new responsibilities in the form of fundraising. If your organization has involved volunteers in minor fundraising roles such as helping at special events or stuffing envelopes, you can ask these volunteers if they have an interest in becoming involved at a deeper

Volunteer Recruitment Steps

✎ Develop a list of the volunteers you need.

✎ Develop a list of potential volunteers.

✎ Find the right person to ask each prospective volunteer.

✎ Prepare a volunteer recruitment packet that includes the position description for the volunteer task you are asking them to accept.

✎ Meet face-to-face with prospective volunteers to discuss their volunteer commitment.

✎ Welcome and orient volunteers to your organization.

✎ Provide education and support for all volunteers, as needed.

✎ Manage the volunteer program, making sure you assign volunteers to roles appropriate for their time and talent.

✎ Acknowledge and recognize volunteers appropriately.

Perspiration!

level, such as soliciting prospective donors through your phone appeal, corporate appeal, or major-gift appeal.

If you have never involved volunteers at all, a good place to start is with those who have already shown an interest in your organization or have ties to it. Alumni are found in many organizations, not just educational institutions. Perhaps your nonprofit has individuals who have participated in a rehabilitation program, taken an art class or donated blood. These are your organization's "alumni." Do not overlook them. They already know your organization and are often very committed to it.

> Even animals can be "alumni." I once worked with a dog rescue group that was engaged in a capital campaign. We decided to run a phonathon as part of the campaign. No, the dogs didn't make phone calls, although the honorary chair's adopted dog did include her paw print on the signature line of the letter that went out to potential donors. But we asked people who had adopted a dog a certain year to call other "parents of alumni" (those who had also adopted a dog in that year) and ask for their gifts to the campaign. Our canine "alumni" were very successful in raising money for this campaign!

Pure Genius!

Volunteers can also be found through local businesses and service or professional organizations, many of which have formal volunteer programs. Also, your board, staff and development committee can often help recruit volunteers for various fundraising roles. Local chambers of commerce are great ways to connect with business persons and entrepreneurs who are looking for opportunities to become more involved in their communities. Many communities also have leadership programs in which community business leaders enroll to learn more about the nonprofit world with the goal of serving on the board of a nonprofit organization. These programs can be a great source of volunteers. You also need to join the "rubber chicken circuit," speaking at meetings of local service and professional associations whose members might be able to volunteer as a group or individually. Check to see if your community has a volunteer center that matches volunteers with organizations and performs much of the screening

Wooing a Prospective Volunteer? Come Prepared!

I was working as director of development in a nonprofit organization. While preparing for our first annual corporate appeal, a new corporate leader moved into town, accepting a position as CEO of one of the area's leading companies. One of my board members suggested I talk to this gentleman about becoming involved with our corporate appeal. I called and was able to schedule an appointment with him. My next step was to put together a volunteer recruitment packet that included a job description, timeline for the corporate appeal, our case for support, a list of other business leaders who had already agreed to serve on our corporate appeal team, a list of our board members, and some additional information about the organization. When I met with this gentleman in his office, he indicated he only had about thirty minutes for the meeting, so after introducing myself and telling him a little about our organization, I produced the volunteer recruitment packet I had prepared for him and explained that we would like him to serve as a team leader in our corporate appeal. I suggested that this would be a great way for him to get to know some of the other corporate leaders in town. I reviewed each piece of the volunteer recruitment packet with him, answering any questions he had. The result: He agreed to serve as a team leader. Before I left his office, however, he said he wanted to tell me why he agreed. "I've been in town all of two weeks, and at least fifteen nonprofit leaders have contacted me to contribute to their cause, serve on their board, or somehow get involved with their organization. But you are the first one who came to see me so well prepared. I know exactly what you expect of me, how much of my time it will take, what the benefits to me and my company will be, and how much of a financial commitment you expect from me. So you are the only one I said 'yes' to." He was an excellent team leader. The following year he chaired our corporate appeal, the next year he was appointed to our board of directors, and soon was chair of our board. All because I went to that first meeting prepared to make the best use of his limited time, to inform him about our expectations, and to listen to his expectation of our organization.

Pure Genius!

of volunteers. This can be another source of volunteers, although the best fundraising volunteers will be those whom you personally recruit and who have a relationship with your organization.

Past donors are an especially good source of volunteers. If they already have supported your organization, it will be easy for them to invite others to join them in this investment. A group of past donors could be invited to a special luncheon at which volunteer opportunities are presented.

Another way to find volunteers is to involve your staff and board members in the identification process. Once you establish volunteer needs and determine the qualities needed to fill each of these volunteer roles, you can have board and staff members brainstorm at a meeting to identify a list of potential volunteers who might have the qualities to fill these roles. Then develop a plan to select those who best meet the needs of your organization and begin to recruit these volunteers.

Recruiting Volunteers

Staff, board or other volunteers can recruit volunteers. Asking volunteers to help you find people such as themselves who share an interest in your mission is the best way for you to recruit additional volunteers.

Possible Sources of Volunteers

✎ Donors

✎ Other volunteers

✎ Clients or users of services

✎ Service clubs—Rotary, Lions, Sertoma, Kiwanis, etc.

✎ Religious institutions

✎ Chambers of commerce

✎ Board members' suggestions

✎ Development committee suggestions

✎ Website visitors

✎ Leadership programs

✎ Volunteer centers

✎ Newsletter readers

✎ Staff contacts

✎ Businesses

✎ Senior citizen centers

✎ Universities

Volunteer position descriptions should include:

✎ Overall responsibilities of volunteers.

✎ Specific tasks to be achieved by this volunteer position.

✎ Experience required or desired.

✎ Supervision provided to the volunteer.

✎ Training provided for this volunteer function.

✎ Time commitment expected, including training time.

✎ Time frame for the event or appeal including starting date, ending dates and meeting dates.

To Summarize

✎ Volunteers can be an invaluable resource for your development program. There are many roles for volunteers in your fundraising program, including planning, research, and the important roles of identifying, cultivating, and soliciting donors.

✎ There are many sources to find volunteers, but the best volunteers will be those who already have a relationship with your organization.

✎ Volunteers need training, education, and support in order to be successful. Recognition of volunteers is essential to keeping them motivated and involved.

Chapter 8

Staffing the Development Office

In This Chapter...

✎ How much staff do we need in our development office?

✎ What is the role of the CEO in fundraising?

✎ Who else in our organization should we involve in our fundraising activities?

Staffing in a nonprofit organization can run the gamut from a part-time development person or a staff person who raises funds, in addition to other duties within the organization, such as public relations or marketing, to a staff of fifty persons or more in a large university. Most organizations need at least one full-time development staff member and some support staff members to assist with the development program.

An organization that does not have at least one full-time staff person will probably not be as successful in its fundraising efforts as one that has staff devoted solely to this function. A study conducted by the California Foundation for Community Colleges shows that among the community colleges studied, those with departments of seven people raise five times as much money per staff person as those with two or fewer staff members in their development programs. An investment in the development office is critical if your organization wants to have an effective development program. The chapter on infrastructure discusses this investment in more detail. For now, though, let's talk about the various roles of the development office and the types of positions that are found in the development office. The number of people you have in your development office will mostly likely depend on the budget of your organization, how much money you need to raise through development efforts, the number of constituents and donors you have, and the amount of time needed to fill the typical functions of a development office.

> ## Size Matters
>
> An interesting study by the Foundation for California Community Colleges showed that a development staff of five or more provides greater efficiency and results, with an even greater efficiency at higher staffing and budget levels. This study cites that the larger development office (seven or more staff) typically raises $1 million a year per staff member, while smaller ones (two or fewer staff persons) raise less than $200,000 per staff member. In order to allow for maximum growth of the development program, the organization must provide the support needed by the development staff.

Development Staff Roles

The Chief Development Officer

The title of the chief development officer (or "CDO") will vary with different organizations. Universities, colleges, and other larger institutions often use the term "institutional advancement," and often have the title of "vice president" for their chief development officer. "Director of development" or "development director" is more common in other types of agencies. Some organizations use the term, "resource development" or "fund

Functions of the Development Office

✎ Researching potential donors

✎ Preparing and implementing the development plan

✎ Directing the efforts of volunteers in the development area

✎ Developing strategies for identifying, cultivating and soliciting donors

✎ Providing stewardship for donors

✎ Developing appropriate recognition strategies

✎ Coordinating all the fundraising activities of the organization

✎ Working with the board and development committee to implement the development plan

✎ Educating your organization's leadership about ethical and legal issues relating to fundraising

✎ Identifying areas of need to be funded and developing a case for support that addresses these needs

✎ Developing appropriate campaign materials to be used for various campaigns and appeals

✎ Preparing the development office budget

The development office often is also responsible for public relations and marketing.

Perspiration!

development" to make it clear that it is a fundraising position. You should use a title that will convey to the public and the internal organization that this is an important position, and that the chief development officer is a member of the management team. If you work for a small organization as a CDO, you will be responsible for all of the functions mentioned earlier. If you are in a larger office, you will direct the efforts of your staff to ensure that these functions are carried out in an ethical and professional manner. I provide a sample job description for a director of development in **Appendix K,** and in **Appendix L** I provide organization charts for both large and small development shops.

Special Events Coordinator/Manager/Director

If your organization runs more than one or two events per year, you might want to hire a special-event manager, particularly if these are large, labor-intense events. What should you look for in a special event manager? Some people just love throwing parties, but there is a lot more involved in running special events than being present at the event itself, including seeking sponsorships, managing the calendar, preparing the budget, and recruiting and working with volunteers. You might have a volunteer who has chaired one of your successful special events who could be a good choice for this position. Because special events can be so labor intensive and draining, staff members who start in this position often seek to move into more integrated fundraising roles where they have an opportunity to work on various fundraising projects in addition to events, so you could find yourself needing to fill this position frequently.

Staff Writer

Plenty of writing is needed in the development office—the development plan, the case for support, grant proposals, direct-mail letters and phonathon scripts. If you are in a one person shop, you will probably be doing all of this yourself. As your program grows, however, you might have a need to hire a grant proposal writer and/or someone who can write a good case for support as well as other fundraising materials developed from the case. You might want to seek someone who has worked in another development office and has done a lot of its writing, or find a journalism major or someone who has worked in the media to fill this position. In a small office, this work is often outsourced to an outside contractor.

Researcher

Many larger organizations have a full-time or at least a part-time researcher, particularly if they have built a major-gifts program. You will want to look for someone with technical skills, good logic and persistence for this development position. Universities and other large organizations generally have a whole department of researchers. Again, in smaller organizations this task usually falls under the chief development officer's duties or might be outsourced or possibly even assigned to a reliable volunteer.

Director of Annual Giving

If you are in a medium sized organization, you might need to hire one person to manage all the annual fund programs. In larger organizations you could need several people to manage each one of the aspects of the annual fund including the direct-mail program, a telephone program and Internet fundraising. While some people think that the annual fund is boring and repetitious, it is the key to developing major donors. A good annual-fund director can help grow the development program significantly. An "annual fund generalist" who works in all aspects of the annual fund might find that one area is particularly appealing and decide to focus even more narrowly on direct mail, for example. As with special events, this is often a position that needs to be filled frequently as development professionals move into other areas.

Director of Corporate Giving

If you have a significant source of funding coming from businesses and corporations or want to expand your reach into these areas you might look for someone just to manage this aspect of your development program. This area of fundraising might include drafting proposals for corporate foundations or organizing an annual business appeal. Many individuals, particularly those who came into the fundraising profession from the corporate world, will find corporate giving challenging and rewarding. Someone from a corporate background might also have good contacts that can prove very valuable to your organization. Some organizations such as large universities have a director of corporate/foundation giving, but these two functions are very different and usually required a different skill set, so you might need a separate director of foundation giving.

Major Gifts

Major gifts are generally defined as a gift at a level that requires special treatment, such as personal solicitation, special recognition, etc. Major gifts levels are defined differently by each organization. In a university or large nonprofit, a major gift could be $100,000 or even $1 million, and in some smaller organizations, a major gift might be $500 or even $100.

definition

Major Gifts Officer

As you grow your development program you will probably need someone who has experience in the major gifts area and who has a track record of success. Note that major gifts are defined very differently for each organization, but in any case, the major gift officer should enjoy meeting face-to-face with individual donors. The person filling this role generally has made a career move into major gifts after years in the development field and experience in closing major gifts. However, your organization could have someone in entry level positions striving to learn as much as possible about major gifts fundraising in order to move into this area. If this person shows potential to deal with major donors, you could be able to fill this position internally. Or you might try recruiting a major-gifts officer from another organization. If you are looking outside the profession for a major-gifts officer, you might try approaching financial planners, attorneys and bankers, who often find this career path attractive, particularly if they have dealt with high income clients in a former career. These professionals will need some education and training in fundraising but will generally have the skill sets and personality traits needed for major gift fundraising.

Director of Planned Giving

Finding someone with experience and expertise in planned giving is usually not easy but if your development office wants to expand this area you need to think about filling this position. If you cannot find someone with specific development experience, there are other professionals who often can easily transition into a planned giving position. This is a career path often chosen by attorneys, financial planners or bankers who want to leave the for-profit world and work in development. While you might not be able to pay at a level to which they are accustomed in a high paying career in law or the financial world, planned giving is generally one of the highest paid positions in the profession of fundraising. Many of these professionals find that, although there is a significant cut in salary compared to the typical earning level of attorneys and financial planners, they enjoy the nonprofit world because of a passion for the mission or just because they want to leave the corporate world behind them. Many attorneys and bankers who have left the corporate world report that they are much happier in the nonprofit community where they feel they are really making a difference.

Planned Giving

The integration of sound personal, financial, and estate planning concepts with the individual donor's plans for lifetime or testamentary giving.

Campaign Specialist/Director/Manager

If your organization is a large one, such as a university, you could be in a campaign mode more often than not, and might need to engage a campaign specialist. Or, if this is a once-in-a-lifetime or very rare occurrence in your organization you will most likely need to hire temporary staff to manage your capital campaign. There are many people who really enjoy the fast-paced world of capital campaigns. You should be able to find someone with experience in capital campaigns in other organizations or even persuade someone to move into your organization from a consulting career. Most organizations embarking on a capital campaign usually involve a consultant even if they have experienced staff people.

Capital Campaign

A campaign to raise substantial funds for a nonprofit organization to finance major building projects, to supplement endowment funds and to meet other needs demanding extensive outlays of capital.

The need for these positions will vary from organization to organization, and the position titles will vary as well. You might opt for variations of any or all of the above positions. The organization charts that you found in **Appendix L** showing the development functions and how they might be distributed in different sized organizations can help. Of course you will need to develop an appropriate organizational structure for *your* development office based on *your* size and *your* needs.

Support Staff

In order to be effective, the chief development officer needs to spend time identifying, cultivating and soliciting the top donors, and should not be spending too much time writing grants, planning events, doing research and tracking donor records. How much staff is needed to support the chief development officer? The answer will depend in part on the size of your organization, the scope of the job, and the dollar goals that have been established for your development program. No matter what the size of your development office, your organization needs to budget for a support staff person to handle the donor database and possibly a second staff person for clerical duties. Very large organizations could have a large number of support staff to support the various professional staff persons. Often small organizations do not see the value of support staff and expect the chief development officer to handle all the clerical work. Looking for an experienced development person to run the program, who also has experience in donor database systems, is a huge mistake. Chief development officers who spend all their time entering data into the system and doing donor research will not have time to build relationships with donors, which is their primary function.

A good database manager is one of the most critical positions of a well-run development office. This position includes preparing development office reports, and sometimes research as well as stewardship of donor records. Individuals interested in technology and the Internet, and who have great organization skills, might be well suited for this position. This is not a task that can be assigned to a support staff person that does not understand development and does not have the skills to make good judgment calls or understand the importance of accuracy in donor records. Hiring a good support staff person, and training that person in the donor database system, and fundraising in general, can assure that the CDO will have time to fill the important functions of identifying, cultivating and soliciting donors.

How We Introduced the Development Director to the Staff

One organization hired its first development director and was wondering how to explain to the rest of its staff what the development officer's role was within the organization. As its consultant, I developed an idea: a Time, Talent and Treasure Hunt. We found a cardboard "treasure chest" and filled it with beads and trinkets, including gold-foil-wrapped candies. Among the "treasures" in the treasure chest were some gift certificates for restaurants, spas, movies, etc. We arranged for presentations at each of the three departmental staff meetings. At these meetings, the development director explained her role in the organization and how she would be raising money for their programs. Then the chair of the development committee told staff members that the development office needed their help. We distributed cards to each staff person with options for them to list gifts of time, talent and treasure they might be able to contribute. Everyone who entered a card in the drawing was eligible for the prizes in the treasure chest. The development office came away from these meetings with a list of potential donors, offers from staff to provide gifts in kind that fit within their talents (such as an offer to do calligraphy on the dinner dance invitations), and more. This was a good start towards cementing relationships between the development office and the rest of the staff, and helping convey the importance of fundraising as "everybody's business."

Pure Genius!

Role of the Executive Director in Fundraising

You should also be certain that your executive director is involved in fundraising. While executive directors are responsible for managing the organization and assuring that it is fulfilling its mission, it is equally important that the CEO spend sufficient time on fundraising. Leadership of the organization must feel comfortable with fundraising. The executive director is the "face" of the organization and most CEOs of businesses and foundations will expect to meet with the CEO of the nonprofit. The CDO should work closely with the executive director to assure the most efficient and effective use of the executive director's time.

The Role of Other Staff Members in Fundraising

Others in your organization also can play a role in development. For example:

- Program people can help with the grant writing process.

- The CFO can be helpful in budgeting for the development office and assuring good stewardship of donor's contributions.

- Program staff members often have contact with potential major donors.

- The receptionist who greets people can set the tone for building a donor's confidence in your organization.

- The public relations or marketing staff can be helpful in preparing fundraising materials.

- Everyone in your organization can play a role in fundraising.

In other words, fundraising is everybody's business. Be sure that the development office has good relations with everyone in the organization and that all employees understand what the development office is all about.

To Summarize

- Fundraising is everybody's business. Involvement of the executive leadership of your organization is critical to a successful fundraising program. Make sure your executive director and your board understand the importance of fundraising as a requirement of the position as leader of your organization.

- As your development office grows, there are many specialty areas that can either be staff positions, or outsourced to consultants. One of the most important things to remember is that your development office needs support staff, including a person to maintain your donor database, which is the gold mine of your office. After all, the database is where all the information about your most precious asset—your donors—is stored.

Where Do We Find the Money?

S o now that you know who raises money and why, the next question is where do you find the money? Many people entering the fundraising arena for the first time think that the solution is grant writing.

In fact, as I write this I just received a "robo-call" telling me there are billions of dollars in grant money available for small businesses. Yeah, right! There is indeed a lot of money available for nonprofits and even for-profit companies from government agencies. A significant amount of money is also given to nonprofits by private foundations. However, looking at the following chart, you can see that only a small portion of the funding received by United States nonprofits comes from foundations. While this chart does not include government funding but rather deals with philanthropic dollars, these facts are often startling to the novice fundraiser.

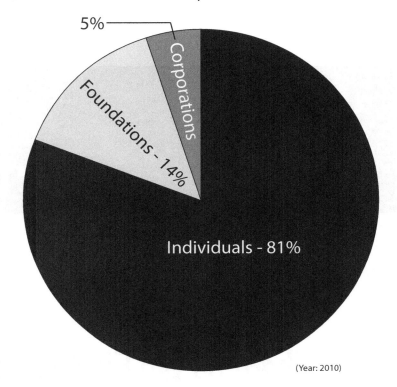

Contributions $290.89 Billion

5%

Corporations

Foundations - 14%

Individuals - 81%

(Year: 2010)

The amount of money given by businesses to fund nonprofit programs is even less than that of foundations. The bulk of the money comes from individuals.

I am not saying to avoid looking for grants, or to avoid seeking donations from businesses and corporations. What I am saying is that you need a well-balanced approach to fundraising. And that your funding streams must be diverse in order to prevent a major tragedy when one funding source dries up. In the following chapters I will discuss the various sources of funding, and I highly recommend that you consider *all* of these ways when preparing your development plan.

Chapter 9

Raising Money from Individuals

Individuals provide most of the contributions to charity in the United States. There are many ways to raise money from individuals, including phonathons, direct mail, Internet fundraising, and major gifts. Each of these is described in the chapters on methods of fundraising. But the first step is identifying potential individual donors and understanding what motivates them to give.

It has often been said that people give for one of two reasons—to change lives or to save lives. And, of course, many people give for the obvious reason—because they were asked. But there are many factors that affect a person's decision to support certain charities and their choice to not support others.

Inspiration: Psychology of Philanthropy (Why People Give)

Following is a list of motivating factors called the "psychology of philanthropy." This list cites some of the popular reasons people give to charitable organizations. Donors give for the following reasons:

- Moral obligation to help
- Personal satisfaction of helping others
- To remove guilt for not giving
- To maintain or improve social status, prestige, respect, or acclaim
- In response to peer pressure
- Out of compassion or empathy
- Personal identification with cause or benefactor
- Self-interest
- Religious influence
- The need to be needed
- Substitution for active participation in good works
- Support for the mission and purpose of the organization
- Personal relationship with the organization
- Appreciation for the organization's mission
- To feel the "glow of emotional virtue"
- As evidence of one's success and ability to give
- To express anger
- To express love
- To express hope (for a cure)

✎ To end fear (of fire, sickness, hell, etc.)

✎ Out of the cause's appeal (cause célèbre)

✎ To be remembered

✎ To gain recognition or attention

✎ To join a worthwhile group, sense of belonging

✎ To preserve the species

✎ To gain immortality

✎ For psychic self-satisfaction

✎ For vicarious self-actualization

✎ Giving to oneself (benefactor seen as an extension of one's self)

✎ Desire to provide public goods one might use themselves

✎ Desire to provide public goods used by others

✎ Desire to provide public goods so others do not try to use one's own goods

✎ Satisfaction derived from the goods themselves

✎ Satisfaction derived for bringing about the result

✎ To fulfill a condition for employment

✎ In response to leadership from respected peers

✎ Desire to be an agent for "public good"

✎ Satisfaction received from seeing others satisfied

✎ Tax benefits

There is a lot written today about the motivation of donors. Some people give because they have been influenced by family attitudes or church doctrine about philanthropy. Some give because of purely altruistic reasons, some because they want to give back, and some because they want their community to be a better place to live. Some even give out of fear or guilt, or because of peer pressure, or the desire to gain status among their peers. There are many reasons people give and many reasons they give to a particular organization.

Most people support organizations about whose mission they feel passionate. Some are dedicated to improving the health and well-being of those less fortunate. Some care about the arts, others about the environment, others about education, and the list goes on. Your key to success is finding the donors who care about your organization and the people you serve.

So, how do you find and reach those donors? Your board, staff, and volunteers must focus their energies on building lasting relationships with major donor prospects. That is why the fundraising process is called "development."

There are several steps to raising major gifts from individuals:

✎ Identifying major donor prospects

✎ Cultivating these prospects

✎ Recruiting the major gifts team

✎ Training the team

✎ Scheduling the appointments

✎ Visiting the prospects

✎ Asking for the gift

The last five items will be discussed in **Chapter 24,** Personal Solicitation, but first let's talk about how you build a list of potential individual donors and how you cultivate relationships with these prospects.

Identifying Major Donor Prospects

You should always start with your board members. Even if you think they are not major donor prospects themselves, you might be surprised at the connections your board has to potential major donors. You can find out just how large their sphere of influence is by starting with a brainstorming session.

Brainstorming is best done in the form of a screening and rating session. There are basically three ways to conduct screening for major donor prospects. For all three methods the screening committee could include:

- Board members

- Development staff

- Executive director

- Development committee members

- Members of your major gifts committee and/or planned giving committee

- Organization volunteers with broad community connections

Select your committee members very carefully and make them aware that the information shared in these meetings is *very confidential.* If your board or committee volunteers have never done screening before, explain to them that this method is used routinely in most organizations and is the best way to determine the key ingredients of a major gift—Linkage, Ability and Interest (the LAI Principle). If you are working with a consultant, the consultant will generally lead the screening meeting. If you do not have a consultant, be sure that the meeting is led by an experienced group facilitator. It will be very important to keep the group on task and explain the methodology and reasons behind the screening meeting to those who are not familiar with the process.

It is also crucial to start with a preliminary list. It is often hard to get a brainstorming session started with a blank slate. Prepare a list of the top 10 percent of donors to your organization or other prospects that you feel might have the potential to make a major gift. List the giving history of these people, with their largest gift and most recent gift. Provide a column for each of the key ingredients—Linkages, Ability and Interest. Be sure to mark the sheets "Highly Confidential." Gifts that have been made anonymously should not be listed.

Now to the three methods:

1. *The Open Screening Session:* Invite the group members to assemble in a quiet room and open the discussion with a brief explanation of the process, its importance to your organization and why they were selected to help with this task. Then distribute the lists and discuss each name on the list, attempting to determine the best linkage—who knows this person best or would be the best person to make the ask. There will often be several linkages and the task of this group is to determine the best solicitation team. Next, try to determine ability—what *could* this person give to the organization if so motivated. Without revealing confidential information, the screening committee members often can estimate the person's net worth and/or income. Then try to determine interest—does this person have knowledge of your organization, is this a cause they are known to support? Is there a specific program of your organization or part of your project that you think would interest them? As each name is discussed, complete the form with the linkages, ability, and interest named. The advantage of this method is that there is discussion and consensus; the disadvantage is that some people feel uncomfortable discussing prospects.

2. *The Closed Session:* This method is very similar to the first, except that instead of discussing each prospect among the group, participants in the session are asked to complete the answers to the Linkage, Ability and Interest sections to the best of their own knowledge. Each person works independently, without discussion among the group. Lists are then collected and the person in charge reviews the lists and determines the consensus of opinion. The advantage of this method is that people might feel freer to comment on prospects if they are doing it confidentially; the disadvantage is that once the lists are collected (each screener should mark the screener's name on the list before turning it in) there is a lot of guesswork and perhaps follow-up to clarify what a screener has written. Without the open discussion, it is sometimes difficult to figure out why one person thought this prospect had the ability to give $1 million and another suggested $10,000.

3. *The Private Screening Session:* This method is similar to the first, except that it is held one-on-one with a staff member and a screening

committee member. The list is reviewed with screening committee members, one at a time, in the privacy of their office or home. The advantages of this method are that it is easier to schedule people at their convenience than getting them all together in one room, and the open discussion takes place at least between the staff and the screening committee member. The disadvantages are that it takes a lot more staff time to meet with screening committee members individually and, again, the lack of open discussion might require follow-up to clarify major differences of opinion.

In all three methods, you should encourage screeners to add their own names to the list. Seeing the list will often jog people to think of other potential donors for your organization.

Whichever method you use, you will most likely uncover some hidden "stars" among your current donors and uncover new prospects along the way.

Cultivating Donors

You should not solicit major gifts from those who are not familiar with both your organization and the volunteer or staff member inviting them to invest in your organization. In some cases, it might take months or even years to cultivate a prospective donor before asking for a major gift.

There are basically two ways to cultivate donors—through cultivation activities and through cultivation events. Cultivation activities can run the gamut from sending a mailing to meeting with the donors in their home.

Cultivation mailings such as program updates, newsletters, annual reports, and surveys are one way to build relationships with your donors. Individuals who care about your organization want to hear from you about your program success and about how their donations have helped the people you serve—and not just when you are asking for money. They want to know what your organization is doing, how it is helping the community, and perhaps even how they can become involved as a volunteer. Donors want, more than anything, to know how you have used the money they contributed or how you will use the money they are being asked to contribute.

How a Church Successfully Cultivated Before the Launch of the Capital Campaign

One church ran a series of informational meetings in selected member homes before officially kicking off a capital campaign, but only after the leadership gifts had been secured. It carefully selected members in various geographic areas to make it convenient for all members of the congregation to attend. Volunteers were chosen on the basis of their location, the size of their home, involvement with the church, history of financial support, and commitment to the campaign. Those who were invited to these informational meetings were not asked to make a pledge that evening but to hear the vision for the church and have the opportunity to ask questions about the campaign. These meetings were very successful so, when it came time for the congregation to be asked, it was ready to support the project whole-heartedly.

Pure Genius!

Once you have a list of prospective major donors, you can develop a plan to cultivate them before asking for a donation. This plan could include the above-mentioned mailings, but should also include more personal approaches for major donor prospects. Some things you might want to do to strengthen the relationship with potential major donors could include inviting them for a tour of your organization, taking them out to lunch (or if appropriate inviting them to lunch on your campus), breakfast, or coffee. You should also plan some personal visits to the donors in their home or place of business. Many development officers have developed close relationships with their donors by treating them special. You might try dropping off a box of candy on Valentine's Day, delivering flowers on the donor's birthday or anniversary, inviting a donor who is an avid boxing fan to a championship boxing match, or just stopping by for a visit with an elderly donor who might not get out much. The possibilities for cementing relationships with personal visits are limitless. Use your imagination!

Cultivation events are planned for groups of donors or prospects, usually smaller groups. Some examples of cultivation events might be a cocktail party hosted by a board member or another volunteer in the host's home, a business leaders' breakfast at your facility, a lunch or breakfast event in a local hotel or other off-site location. Cultivation events should be focused on a specific audience and have a planned, but brief, agenda. For example you might decide to host an event for local business leaders, or you might narrow your audience to members of the banking and financial community, realtors, insurance company leaders, etc. Or you might want to invite local foundation leaders, political leaders, or clergy members, depending on your target audience. Identifying your audience is the first step in a successful cultivation event. Once you determine the audience, you can then select the right event for that audience. For example, business persons usually prefer a breakfast meeting. On the other hand, a group of local philanthropists might enjoy a cocktail party in the home of a board member, and members of the clergy might prefer a lunch event.

One of the secrets of a successful cultivation event is having the right person host the event and having that person sign the invitations. Most people respond better to an invitation from a peer than from the organization. If possible, send the invitation on the host's personal or business letterhead. The invitation should clearly state that you are not asking for money at this event. Rather, explain that it is a way for guests to get to know your organization better and to lend their insights to your organization about how you might better serve the community.

The agenda should include introductions, a short presentation about your organization (a video, DVD, or PowerPoint is usually effective, if it is brief), and a testimonial if possible from a client or user of your services. You will want to leave ample time for questions and answers and/or discussion. And you should ask for input about how you can better meet the needs of the community.

To Summarize

✎ Major donors, whether individual or corporate, need to be identified and cultivated before being asked to contribute to your organization. Identifying major donors is best done through screening and rating meetings, in which board members, staff, and volunteers review lists of potential donors with the aim of identifying linkages, ability and interest in the organization. Once you've identified these donors, some of them might not be very familiar with your organization, so you will need to plan ways to cultivate the relationship before soliciting for a donation.

✎ You can use numerous activities and events to cultivate donors. These activities could include personal invitations to a tour or a private lunch meeting with your organization's leadership, or events such as a business leaders' breakfast or cocktail party.

Chapter 10

Raising Money from Foundations

In This Chapter...

✎ What types of foundations are potential funders for your organization?

✎ What is the best way to find these foundations?

✎ How much time is needed to research all the possible sources of foundation funding?

About 12 to 14 percent of philanthropic donations in the U.S. typically comes from foundations, representing a significant source of program funding in the form of grants. While I do not delve into the world of government grants, I'll briefly mention a source you can use to find such grants as well.

First let's talk about types of foundations. There are a number of types of foundations that you can approach for funding. These include:

✎ Large private foundations, usually started by a major philanthropist such as the Kellogg Foundation, the Ford Foundation or the Kresge Foundation, that often fund national and international projects and organizations.

✎ Small- to medium-sized family foundations that usually focus on local or regional giving.

✎ Corporate foundations, which can be large and national in scope such as the Bank of America Foundation, or smaller corporate foundations that are local or regional in scope.

✎ Operating foundations which are formed for the purpose of supporting a single organization such as a hospital, university or museum.

✎ Community foundations which are usually funded by individual philanthropists in a community to fund local causes.

It is important to understand these differences since the way you will approach each foundation will often be quite different. So, how do you start research and when do you find the time to do adequate research when there is so much on your plate? The answer is you have to make time. The good news is there are a number of great tools to help you. These include:

✎ http://www.grants.gov, the ultimate source of all government funding. This website is arranged by department, such as Health and Human Services, Department of Justice, etc. You can also search by topic such as mentoring for children of prisoners or feeding the hungry. It will probably require a great deal of time to search all the grants available on the federal level, but you might be able to find a volunteer to help with this who is computer savvy and likes research.

✎ http://www.grantstation.com is a paid service to which you can subscribe. One of the advantages of this service is that it covers both government funding, private foundations and corporate funding sources. Grant Station also sends out a weekly update to its members featuring current information on funding sources and deadlines.

✎ http://www.foundationcenter.com, which also involves a fee, is an excellent source of funding information about private foundations and large corporate foundations.

Informal research will be especially useful with smaller local family foundations which are usually governed by family members or a small group of trustees. Often the personal contact your board members and volunteers have with trustees can provide the best research information for these foundations.

When researching foundations, you will find that there are many differences among the various types of foundations. Many private foundations are organizations that have been funded by wealthy individuals who have a specific type of nonprofit organization they tend to support. Larger private foundations often fund a variety of causes and usually have program officers in each area—i.e. arts and culture, health care, education, youth programs. Some foundations are started by businesses as a vehicle to provide charitable donations rather than give from their corporate budget. These can be large or small and might fund a variety of projects and

Do Your Homework!

You need to do your homework! In a former life, I worked for a bank that was very socially responsible. My office was directly across from the community relations director, who made the decisions about which organizations the bank would fund. I knew that the director of this department was very concerned about environmental issues and the bank had funded several organizations that helped to preserve the environment. When I launched my consulting career a number of years after leaving the bank, one of my first clients was an environmental group that had previously been funded by this bank. It seemed like an easy ask so I suggested it ask the bank for a substantial contribution. It turned out that after I left the bank it became more strategic in its giving and focused its contributions in a few select areas each year. That year it was health, hunger and homelessness, so my client didn't get a gift. Lesson learned! Don't forget to do your research. Circumstances and priorities often change.

Perspiration!

causes although they generally do not fund religious organizations. Other foundations are started by individuals, some of which have been under provisions established in their wills. These foundations are often managed by family members and are rather informal. Community foundations have been established to raise money from donors and disperse them to community groups. Other foundations, known as operating foundations, are set up to fund a specific nonprofit or a specific area such as research or education and do not accept applications for funding from organizations other than the pre-approved ones they were formed to support.

Information about foundations is usually available on their websites. Some smaller foundations might not have a website, but most foundations do publish annual reports. All United States foundations are required to fill out a report annually with the Internal Revenue Service (990-PF). That information is public knowledge and can be found on http://www.guidestar.org.

It is essential to learn what types of organizations the foundation funds. Corporate, large private and community foundations often change their priorities so it is important to keep abreast of their current guidelines and interests. New needs often arise in a community and most foundations will attempt to address these needs when establishing grant priorities.

I provide a worksheet to track foundation prospects in **Appendix M.** In the next appendix, **Appendix N,** I provide sample prospect worksheets for foundation research, corporate research, and individual research.

You can find information about grant sources in numerous locations. Some of these include online research tools, subscriptions to which can either be purchased by your organization or used for free at your local library. A tremendous amount of free information exists on the Internet using search engines such as Google, going to the website of the funder, or searching http://www.guidestar.org or http://www.grants.gov. However, all of this research takes time. If you've ever researched anything on the Internet, from finding a recipe for cheesecake to looking for a good hotel rate or airfare, you know the amount of time that can be involved with even a simple search. Imagine searching the tens of thousands foundations that exist in the United States. Of course you will want to start by limiting your research to those foundations that fund organizations in your geographic

Researching Foundations

When researching a foundation, some questions you should try to answer include:

- What types of programs does this foundation fund—operating expenses, programs, capital, or endowment?

- What are the typical size and purpose of grants it has awarded? The foundation's 990 form will list this information.

- What are the application deadlines?

- Do the guidelines as to types of funding this foundation provides— annual, capital, endowment, etc.—fit the needs of our organization?

- Does it fund our type of organization—arts, healthcare, education, etc.?

Perspiration!

area and your type of organization, which will eliminate most of these tens of thousands. But even after you've narrowed your search to a dozen or so that fit your criteria, your research must be thorough. You need to know the guidelines, the deadlines, the amount of funding, and the types of funding each foundation does, so it could easily be a full-time job in an organization that does a lot of grant writing. After weighing the costs and time involved for research, and the potential return, you must develop your own plan for researching various sources of grant funds. Other sources that have foundation information are http://www.bigonlinedatabase.com and http://www.grantstation.com. However, most of these sources require fees to use their services. If you cannot afford to purchase these research tools such as the Foundation Center or Grant Station directories, a good starting point is to visit your local library. Some libraries have been designated as Foundation Center Cooperating Libraries. These grant center libraries have special materials for grant seekers, both online and in print.

If possible, you should try to arrange a meeting with a representative of the foundation to obtain information about the grants they provide. Larger foundations have program officers, some of whom might focus on specific areas such as education, health, or the arts. Program officers are usually willing to meet with potential grantees. However, small private foundations might not have staff or even an office and often the trustees meet sporadically when there are proposals to be considered.

One way to hone in on the foundations with which you will have the most success is to determine if your organization has any linkages to these foundations. Using a form such as the one in **Appendix M,** you can develop a list of potential funders and list the foundations' trustees on this form along with the other information. Share this list with your board, staff and development committee to see if any of them have a connection to the foundation's trustees or officers. This will help open the door to building a relationship with this foundation.

To Summarize

✎ Although foundation funding is not the largest source of philanthropic dollars, there are a lot of different foundations in almost every community and a number of national funders that might be interested in your programs or projects. These include large private foundations, corporate foundations, small family foundations and community foundations in addition to government sources for grants.

✎ Do your research to find out which of these might be likely funders for your organization. Using various research tools that are available, you will need to determine what types of organizations these foundations fund, what types of programs they will consider funding, how much they typically give and what the deadlines are along with any other special guidelines this foundation might have.

✎ Involve your staff, board and other volunteers in the process of determining any linkages you might have with this foundation before submitting a proposal.

Chapter 11

Raising Money from Businesses

The amount of funding that actually comes from businesses and corporations is even more dismal than that coming from foundations. Anywhere from 4 to 6 percent of all contributions in the United States typically comes from the corporate world. So does this mean you shouldn't bother with businesses and corporations? No!

Building relationships with your local business community is important for many reasons. While the amount of charitable funding is relatively small, there are other opportunities that you should take advantage:

✎ There can be corporate sponsorship or funding available from the marketing department of the corporation. (These dollars are not included in the chart in the introduction to **Part 3**, which only includes "philanthropic" dollars).

✎ You will have an opportunity to recruit corporate volunteers.

✎ There is an opportunity to build relationships with corporate leaders who are often individual philanthropists and who can contribute to your organization.

✎ During a capital campaign you are likely to receive a much larger percentage of gifts from corporations than the overall 5-6 percent shown in the chart in the introduction to **Part 3**.

So how do you start building corporate relationships that can benefit your organization?

Some large nonprofit organizations such as universities lump together businesses with foundations and set up a corporate and foundation gifts department within their development offices. I think this is a huge mistake! The two entities are very different and, therefore, the approaches to them must be very different. Foundations are in business to give away money while corporations are in business to make money for their stockholders. It is as simple as that! Even a small business owner who might not have stockholders has set up the business with the goal of showing a profit. This is sometimes a simple concept that nonprofits find hard to grasp, particularly if most of their previous fundraising efforts have been focused on government or foundation grants. Remember that foundations are in the business of giving away money (and, in fact, are required to give away a certain percentage of their assets annually); businesses are in the business of making money for their stockholders or owners!

Asking for Advice

There is a saying in fundraising: "If you want advice, ask for money; if you want money, ask for advice." This adage is especially true when it comes to raising funds from your local business community.

Inspiration!

Does this mean that businesses and corporations are uncharitable or selfish? No. They are a vital part of every community, creating jobs, bringing tourists or other businesses into the community and generating tax revenues. Remember, most individuals, including business owners, care very deeply about their communities. Many businesses are socially conscious, and even those that are not as altruistic will often give to nonprofits because of the direct or indirect benefit to their company or their employees.

So, how can you find out what motivates businesses in your community to give to charitable causes? Ask them! Asking for the advice of local business leaders before asking for money is one of the keys to success. And, as with all fundraising, corporate and business fundraising is built on the three key words in fundraising: relationships, relationships, relationships.

How to Approach Your Business Community

In order to be successful at raising money from your local business, you need to:

- Find out who the decision makers are within the company.

- Build relationships with leaders of your business community.

- Identify the advantages to the business of making a contribution to your organization and explain these advantages to business decision makers.

- Approach businesses by visiting decision makers individually and personally.

- Solicit businesses only after proper research.

- Provide concise but persuasive information on the programs/ projects for which you are seeking funding.

Perspiration!

Begin by identifying businesses in your community that could be potential donors for your organization. These could be:

- ✎ Chamber of commerce members

- ✎ Vendors from whom you purchase goods and services

- ✎ Employers of your board members

- ✎ Employers of staff members' spouses and relatives

- ✎ Companies that have given to other nonprofits

- ✎ Companies that have an affiliation to or an interest in the services your nonprofit provides

Your local chamber of commerce can be very helpful in identifying local businesses. Becoming active in the chamber is a great way to build relationships with the business community. Likewise, local service clubs such as Rotary or Kiwanis can be helpful in building relationships with local business owners who are members of the organization.

The best way to obtain funding from a business is to begin by informing

Keys to Obtaining Gifts from Corporations and Businesses

- ✎ *Identify*—Determine who the corporations in your community are that might have an interest in supporting your organization.

- ✎ *Inform*—Provide them an annual report, newsletter, a quality website.

- ✎ *Invite*—Host a series of cultivation events for local businesses, and invite corporate leaders to attend.

- ✎ *Involve*—Ask business leaders to serve on your board, development committee, or advisory council.

- ✎ *Invest*—Only after all the other steps have been reached, invite these corporations and businesses to invest in your organization.

Perspiration!

A Former Client of the Agency Was a Powerful Choice!

One successful cultivation event turned out even better than we had hoped it would. A community homeless shelter was planning its first corporate annual appeal but realized that most of the business leaders in the community did not know much about the shelter and all the programs it offered. We recommended holding a cultivation event first in the form of a business leaders' breakfast meeting. One of the board members suggested we invite the CEO of the county's largest manufacturing company to host the event. Once the board member and the executive director paid a visit to the CEO and explained how they needed his help, he agreed and was very enthused about supporting this organization. He agreed to review the invitation list and refine it, adding several of his own business contacts to the list. We wrote the letter for him and, after he approved it, he agreed to have his office send it out on his letterhead. We invited about seventy-five businesses leaders, expecting to have about a dozen attend. Because of the invitation from such an influential community leader, we had about fifty key community leaders attend the event.

What really made this event successful, in addition to the host and his role in the invitation process, was the agenda for the day. After brief introductions by the board chair (most of the board attended in addition to the fifty guests), breakfast with the shelter clients, and a brief talk about the shelter by the executive director, we invited the guests to take a tour of the shelter.

The gentleman who led the tour was carefully selected. He was a shelter employee but had actually been a client in the shelter himself. He now held a job at the shelter, had his own apartment, and was getting his life together. Having him lead the tour, pointing out "this was the bed I slept in when I was a guest here" and other firsthand knowledge about how the shelter's program worked, was a stroke of pure genius! When these business leaders were later approached to help with our annual business appeal, they responded with both their volunteer time and their business and personal contributions. The appeal was a huge success!

Pure Genius!

the businessperson about the services of your organization. This can be done in many ways:

- Invite business leaders to serve on your business advisory committee.

- Send these leaders information about your organization, such as your annual report, on a regular basis.

- Invite the decision makers of your business community to an open house at your organization, to take part in a focus group or to attend a cultivation event.

- Research the business to find out what types of goods and services they offer to see if there might be a natural affiliation with your mission.

- Invite business leaders to a meeting with your executive director and a tour of your facility.

One great way to involve your local business leaders is to invite them to attend a focus group session where you provide information about your organization and then ask for their input. The key to successful business gatherings of this type is the invitation process. Ask a prominent local business leader with whom your organization already has an established relationship to invite some peers to attend a brief meeting. Provide this person with a list of business leaders you plan to invite and ask the host to review and add to the list. Often breakfast meetings are best for business persons so they can arrive early, perhaps 7:00 a.m. or 7:30 a.m., and still get to their places of business by 8:30 a.m. or 9:00 a.m.

You need to make sure that your meetings do not run more than an hour and a quarter. Inviting about twenty-five to thirty people will usually result in attendance of about a dozen or so business persons. If possible, take them for a brief tour of your facility or a virtual tour by video or PowerPoint presentation. Have current clients talk about your organization and what your programs and services mean to them. Then invite the participants to have an open discussion, soliciting their advice on questions such as how to market your organization's services more effectively, how to improve your fundraising program and how their company might be able to partner with your organization in some way. Give them a *brief* form to complete or have someone take careful notes of the discussion. Do *not* ask for money at this event. Ask for advice!

Most organizations that try this approach leave the event with at least one or two leads of local business persons who are really enthused and interested in the organization's mission and programs and who want to develop a further relationship with the organization. You need to have a plan in place to follow up with those who have attended your event. First, send all attendees a personal note thanking them for attending and for providing input. For those who mentioned something specific that needs to be followed up on, be sure you follow through and provide the requested information. For example, if they asked for more detailed program information, you can send an annual budget, a list of who is on the board, or information about a specific program.

You can invite those who seem eager to become involved to serve on a committee—the development committee, finance committee, marketing committee, or program committee, depending on where their expertise and interests lie. You can invite attendees to lunch with your executive director and/or your board chair, especially if this person could be a potential board member. Be sure to add attendees to your newsletter list and invite them to events your organization is holding.

If any of your volunteers are employed by a company or organization, seek out ways your organization can provide some service for the company's employees.

Avoid Direct Mail in Wooing Business Leaders

One thing you should be cautious about—going to your local chamber of commerce, asking for the list of all its members and sending a direct-mail appeal out to its members. Most business leaders do not read fundraising requests they receive from nonprofits. In fact, the mail is usually screened by a secretary or assistant who might toss it in the trash before it even lands on the decision maker's desk.

Uninspired

Determining How Many Volunteers You Need

A good rule of thumb when personally soliciting businesses is to ask each volunteer to make no more than five visits. If volunteers are expected to make more than five calls, they will often get frustrated, feel overwhelmed, and will not even make one visit.

Inspiration!

For example, if you are with a disease-fighting organization, you could talk to their employees about the effects of blindness, lung disease, or narcolepsy. Do not mention money to them yet! This is all part of the relationship-building process. Remember, "Ask for money, and you will get advice, ask for advice, and eventually you will get the money."

Before soliciting any business for funding, some additional research will be helpful. The company's annual report and website are two excellent sources of the information you will want to know:

- Is the company locally owned or part of a national or international company with headquarters outside of your community?

- What types of profits or losses did the company experience in the past year?

- If there is a corporate foundation, what are the foundation's grant application procedures and guidelines?

- What nonprofits has the company funded in the last several years, and what were the amounts of the contributions?

- Are decisions about contributions made by an individual, a department, or a committee?

- In addition to philanthropic contributions, how does this company give sponsorships or gifts in kind? Does it give through its marketing department for awareness purposes?

- Does the company have a formal employee volunteer program?

Instead of appealing to businesses through the mail, establish a peer-to-peer solicitation program. Start with one or two business leaders who are already involved with your organization, either serving on a committee or on the board. Select a chair and vice chair or co-chairs who have a passion for your mission and who have already made a financial commitment. These leaders will then help build a team of other business persons who can talk to their friends and business associates about a contribution.

A Good Tool for Your Business Appeal

A simple but professional-looking annual report is a great tool to which business persons can relate. After all, most businesses produce their own annual report, so this is a piece with which they will be familiar. The annual report displays your financial picture at a glance, shows the community impact your programs have, and lists other companies and individuals who support your organization, all things that will help make the case to potential corporate donors.

Perspiration!

In order to determine how many volunteers you need for your business appeal, first make a list of all the companies you would like to solicit. Then divide that list by five. Start small! You might have hundreds of businesses in the community, but select the ones with whom you think you will have the best chance of being successful. Select companies that are involved in or connected to your organization. For example, maybe one or more of the local banks had teams in your golf tournament or bowl-a-thon. You should always include your vendors. And include companies whose products have a natural connection to your mission. For example, if you work for a health care facility, plan to contact any local manufacturers of medical supplies or pharmaceuticals.

You can ask your staff and board members for a list of companies with whom they do business or where they or their spouses work. You should select businesses with a track record of contributing to nonprofits. You can search donor lists of community groups such as the symphony, hospital, United Way, and universities, which generally publish lists of their donors.

Your chances for success increase dramatically if the company already knows about your organization. This is the time to approach those businesses who attended your advice-giving focus groups and cultivation events. From this list of potential donors, identify potential volunteers.

Remember that many businesses only support nonprofits with which their employees are involved, so selecting the right volunteers is the key to the process. The more volunteers, the more companies you can approach. Once the program expands to what seems to be an unmanageable size, divide the volunteers into teams of five people, and work with team leaders.

Your volunteers will need a training session in which they will learn how to make the "case" for your organization and how to ask for a gift. If this is the first time these volunteers have been involved with an appeal of this type, they might need more intense training on topics such as how to schedule a meeting. However, if the volunteers are fairly sophisticated and will be calling on their friends and peers, they might not need as much training.

At this training, be sure to provide your volunteers with information about your organization that they can give to prospective donors. But remember, these are business persons, not foundation officers. They do not have the

---

Competition between Donors: A Development Officer's Dream!

One of my clients was engaged in a capital campaign. We had assembled a great team of volunteers who represented the local business community leadership, including the presidents of the four major banks in the community. At one campaign cabinet meeting, one of the bankers was boasting about a recent bank acquisition that now made his bank four times the size of his colleague's institution. The colleague very quickly responded with, "Oh good, our bank is pledging $250,000 to the campaign, so I am sure your bank will now give $1 million."

Pure Genius!

time, or perhaps even the interest, to read volumes of materials. A simple one-page fact sheet can be very helpful. Give the volunteers additional information such as brochures or annual reports for those prospects who request more detailed information.

If possible, focus your appeal on a specific project or program, such as a scholarship program for people who cannot afford your services. Your solicitation materials should clearly make a compelling case, answering the question why your local business community should support this program or project. Remember that a top-notch website is essential. Many business persons would rather search the website than read printed materials.

Be as specific as possible about why giving to your agency will help their business. Some tips to help you do this include:

✎ Learn the federal and state tax advantages for businesses giving to your organization, such as tax credit programs.

✎ Indicate how lowering crime, increasing education, improving health of your community's people (or whatever service your organization provides) helps your entire community.

✎ Inform the business about how its contribution will be recognized and publicized, thus leading to good will for that business in the community.

✎ Make the point that a strong community will result in the ability for them to recruit more qualified employees to work and live in that community.

Business leaders will be able to identify with terms such as "ROI" (return on investment), "economic impact" and "bottom line." It might be beneficial for you to do an economic impact study proving that your organization saves tax dollars and/or brings in dollars to your community. Also citing credentials of your staff and board can be impressive to the business leaders with whom you are talking.

Always begin with a kickoff meeting where you will provide your volunteers with information packets containing all the materials you have developed. You will want to be sure that you answer any questions about your organization and its programs. You will want to provide training or a refresher in making the ask. A key part of this kickoff meeting will be an inspirational talk; if you can invite a client who is receiving services from your organization, this talk will have even greater impact.

Report meetings will also be important so your volunteers can celebrate success, provide feedback on how the program is going and receive hints from other volunteers on how to approach their prospects. Sometimes these report meetings can be very effective in motivating those volunteers who are not doing well by providing them an opportunity to hear from other volunteers who are successful with their visits. And, of course, if your volunteers have a healthy sense of competition, this might be the time to encourage some competitive interaction.

To Summarize

✎ Although charitable giving from businesses and corporations is not the main source of funding in the United States, many organizations can benefit greatly from building strong relationships with their business community.

✎ In order to raise money from businesses, direct mail is not the answer. You need to recruit volunteers from the business leaders who can open doors to other business leaders, provide funding from their own business, and solicit their peers for donations. Involving these business leaders on your board, development committee, or annual corporate appeal committee is an effective way to keep them involved in your organization.

✎ Remember the adage, "Ask for money and you will get advice; ask for advice and you will get the money."

Chapter 12

Raising Money from Organizations

In This Chapter...

✎ From what type of organizations in the community can you seek funding?

✎ How do you find these organizations?

✎ What is the best way to approach these organizations for funding?

Although not specifically broken out in the chart at the beginning of Part 3, there are in most communities a significant number of professional and service groups, many of which contribute to nonprofit organizations. Most of these groups have weekly or monthly meetings to which they invite guest speakers. Since many of these groups need a speaker every week, you can easily make a friend of the program chair by offering to speak at one or more meetings each year.

Start by developing a list of service and professional groups in your community. You can begin this process by asking your board members, volunteers, and other constituents to which groups they belong. Sometimes you can find these organizations in the phone book or through their websites.

There are several reasons why you should consider speaking to these service and professional clubs:

- ✎ Service clubs, such as Rotary, Lions Clubs, Soroptomists, and others typically have as a primary goal to raise money for charity.

- ✎ Professional clubs such as the National Association of Women Business Owners might not have philanthropy as their top priority, but often do make contributions to various nonprofits from the club's treasury.

- ✎ Business leaders often "hang out" at these associations and clubs.

- ✎ Members of associations and clubs tend to be "joiners," and therefore potential volunteers and donors for your organization.

- ✎ Usually there is a national or international association to which local chapters belong. These parent associations often have charitable foundations.

- ✎ Many of these groups have numerous chapters within your region and if you make a favorable impression on one chapter, leaders of that chapter might be willing to introduce you to other chapters or suggest a joint chapter project to benefit your organization.

One thing you need to become accustomed to as a development officer is the "rubber chicken circuit." Attend as many events of your local service and professional groups as possible. Most of these groups meet weekly or monthly and need a speaker at each meeting, so there are thousands of opportunities for your organization to get in front of these groups. Once you have identified the groups that are active in your area, you need to develop a list of the organizations, a contact person within the organization (either the president or the program chair is the best person to start with), and their contact information. You can then develop a list of all these groups with their contact person, the dates and times of their meetings, and any other information you can find about them such as their giving history and areas of special interests. Once you have the list put together, review this list with your board to see if any of them are members of these groups or know someone who is. You should also review the list with staff members and with your development committee.

Before approaching any service or professional group, it is important to research their giving history. How do they raise money? Have they given to your organization before and, if so, how much and for what purpose? What have they given to other organizations in the community, and for what purposes was this money given? What are the restrictions under which they operate? What is their area of interest? For example, Lions Clubs often support the visually impaired, while Sertoma clubs help the hearing impaired. Many other groups have their own particular areas of interest. Even if your organization does not fit into their primary area of interest, some service groups might still fund a project because it helps the local community.

How Being Creative Paid Off!

One organization that served people with mental disabilities approached its local Sertoma Club, whose interest was in helping the hearing impaired. It seemed like quite a stretch for the organization to get funding from its local Sertoma Club. The organization, however, found a program that would meet the interests of Sertoma: Its summer camp was attended by a number of children who had both physical and mental challenges, among them a number of campers who had hearing impairments and needed some special equipment. The Sertoma Club, when approached to fund this project, not only pitched in with a nice gift from its chapter treasury, but was able to secure a matching grant from the national Sertoma Foundation.

Pure Genius!

So what type of presentations do you make to these groups? The members typically are looking for information that will help them or their family members, or impact the community. Rather than asking directly for money at these presentations, think of them as a cultivation tool. You can prepare a PowerPoint presentation, slide show, or video that shows your organization in action. If feasible, bring a client or user of your services along to "make the pitch" for how great your organization is.

While it might not be feasible for you to bring a client or alumnus of your program to a presentation, you can show and tell your story in a variety of ways. If you can offer members something that is of direct interest to them, such as health tips, ways to save the environment, how your employees can help their employees, or something similar, you will make an impression on them as an organization that is more concerned with creating win-win collaborations than one that is coming to them with its hand out!

Always have a take-away for members of the audience: a fact sheet about your programs, an annual report, a promotional give-away item with your name and logo, or something similar. Also, don't forget to bring enough of your business cards for each member of the club.

You should always plan enough time for questions and answers at the end and try to engage the members in dialogue. Ask them, for example, if there are ways they could see themselves becoming involved with your organization (as a group or individually), or other groups they think you should speak to, or if your program is something their national or international organizations might be interested in. You can also ask if any individual members would like to be added to your mailing list to receive newsletters, invitations to events, and so on. Be sure to collect business cards from those interested members.

Have Clients Address the Group!

I attended one such presentation for a mentoring group, in which it brought one of its former "mentees," a young man from a very rough neighborhood of a major gang-infested urban area. The mentee was now a college student and came nicely dressed in a suit and tie. He gave a not-well-polished but very emotionally powerful story about how his mentor helped him stay out of trouble and excel in school. Although his was not at all a professional presentation, it did the trick! Members of the audience were visibly moved by his story and immediately wanted to know how they could become involved.

Pure Genius!

To Summarize

In most communities there are a large number of service and professional organizations, many of which have a philanthropic purpose. Many of these groups have a specific area of interest, such as funding agencies that work with young people or funding research for a specific disease. However, you might be able to find a program that would interest some of these groups, even if their areas of interest are not specifically your mission.

The best way to reach these organizations is to develop an approach strategy that offers to speak at their meetings about your organization. Attending functions of local professional clubs and even other nonprofit organizations can help you develop relationships with the organization that could be long lasting and a win-win situation for both you and the community organization.

Part 4

What Do We Need in Place Before We Can Effectively Raise Funds?

Now that you know why you need to raise money, who raises money, and who to raise money from, you probably think you're ready to go. Not quite yet! (I did warn you this was a long-term process, didn't I?)

There are some things you need to have in place before you are ready to start asking for donations. Most of these fall under what I term "infrastructure." Without these basic fundamental things in place, you might be somewhat successful for a while, but will not reach your true potential and, in many cases, your development program could crash and burn. It is like building a house without laying the foundation first. So, be patient, and let's see if you are ready to start raising money.

Chapter 13

Strategic Organizational Planning

In This Chapter...

✎ What is strategic planning and why is it important to fundraising?

✎ What is the difference between mission, vision, and values, and how do they fit into our fundraising plan?

✎ How do you get your organization engaged in strategic planning?

In today's fast-paced world of change, a long-range strategic plan can no longer be developed for five to ten years down the road. Most strategic planning today looks at a three-year time period. The board and staff develop the strategic plan, with input from the various constituencies.

A strategic plan will take several months to develop and a planning committee needs to be established. This committee should include board members, staff from each department of your organization, and representatives of your various constituencies, such as users of your services, alumni, parents, funders, and community leaders. The strategic plan needs to cover all aspects of your organization—program,

Strategic Planning

A program incorporating a strategy for achieving organizational goals and objectives within a specific timeframe and with substantive support in the form of methods, priorities, and resources.

finance, facilities, marketing and development. The plan includes goals and objectives, as well as strategies to reach these goals and objectives. Goals are the broad based aspects of the plan.

Each department then develops its own action plan, which includes timelines, budgets, and responsibilities. The plan will be meaningless if it doesn't answer these questions: How much it will cost? When will it be done? Who is responsible for implementing this strategy?

The plan should also include a process for evaluation, at least quarterly, to measure progress. The best plan in the world doesn't work if it sits in a drawer. It must be dynamic and flexible.

Mission Statement

All strategic planning must begin with the mission statement. A good mission statement should be just a few sentences and should tell what the organization does and who it serves.

If your mission statement does not fit on the back of your business card, it is probably too lengthy. Often the mission statement is developed or

A good example of a mission statement:

"Big Brothers Big Sisters of Nevada... enhancing children's lives through exceptional mentoring relationships."

Pure Genius!

revised during a strategic planning process. Your board needs to approve the mission statement, and one of the board's major roles is to assure that programs and all operations are accomplished in relationship to the mission of the organization. If there is no mission statement in place, start with the purpose of your organization listed in your Articles of Incorporation. Because an attorney most likely

Places You Should Publish Your Mission

✎ Your organization letterhead

✎ Framed copies in public areas and staff offices

✎ Screen saver on office computers

✎ At the top of every board meeting agenda

✎ In the minutes of all board meetings

✎ In your annual report

✎ In every newsletter

✎ On all agency brochures

✎ In videos/DVDs/PowerPoint presentations

✎ In all grant proposals

✎ On pre-printed directions to your organization

✎ On your postmark

✎ On voice mail messages

✎ On the home page and every page of your website and Facebook page

✎ In all employees' email signatures

✎ On your agency checks

✎ On your invoices

✎ On the back of all employees' business cards

✎ On response envelopes used in appeals

Perspiration!

wrote this purpose, it is probably an accurate description of your organization's purpose, but will most likely need to be fine-tuned by the board so that it is clear, concise, and meaningful to the public. The most persuasive reason that people give to an organization is because they believe in its mission; therefore, your mission statement should be communicated to donors and your constituency as often and in as many ways as possible. Put the mission statement on all your business cards, newsletters, brochures, and other communications, including your website. Remind board members of the reason they serve the organization by putting the mission statement at the top of every board meeting agenda.

Strategies

Examples of strategies the organization might use to reach the objective of developing an interactive website might include selecting a website designer, determining the content desired by visitors to the website, developing a plan to regularly update the content of the web pages, etc.

Inspiration!

Goals and Objectives

A goal might be to increase awareness of your organization in the community. An objective, on the other hand, needs to be measurable, attainable, and specific. An example of an objective might be to develop an interactive website by June 20XX.

Inspiration!

Vision Statement

Unlike the mission, which is a good snapshot of where your organization is right now, the vision statement is a statement of where you want to be. This is the place to dream. The vision statement talks about where your organization wants to be in the future and, more importantly, how you envision your community's future. Sometimes the vision is to cease to exist because there is no longer a need for your organization.

Your vision statement is important because your organization needs to know both where it is now and where it is going before developing a plan on how to get there. Not having a vision statement is like starting a trip without a final destination. The vision, as with the mission, needs to be adopted and approved by your board of directors as well as your staff. Everyone can work toward a common vision once it is confirmed by your organization as a whole.

Values

Values are the things your organization holds near and dear, the things on which it will not compromise. You could think of your values as your "line in the sand."

Some examples of values might include a commitment to excellent services, innovation, diversity, creativity, honesty, integrity, and so on. Values might include more specific beliefs such as: "Eating vegetables is more economically efficient and ecologically responsible than eating beef." (Vegetarian Association.)

The Importance of Planning

Every nonprofit must engage in planning in order to develop written goals and objectives, solidify its mission, vision and values, and set the strategy in motion that will drive its action plan in the years ahead. Does planning really matter in the nonprofit world?

The Cheshire cat was a wise strategist. He knew that Alice was bound to wander aimlessly if she didn't have a clear sense

Does Planning Matter?

"Cheshire Puss," Alice began, "Would you tell me please which way I ought to go from here?"

"That depends a great deal on where you want to get to," said the cat.

"I don't much care where," said Alice, "so long as I get somewhere," Alice added.

"Then it doesn't matter which way you go," said the cat.

—Lewis Carroll

Inspiration!

of where she was and where she was headed.

Nonprofit leaders cannot be prepared for all the unexpected "rabbit holes" we sometimes find ourselves tumbling down. But strategic planning can help your organization and you, as a nonprofit leader, to prepare for these unexpected turns. You can anticipate the best outcomes but be prepared for the worst, if you have a strategic plan.

You might hear planning referred to by a number of terms—long-term planning, strategic planning business planning and the like. The terminology is not as important as the process and the product.

Your board and leadership staff must participate in planning. You need to get input from key stakeholders (the process). You need to set clear goals and objectives. You need to be able to measure success and adjust strategies when these goals and objectives are not being met.

A facilitator to help guide the planning process is critical. An objective outside facilitator will keep the process on track and help you create a product (the planning document) that will be used to guide your board and staff in achieving goals.

There are a lot of books out there that can help you with the strategic planning process. Some of these books are listed in Suggested Reading, **Appendix EE.**

An example of a vision statement

"No child in our city will go hungry to bed in the evening."

Inspiration!

SWOT

An analysis of an organization that looks at both the internal and external environments of the organization. The acronym SWOT stands for Strengths, Weaknesses, Opportunities, and Threats; strengths and weaknesses being internal, and opportunities and threats being external.

Inspiration!

How Can Strategic Planning Help Fundraising?

Too often, even organizations that understand the value of long-range planning and strategic planning on an overall organizational basis fail to utilize these same strategies in their development program. Development and fundraising is often handled in a haphazard way because, as with Alice, the development officer sometimes has no idea where the organization wants to be. Organizations can be caught up in the day-to-day management of a myriad of fundraising activities, many of which are often unproductive or counter-productive to building lasting donor relationships.

Before planning how to reach your vision, you must first define where you are now. As with Alice, you must take stock of your current situation,

Insanity

The definition of insanity is doing the same thing over and over again and expecting different results.

—Albert Einstein

Some pitfalls that can stagnate your planning process:

✎ Lack of cohesiveness and consensus among staff, board and other constituents

✎ Establishing too many goals, or unrealistic goals

✎ Not understanding the difference between goals and objectives

✎ Not developing strategies to implement goals and objectives

✎ Not assigning areas of responsibility, budgets or timelines to the action steps needed to implement goals and objectives

Uninspired

and then find the right path to success through strategic planning.

Your organizational leadership must take the time to plan strategically; otherwise your organization will be left behind in the dynamic and ever-evolving world of the nonprofit sector. Your leadership must consider the return on investment of careful, strategic planning.

> *The future has several names.*
>
> *For the weak, it is impossible,*
>
> *For the fainthearted, it is unknown.*
>
> *For the thoughtful and the valiant, it is ideal.*
>
> *The challenge is urgent, the task is large, the time is now.*
>
> —Victor Hugo

Inspiration!

How do you assure that your plans are truly strategic and that they will be implemented?

To be strategic, you must consider how each goal will be implemented, build consensus among your key stakeholders, and develop evaluation systems to measure performance at critical intervals along the way.

A system to monitor your plan is critical. A key person, often the vice president of the board, must be assigned to monitor the plan on a regular basis, holding accountable all those involved in plan implementation, and being prepared to make adjustments to the plan when necessary. Assuring that your plan is future-focused at each step of the process is essential. Using tools such as those provided in **Appendixes O** and **P** can help you monitor both your strategic plan and your development plan.

To Summarize

✎ Organizational strategic planning is critical to fundraising efforts. Your entire organization, board, and management staff must be involved in the strategic planning process. The plan starts with an assessment of where you are now. This is accomplished through a SWOT analysis, an environmental scan and a careful review of your mission statement. Your mission is the major reason donors support your organization, so you need to have a clear, concise mission statement.

✎ The next step is to determine where you want to be—your vision. You need a vision statement that is truly *visionary*—what is it your organization plans to accomplish? Values are also important. What are the values your organization holds firmly to and on which it will not compromise?

✎ The strategic plan is your road map, your GPS system, so to speak. It tells you how to attain your vision, and it must be evaluated on a regular basis so you don't stray from your goals. It is critical to have a strategic plan in order to help you create a development plan that will allow you to attain the funding necessary to fulfill your mission and reach your vision.

Chapter 14

Your Development Plan

How many times has a well-meaning board member or volunteer come to one of your board or development committee meetings and offered this sage advice? "We should do a (golf tournament, gala dinner dance, art auction, walkathon, etc., etc.) because (Girl Scouts, Boy Scouts, the hospital, etc.) did one and raised $100,000."

Before the meeting ends, the whole board or committee is caught up in "event fever" and has the invitations designed, the flowers ordered, and the T-shirt sponsors listed. And there you are, the frustrated development officer, trying to meet grant deadlines, straighten out your donor database that is a mess, and organize the other events that your organization is currently conducting. So what do you do when the board is bitten by the "event bug?" Have a development plan!

Another fatal mistake that many organizations make is relying solely on a grant writer to raise all the money needed for programs and operations. Given the fact that, as we've seen, foundation grants only account for approximately 12 to 14 percent of all philanthropic giving in the United States, this approach seems equally as foolhardy as depending mainly on events to raise money for your organization. While both grants and events are important parts of a well-rounded development program, they should not be the *only* methods of fundraising you use. So how do you handle these board suggestions or (in some cases) mandates? Again, the development plan is the answer.

Boards and volunteers often do not realize that events and grant research can be costly, not only in terms of hard costs, but in "opportunity costs." In other words, what activities must you give up in order to focus your limited time on this proposed new activity? Your first reaction to the board or development committee that suggests either of these approaches should be, "Well, let's pull out our development plan and see if this event/grant is part of our plan; if not, what other activities must we drop in order to concentrate on this event/grant?" However, many organizations do not have a development plan to reference. If your organization is one of those, this is one good reason why you should have a development plan. Other reasons include the fact that the development plan provides:

- ✎ A way to measure success of your development activities.

- ✎ Assurance that your development activities provide a balanced approach—in other words "Don't put all your eggs in one basket."

- ✎ A way to determine the appropriate budget for the development office.

- ✎ Assurance that you have the human resources to implement the development activities that are planned.

- ✎ Timelines that allow the development office to best utilize staff time.

If you have a development plan complete with timelines, areas of responsibility and budgets, you will be more successful at keeping your staff, board, and volunteers focused on the activities that are most cost effective and produce the best results.

As with strategic planning, a SWOT (Strengths, Weaknesses, Opportunities and Threats) analysis of the development office is a good place to start, analyzing the internal strengths and weaknesses of your development office, and evaluating the external threats and opportunities for development. A full-blown development audit is often the most useful tool in evaluating past successes and assessing future opportunities. The audit can also provide comparisons with national, regional, or local statistics of similar organizations and provide benchmarks by which to measure success of your development plan.

Building consensus, a vital part of strategic planning, is also critical in the development planning process. Involving key stakeholders in the development program—board members, volunteers, management staff, program staff, donors, and the entire development staff, is critical.

Just as in strategic planning, your development plan must be focused on the mission and vision of the organization. Each development goal should be assessed in light of its relevance to your organization's mission and vision.

As with strategic planning, your development plan should focus on a limited number of goals in different areas and SMART (Specific, Measurable, Action-oriented, Realistic, and Time-defined) objectives should be listed for each goal. Your operational development plan also needs to contain strategies and action steps for each objective. A measurement system must be established and someone must be responsible for the implementation and monitoring of the plan.

Does your organization resist allocating the time necessary to development planning?

CEOs and development officers are often under a great deal of pressure to raise money quickly. Entrepreneurial board members who are shrewd business persons are often accustomed to working on the basis of instant decisions, and might want the development office to just "go out and do it" without adequate planning. Development officers might be so caught up in keeping their heads above water that they do not have the time to plan. You need to resist the urge to skip the planning phase! Eliminating this important step is like getting in your car and starting to drive without knowing where you are and where you are going. The GPS system won't do you much good without this needed information.

The development plan is an outgrowth of your strategic plan. Once goals and objectives are established for the development program and approved by the board, the development office then has the task of designing its annual plan, as all other departments will do within their areas. The annual development plan covers all aspects of the fundraising program. If there is not a separate public relations plan, this area is covered in the development plan since good public relations are critical to development. The plan is written from the viewpoint of having an integrated development program. Building on sound public relations to create awareness, your plan should include components of annual giving, major giving, capital needs, and planned giving. Human resources and infrastructure also need to be addressed in your plan. The plan will include various fundraising techniques, such as:

- Research

- Proposal writing

- Special events

- Direct mail

- Internet fundraising

- Telephone fundraising

- Personal solicitations

- Acknowledgement

- Recognition

- Stewardship

Development of an action plan will assure implementation of the plan—budgeting for development; areas of responsibility: who is responsible for each task—staff, board, volunteers; and timelines for implementation of each step.

What Should Your Development Plan Include?

Your development plan should start with an analysis of your current development activities. Some questions to ask:

✎ What has been the history of this activity; have results increased or decreased over the years?

✎ What are the costs of this activity, both hard costs, staff time, and opportunity costs?

✎ Do we have the human resources to manage this activity?

✎ Do we have the technology needed to manage this activity?

✎ What are the subsidiary benefits of this activity, i.e., if the activity is a cultivation or awareness-raising event, should we continue the activity even if it does not raise money?

✎ How do current trends affect this activity?

✎ Are there ways we can increase the effectiveness of this activity?

Once you've analyzed current activities, you can decide whether you want to keep them status quo, focus more time and energy on them, or drop them.

An effective development plan lists goals and objectives for each activity. Goals and objectives do not always have to be monetary. For example, a goal could be to raise awareness of your organization in the community. An objective might be to raise constituent participation by 5 percent this year, increase the size of the development committee by four people, and to personally visit three major donors each month. Without specific goals, it will be impossible next year to measure the success of the plan. A development plan also helps your development office justify its budget, provides measurement tools to use in performance appraisals, and provides donors with a sense of confidence in your organization. So, is there any reason your organization does not need a development plan?

Some Reasons Your Organization Might Fail at Fundraising

Planning is critical in all aspects of managing a nonprofit organization. However, even organizations that understand the value of organization-wide, long-range strategic planning often fail to use these same strategies in their development program. Fundraising is often pursued in a haphazard way because, as with Alice, novices sometimes have no idea where they want to be. They are caught up in the day-to-day management of myriad fundraising activities, many of which are often unproductive or counter-productive to building lasting donor relationships.

You might be in a situation where undue pressure is applied to your fundraising staff or volunteers by boards and executive management who think of fundraising as a "necessary evil." Despite the extensive body of knowledge on the subject of fundraising, these leaders still approach fundraising with a "tin-cup" mentality. They often refuse to make the necessary financial investment in a professional development office or the time commitment to develop an agency-wide, comprehensive development plan.

Questions to Ask About Your Development Program

✎ Does your organization have a base of donors who faithfully support the organization?

✎ Do you have enough staff members to plan and implement all your fundraising activities?

✎ Do you have a compelling case for support?

✎ How committed is your board?

✎ How many volunteers are available to help plan and implement your fundraising activities?

Perspiration!

How to Develop Your Plan

Usually the chief development officer has the primary responsibility of putting together the development plan. If you have a development committee, members of this committee should also be involved. Some additional people to get involved in the process might include:

- ✎ Key board members, especially the board chair

- ✎ Your executive director (the CEO's involvement in development is critical)

- ✎ Other staff members who might have input into developing the case for support, identifying prospective donors or fundraising techniques, or providing budget information

- ✎ Major donors who might encourage other prospective donors to become involved

Goals and Objectives

Goals are broad-based.

Objectives must be SMART

- ✎ **S**pecific

- ✎ **M**easurable

- ✎ **A**ction-oriented

- ✎ **R**ealistic

- ✎ **T**ime-defined

Without specific objectives, it will be impossible to measure success of your plan at the end of the year and to plan for the future.

Inspiration!

First, your organization must commit to strategic planning at an organizational level if your development planning is to be successful. Second, as the organization grows, it must allocate sufficient funding for a development office, allowing you to hire staff that has the ability to plan and interest in planning, for fundraising. If your organization is too small to have staff members devoted to development, an experienced volunteer or group of volunteers must be committed to developing a fundraising plan.

Who Develops and Implements the Plan?

How do you find time for planning? Who will implement the plan once it is approved by the board? By involving the right individuals in developing the plan and then implementing it, you can move forward in a timely manner and provide a framework for evaluating your development program.

Typically, these are the individuals involved in the fundraising planning process and in implementing the plan:

Chief Development Officer

If you are the chief fundraiser for the organization, you will have the primary responsibility for the plan. You will create a detailed fundraising budget. You will also assign responsibilities to those who will implement the plan. You will be held responsible for implementing the plan, evaluating the plan's success and adapting the plan, as needed.

Other Development Staff

If you have additional development team members, they should be involved with the planning process and will implement the various segments of the plan that pertain to their duties. It is important to include support staff in the planning process. Your goals can suffer serious delays if not enough support staff and technology is available to implement the strategies that meet your objectives.

Non-Development Staff

The chief executive officer (the executive director, pastor, administrator, etc.) of your organization is, in reality, the chief fundraiser. Your top leadership should be involved in setting the goals of the development program. The CEO's role in implementing the plan, particularly the identification, cultivation, and solicitation of major-gift prospects, will be critical in the plan's success. Therefore, the CEO must be willing to support the plan and to fulfill an important role in the process. The chief financial officer (CFO) (this might be your accountant or bookkeeper) must also be involved in the plan, particularly to budget for additional staff, technology or other resources that will be needed to implement the plan. For some organizations, other staff members might be involved, such as program staff members who should be consulted regarding their funding requests, and facility managers who might have capital needs that require funding.

Board Members

Board members are instrumental in developing the strategic plan for your organization and should be involved in the development planning as well. Their role in developing all the details of the plan might be less intense than that of your development staff or development committee, but the board must be involved in establishing goals and objectives. If you have no development staff, your board will be more involved in the details of the plan. In any size organization, the board's role in implementing the plan will be critical. As with the CEO, board members will have a key role to play in identifying, cultivating, and soliciting donors, so they must, at the very least, help establish goals and objectives.

Development Committee

Development committee members will have a larger role in the planning process than the full board since this is their area of focus. This committee should include several board members and is usually chaired by a board member. However, it is important to expand the development committee beyond the board and involve community members—especially those with community contacts and specific skills and talents that can be useful to the committee. Include individuals such as an estate planning attorney, financial planner, or an accountant who can help with planned giving. This committee, along with your staff, will play a key role in implementing the plan.

Other Volunteers

If other volunteers, such as a parent group, auxiliary, alumni association, planned giving committee, or events committee are involved in the fundraising program, they might also be invited to review and provide input into the parts of your plan that pertain to their activities.

Consultants

A consultant is often involved in the planning process, particularly in the assessment phase. Many organizations engage a consultant to conduct an assessment of their past fundraising performance before establishing goals for the current plan. A consultant can provide an objective view of your organization's fundraising program and help establish realistic objectives, as well as recommend strategies for the plan. If you have no development staff or volunteer experienced in fundraising, a consultant may be called in to assist in preparing the plan.

Goals and Objectives in the Development Plan

As we've already discussed in **Chapter 13,** Strategic Organizational Planning, goals are broad-based items. For example, goals for your development plan might include: "Raise public awareness of our organization," "Develop a more effective board of directors," or "Increase donor participation."

Remember that objectives, on the other hand, are more specific and must be SMART:

- **S**pecific

- **M**easurable

- **A**ction-oriented

- **R**ealistic

- **T**ime-defined

Objectives for the above stated goals might be:

- To develop a website that, by the end of the year, is frequented by one-hundred potential donors each month.

- To increase the size of the board from nine to eighteen individuals, over a period of three years, adding three individuals each year.

- To increase the percentage of donors who contribute through the annual phonathon from 14 percent to 25 percent over the next two years.

Pure Genius!

How do you convince your CEO and board members that they need to be part of the development planning process?

Successful organizations have visionary leaders who understand the importance of planning. But if your leaders do not understand the importance of planning you might need to enlist outside help. One way to convince leaders of the importance of strategic planning for development is by having them interact with key nonprofit leaders in their community. A CEO or board chair from a highly respected and successful nonprofit can often convince a struggling CEO of the value of strategic planning for development, as well as organization-wide strategic planning. Sometimes a consultant can help convince leadership of the importance of planning for development.

Your leaders might feel that development is not their area of expertise and might want to spend their time on organizational planning with which they are generally more comfortable. You need to help your organization's leaders reach a comfort level with development and philanthropy and convince them that their insights as the organization's leaders are critical to a successful development program.

How do you prepare your development office for a rapidly changing environment?

Involving community leaders in the philanthropic process and the development planning process is one good way to assure that community concerns and changing environments are incorporated into your development planning process.

Marketing people, key business leaders, and political personalities are generally in tune with environmental factors that could affect your organization's development program, and should be invited to participate in the philanthropic planning process.

What Should Your Finished Plan Look Like?

One thing you need to remember about the plan is that it is more than simply a document! Both the process and the product are important. While it is important to discuss who should be involved in the planning process and why the process itself is important, it is equally important that you produce a written document. The document itself will be critical to your evaluation process.

The plan should start with an analysis of prior fundraising efforts (assuming, of course, that your organization has engaged in fundraising in the past). It should also state the mission and vision of your organization, because the mission and vision should drive all your development efforts. The plan should then list the broad based goals of the plan, specific objectives under each goal, and the strategies and action steps that will be used to implement the objectives. It also needs to contain benchmarks and an evaluation system.

The Action Plan

Each of your objectives should include specific strategies and action steps to accomplish your objectives. It is critical to address these four questions for each objective in your development plan:

✎ Who is going to do it?

✎ When will it be completed?

✎ How much will it cost?

✎ How much will it raise?

All areas of fundraising should be covered in your plan including various fundraising approaches such as direct mail, grants, and special events, telephone fundraising, and personal solicitation. The plan should also address the various constituencies that will be approached, such as foundations, corporations, individuals—who may include alumni, parents, organization members, present clients, past clients, and community members—as well as organizations such as businesses, religious institutions, and service clubs.

The development plan, especially for organizations new to fundraising, should also focus on infrastructure that is needed to manage a fundraising program—technology, communications, research, cultivation, stewardship, human resources (including board, staff, and volunteers), policies, and procedures.

Each objective must include the strategies and action steps to accomplish it, as well as timelines, areas of responsibility, and budgeted costs and income. In setting goals and objectives, be sure to think about the SMART objectives mentioned earlier. Each objective must be measurable— you must be able to determine if you have accomplished this step. For example, did the board identify ten potential development committee members by August 31? Did your year-end mail appeal net $10,000? Have seventy-five individuals increased pledges during the phonathon? Did 200 individuals attend your annual dinner? Did you increase results in your annual fund by 10 percent? Your objectives must be action oriented, outlining a specific action that will be taken to achieve this objective. They must be realistic, yet visionary, and not too easy to accomplish.

Neither in Stone Nor Disappearing Ink

One thing to remember is that the plan is not written in stone, but neither is it written in disappearing ink! It should be flexible, but not *too* flexible.

practical tip

The planning document should be easy to follow, referred to often, and evaluated regularly. One of the biggest problems with many plans is that they sit on a shelf gathering dust. If the plan has all the necessary components, it should be easy to implement and easily measurable. Your plan could fail if your organization is good at setting goals and objectives, but not always as diligent when it comes to establishing the action steps necessary to implement your goals. Your plan must be monitored on a regular basis and evaluated on the basis of its objectives.

Before your plan is complete, you need to have this evaluation process in place. This process must include assigning an individual, usually the chief development officer, to monitor the plan on a regular basis. The plan should also include a section that lists all the action steps in chronological order, a section that lists each step that has a budget impact, and a section that outlines tasks by who is responsible for implementing that action step.

If each individual, committee or department that is responsible for implementing the plan has an easy tool to measure progress, it is much more likely that they will follow the plan. Similarly, the budget will be helpful when presenting the plan to the CEO, the CFO, or the board that must approve expenditures needed to implement the plan. Finally, the timeline, in chronological order, will make it easier for the chief development officer to measure progress on a monthly or even weekly basis. Samples of the benchmarking tools are included in **Appendixes O** and **P.**

Monitoring the Plan

At every development committee meeting, your plan should be reviewed, especially in relation to the timeline and the areas of responsibility. It should also be reviewed at board meetings and at staff meetings. The chief development officer should not use the plan to criticize staff members or volunteers who are falling behind in carrying out their parts of the plan. Rather, the plan should be used as a tool to celebrate progress and discuss issues that might be impeding progress. Often segments of your plan are not accomplished according to the timeline. However, circumstances might justify this deviation. For example, a direct-mail piece might not have been sent on time because a major grant application took precedence.

The board, which also has a major responsibility for certain segments of the plan, should review the plan periodically to assess progress and help establish goals for the next planning year. The development staff should discuss the plan with the CEO and the board to outline progress made and areas that might be hindering implementation of the plan, such as lack of technology, inadequate board or staff involvement, or budget constraints.

It is important to follow established guidelines for the various fundraising components that can help compare your organization's progress with acceptable standards in each area. Remember that some non-monetary goals should also be established in your plan, particularly if your organization is new to fundraising. Be sure to celebrate progress made on these goals, as well. It is not always just about the money!

Try to not become discouraged if all your objectives are not met. Monitoring your plan on a regular basis will assure that some objectives are not totally ignored while pursuing other areas. Staff, board and volunteers must not be led astray by delving into areas that are not in the plan. If a good idea is presented that is not in the plan, the chief development officer should suggest that the idea be investigated further and possibly incorporated into the next plan. If the opportunity is immediate and your organization feels compelled to pursue it, then those involved in this decision need to examine the plan to see what area might have to be revised in the current plan in order to pursue this new opportunity.

To Summarize

✎ The development plan is the foundation of fundraising success. You need to have a development plan that is part of your strategic plan. As with the strategic plans, it needs to have goals, objectives, strategies, and action steps that include timelines, budgets, and areas of responsibility.

✎ Board members, development staff, and non-development staff need to be involved in developing the plan. The plan should include both monetary and non-monetary goals. Objectives must be SMART—specific, measurable, action-oriented, realistic, and time-defined.

✎ Be sure to establish a person to monitor the plan and benchmarks so the plan can be evaluated on a regular basis.

Chapter 15

Understanding Philanthropy and Fundraising Methods

In This Chapter...

✎ Why do donors give or not give to nonprofits?

✎ What strategies can you use to move donors up the donor pyramid?

✎ How do you find the donor's "hot button?"

Before approaching prospective donors to ask for their contribution, you must first understand the reasons why they might give to your organization and why they might not give, and then you can design an approach to them based on their individual reasons for supporting your organization. You must know how to develop a case for support that is donor-centered and that shows donors how they can be a part of the solution and how their gifts will truly make a difference in their community.

As we've seen in **Chapter 9,** there are many reasons people give. Sometimes the most obvious ones, such as tax benefits, are not nearly as influential to a donor's decision as people think. In fact, tax benefits generally rank very low on the scale of why people give, although they often affect *when* and *how* a donor gives. Research shows that the most compelling reason people give is because they believe in the mission of the organization—a good reason to have a compelling mission statement and to promote your mission everywhere.

Finding What Motivates Your Donors to Give

There are several ways you can determine what motivates your donors to give. First, ask them! During the preparation for a capital campaign, most organizations conduct a feasibility or planning study whereby a consultant talks to donors about the likelihood of their supporting the organization. But if you are not in a situation where a study is appropriate, you can hold focus groups to find out what motivates your donors. Or you can survey them informally on a one-to-one basis. During the personal solicitation process for major gifts, team members making the solicitation calls should always probe for the reasons why a prospective donor chooses to give or not to give. These reasons can be helpful when approaching this prospective donor in the future or approaching other donors who might have similar motivations.

Why Donors Don't Give, or Stop Giving

There are many reasons donors do not give, as well. One of these is that they do not trust the organization to use its money wisely. Another reason donors do not support certain organizations is because they are not convinced the need is urgent and compelling. Or, perhaps they feel there are other organizations doing similar work, and they are either more familiar with these other organizations or they think the other organizations are doing a better job of addressing the needs they feel are important. This is why having a compelling and well-written case for support is so important.

People stop giving to nonprofits for a variety of reasons, as well. Occasionally, donors die or move away and must be replaced with newly-acquired donors. In a mobile society, donors moving out of the area is a common reason organizations lose their support. Sometimes donors are upset with an organization because their gifts were not reported accurately or recognized properly, or they have a falling out with a staff or a board member. You can be assured that every person who is unhappy with your organization will tell at least fifteen persons about their concerns and, if these fifteen tell fifteen more, your organization can lose support dramatically. The most compelling of the reasons donors stop supporting organizations, believe it or not, is because they think the organization does not care about them as an individual.

Once you understand your donors' motivations to give, reasons they don't give, and the kind of things that make them stop giving, you can better plan how to approach them, what you need to have in place when inviting donors to contribute, and what you need to do to properly steward their gifts.

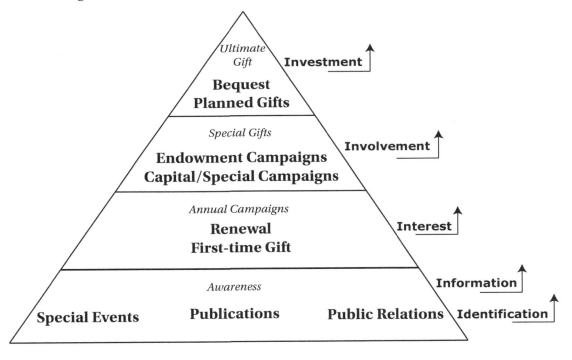

Moving Donors Up the Donor Pyramid

Anyone who has been involved in fundraising for any length of time has probably seen some version of the donor pyramid, above. Basically this concept tells us that in any fundraising efforts there will many steps that have to take place before a donor is willing to make the final commitment of the "ultimate gift."

You might think about this as you would a courtship. Most of us don't meet the "love of our lives," decide "this is the one," and immediately make a commitment to spend the rest of our lives together. If you have someone significant in your life, you probably met, maybe casually, maybe even over the Internet. Then a friendship started which, as it became more serious, involved more commitment on the part of both parties. Eventually after a period of "courtship" for months or maybe several years, there was a formal commitment made, maybe in the form of an engagement. And then perhaps more months or years went by and eventually the final commitment of a life-long relationship took place. Even so, many things can go wrong to end this commitment. The ever-growing divorce rate proves this!

Your relationship with your donors is a lot like this. First you "met" the donor, through the awareness you created through public relations, your website, a special event, direct mail, or the Internet. As the donor became more involved with your organization there was more of a sense of commitment. The donor made a first annual gift and, if you did everything right, there were multiple renewed gifts, upgraded gifts and maybe even a special (major) gift to a campaign. The more involved the donor becomes, the more investment is apparent. And only after a period of "getting to know each other" is the donor ready to "pop the question," "is this the organization to which I want to commit an ultimate gift?" And, as with personal relationships, a lot can go wrong in the donor relationship process if we're not careful.

The donor pyramid shows how people become more engaged in your organization by gradually moving up the donor pyramid based on the "I" words. We have already talked about identifying potential donors and providing them with information about your organization so they can become familiar enough with you to make a first-time annual gift. In the chapters ahead, I talk more about encouraging and cultivating the interest of your donors and about moving your donors into more involvement in your organization by making a major gift and, finally, about how to reach the ultimate investment through planned giving.

Think about the bottom of the pyramid first, creating awareness. How do you get donors to notice you among the hundreds or thousands of nonprofits that might be in your community? Are you a small fish in a small pond, a big fish in a small pond, a small fish in a big pond, or a big fish in a big pond? What is your market position? How do you make your case? How do you use free or cheap methods to create awareness of your organization?

Next, think about making that initial approach to a donor—whether through direct mail, telephone or the Internet. Which of these methods is the most cost effective? Which ones reach the most people? How can you sift through these mass media contacts and find the people that could move to the next level?

As your donors move up the donor pyramid, how do you know when they are ready for the "big ask?" How do you know when it is time for the "ultimate gift"? What are the options through which a donor can make an ultimate gift? Each of these will be explored in more detail in the chapters ahead.

No matter where your donors are in the donor pyramid, the one sure way to make certain they get "stuck" at that level or even drop to a lower level (maybe even a "zero level") is to not steward your donors' gifts properly. It is critical that you are good stewards of your donors' gifts, follow ethical and professional standards, and properly recognize gifts. All these steps will be necessary to inch your donors up the donor pyramid to the ultimate gift.

To Summarize

✎ There are many reasons people give to some nonprofits and not to others. Among the most compelling reason donors will support your organization is that they believe in the mission and vision of your organization. However, even when people support your mission, donors can be very fickle. If you do not acknowledge and recognize their gifts, do not show them that their contributions really make a difference, and/or tell them how you've spent their money, they may be tempted to move on to another organization that treats them with more respect, provides them with a more compelling story, and/or reaches out to them to make a connection between the organization's needs and their own needs and desires.

✎ As many reasons there are that motivate people to give, there are an equally significant number of ways in which donors can be approached. Remember that all fundraising is really about moving donors up the donor pyramid to the point where they are inspired to make an investment in your organization. You need to start at the bottom of this donor pyramid and plan carefully the right moves to help donors make the ultimate gift.

Chapter 16

Infrastructure

In This Chapter...

✎ How important is it for fundraising to have a donor database system?

✎ What kind of policies and procedures do you need to have in place to do effective fundraising?

✎ What kind of a budget do you need to support development efforts?

Infrastructure in the development program is much like infrastructure in a city, county, state, or country. You cannot have a great community if you don't have roads, bridges, a cable system, and other utilities to support the community. Likewise, you cannot have a strong development program without adequate software systems, policies, and procedures in place. Let's talk about some of the things every development office should have before you start to raise money.

Among the items that help lay the foundation of a vibrant and thriving development program are policies and procedures, having a strong case for support, and adequate staffing of the development department. Policies affect how your organization deals with donors, such as how you acknowledge and recognize their gifts and what types of gifts are acceptable to your organization. Policies are usually developed by the staff but approved by the board. Procedures are internal to the organization and are usually developed and approved by staff.

Gift Acceptance Policies

One document you need before you can begin fundraising is a gift acceptance policy. These policies should be developed by development staff and approved by your board of directors. Policies should address questions such as:

- What types of gifts will we accept?

- From whom will we accept gifts?

- How will we dispose of those gifts?

- What types of recognition will we give donors?

- How will we invest donor contributions to our endowment fund?

- What percentage, if any, of our endowment fund will we use for operational expenses?

Some issues that could come up in major gift appeals, capital campaigns, and planned giving programs that can be resolved by having gift acceptance policies before the solicitations take place might include:

To Accept a Donation from a Brothel? That is the Question

One organization based in Nevada was offered a gift from a brothel, a legal business in its county. Since there were no gift acceptance policies in place, this organization spent four hours at a board meeting debating whether it should accept this gift. It finally came down to a 60 percent/40 percent vote to not accept the gift because a slim majority of board members felt this gift did not fit in with the mission of the organization, a domestic violence shelter. If this organization had gift acceptance policies in place, the board and staff would not have needed to spend four contentious hours discussing whether to accept the gift.

Uninspired

- A thirty-year-old donor wishes to give your organization a gift of an insurance policy; how will you handle and recognize this gift?

- A prospective donor wants to give your organization a gift of real estate; what stipulations should be made before accepting the gift? Suppose the real estate has an underground oil tank or asbestos? Can you afford to remediate these issues? Does your organization want to be a real estate manager?

- How much must donors give to have a building or area designated in their name or the name of a loved one?

- If a donor gives a gift of appreciated stock, does your organization keep it in its portfolio or sell it and convert it into available cash?

Gift Acceptance Policies Save the Day!

One environmental organization faced an interesting dilemma. One day a gentleman who ran a company that was guilty of polluting the environment stopped into the organization's office with a check for $350. The executive director was surprised when the receptionist told her about this unexpected "gift." Upon some further investigation it was discovered that the check was to cover ten $35 memberships in the organization. The astute executive director quickly figured out what was happening. There was a public hearing scheduled for the following week, and it became clear that this gentleman planned to show up at the meeting with ten of his friends or employees who would then be members of this organization to protest its viewpoint on the subject of the hearing. After calling the organization's attorney to make sure it could refuse the gift on the basis that members sign a pledge form saying they support the mission of the organization, the executive director called the "donor" and told him it would be returning his check. Disaster averted, thanks to gift acceptance policies!

Pure Genius!

✎ A company that is known as a polluter of the environment or a distributor of a socially unacceptable product or service wishes to make a gift—do you accept it?

These and many other questions can be handled legally, ethically, and tactfully with proper gift acceptance policies.

Procedure Manual

Unlike the gift acceptance policies, procedures are developed and approved by your staff. The procedure manual is important in that it enables anyone in your development office to handle routine day-to-day procedural items. Some areas covered in the procedure manual are:

✎ How soon does an acknowledgment letter get mailed after the gift is received? Twenty-four hours is ideal, forty-eight hours is the maximum amount of time it should take to thank a donor.

✎ Who signs donor thank-you letters? Often, letters to major donors are signed by the chair of the board, with the CEO signing the next level of donors, and the CDO signing the letters to smaller donors. There is no hard and fast rule about this. Your organization must establish its own guidelines in the form of written procedures.

✎ Who receives gifts? Some organizations have all checks going directly to the finance department. In others, the development office receives donations first, facilitating proper acknowledgement and recognition. Then, after copying, checks are sent to the finance office. Unless the finance office is completely faithful about sending check copies to the development office within twenty-four hours, it is best for your development office to receive gifts, make copies of the checks or other instruments, and *promptly* send them to the finance office for deposit.

Procedure manuals can also outline the coding structure for various donors and prospects as well as list routine reports that need to be generated from your donor database system.

Having a procedure manual in place will help temporary staff and volunteers fill in when a key staff member is out of the office and will also help evaluate your staff on the basis of how well procedures are followed.

Donor Software

It is important to have a good donor database system in place before beginning any major fundraising effort; this is the foundation for any fundraising/development program. A dynamic database is the heart of a successful development office. The information contained in the database will be used for many purposes, and must be available in a format that allows access, manipulation, and analysis. *A database is more than just a mailing list.* Similar to for-profit businesses gathering data about customers, the nonprofit organization must track information about its constituents, too—volunteers, clients, potential supporters, current donors, ticket-buyers, event attendees, etc. It is also important to gather and store research information about foundations and corporations.

The world is populated with prospective donors. Before you solicit these prospects, you must create relationships with them and help them to become familiar with your work and involved with

Donor Database Strategies

Some things to keep in mind when you set up your donor database:

✎ Coding is essential; be sure to have your coding plan in mind before you start entering names.

✎ Study your donor database to understand and plan extraction strategies for the codes so you know if you will be able to access the information you need by those codes.

✎ Involve all active users in the code planning process. A user could include your development director, membership manager, data entry persons, or accountant, and is not limited to those sitting at the keyboard.

✎ Write a description for each code, its relationship to other codes and its function in the database— recommended reading for data entry persons.

practical tip

your staff. Donors will invest in your cause, if they believe in your vision. In order to target different segments of the population with appropriate messages and maintain a flow of information and appreciation to your prospects and donors, you need to build your donor database and identify investors. That's where fundraising software can help. The effective use of a fundraising software system will help identify donors, track donor activity, process and acknowledge gifts, and analyze results to find areas of success.

Fundraising Software

What is a fundraising software system? It is a software application that provides you with a tool to increase the effectiveness of your fundraising efforts. As with other tools, fundraising systems come in a variety of sizes, shapes, and prices. The right software will provide an undeniable return on investment. In some cases, the return comes from areas of increased efficiency, such as mailing or gift processing. You will also see savings through the increased efficiency the software system allows. You should see cost savings such as lowered postage and printing costs by avoiding duplicate mailings to the same donor. A software system also allows you to track important information about donors and prospective donors that will help you build lasting relationships.

Why I Stopped Supporting this Organization

I stopped supporting one nonprofit organization—one I cared deeply about—because after numerous phone calls about this issue I was still receiving three of its newsletters, each addressed to me in the same way. I decided if it could not efficiently handle its mailing list, it might not be efficiently handling my donations either.

Uninspired

Improved Efficiencies

An effective fundraising software system will provide your support with the tools to do their jobs more efficiently and more effectively. Increasing the productivity of the office staff ultimately saves your organization money.

Many tasks and functions become simplified when the full capabilities of a system are utilized.

Gift processing is traditionally an aspect of development that is time consuming but needs to be done on a daily basis. Crediting the donor and immediately sending a personalized thank you letter is critical to fundraising success. A good development software system makes this process faster and easier. However, your donor database also provides your professional staff a tool to help with the process of cultivating and soliciting donors.

So, what are some of the ways your database can help you save time?

- ✎ Special events—the use of software designed exclusively to manage the logistics and reporting can reduce the number of staff hours it takes to coordinate events. It will also help with follow-up tasks and analysis of each event.

- ✎ Once your development office processes gifts, the checks will then be given to the accounting office. Many times, the accounting office must process the same gifts but allocate the monies to the specific general ledger accounts. Through the use of a fundraising system that allows for links to accounting and spreadsheet applications, the double entry work is eliminated.

- ✎ Reporting—reports are used to track the status of a particular appeal, enabling you to include certain information in your annual report or to identify in your database those individuals with specific characteristics. Through the use of fundraising software system reports, this information can be generated quickly and according to your needs.

Decreased Costs

By purchasing and implementing an effective fundraising software system, you can realize significant savings on common expenditures. For instance, mailing costs are sometimes a large portion of your development office's budget, so efficient mailing systems are an important aspect of your development program. Unfortunately, a great deal of money is wasted in this area. A software system will reduce costs in all aspects of your office's mailings by helping you eliminate duplicate records.

✎ For targeted mailings, your donor database will give you the capacity to mail to selected segments within the entire database quickly and easily, if the segmentation codes have been carefully planned.

✎ Many people prefer to receive their membership or events information by email. A system that allows individualized, bulk emails is an efficient and cost-effective way to reduce postage and printing costs.

✎ Efficient checks for duplicate or bad addresses can result in significant savings in mailings.

Capturing Lost Opportunity

One of the areas in which fundraising software can be of the biggest help is in capturing lost opportunity. For instance, many donors have the ability to give much more than you typically ask them for. And, each year, organizations lose money from the people who don't, for one reason or another, renew their support. As your database grows, the fundraising software system will help you find these people. Here are some ways you can use a system to help capture otherwise lost opportunity:

✎ Run reports to track people who have given at some previous time, but who have not given this year. Once these people are found, you can apply appropriate strategies to encourage them to contribute again.

✎ Tickler files help make sure nothing falls through the cracks. If they aren't asked, or asked in their preferred way, people will not contribute.

✎ Analysis reports help to identify fundraising initiatives that are or are not working. They also help determine appropriate goal levels for specific campaigns.

✎ Good fundraising software allows you to gather and store important information about individual donors and grantmaking organizations, so that you can cultivate productive relationships with them.

The chart below demonstrates the types of contact you will want to make with current or potential sources of funding, both individual and organizational. Good fundraising software will help with these efforts in many ways.

	Suspects	Prospects	Donors	Investors
Planned Gifts			Visits with personal follow-up	Visits with personal follow-up
Major Gifts			Mail, calls with follow-up	Visits with personal follow-up
Capital Campaign			Mail, calls with follow-up	Visits with personal follow-up
Grants		Mail with follow-up	Proposals with scheduled follow-up	Proposals
Corporate Gifts		Proposals	Proposals	Visits, calls & proposals
Membership		Proposals	Mail	Mail & calls
Special Events	Mail	Mail	Mail	Mail & calls
Annual Appeal	Mail	Mail	Mail	

The person who actually enters the data needs to understand the importance of accuracy for the development office. Donors can become very offended if their information is not correct. Some things to keep in mind include:

✎ Middle initials are important.

✎ Phone numbers are important.

✎ Email addresses are important.

✎ Have proper reference materials handy, such as phone book, zip directory, etc.

✎ Use your donor database's duplicate avoidance procedure.

✎ Never remove records with donation or membership history. Develop "Inactive" and "Deceased" codes to handle inactive accounts.

✎ Remove prospects after a predetermined number of years with no response.

✎ Birthdates are helpful for the planned giving effort and general cultivation.

✎ Backup daily or before mission-critical procedures such as merging records or making global changes.

✎ Donor privacy is very important. A few hints to help you use donor data ethically:

❖ Know and share the "Donor Bill of Rights" with your donors, stakeholders, and anyone who works on your database.

❖ Do not share pledge/gift reports with board members, volunteers, staff, reporters, etc. without proper clearance—as they say, "Loose lips sink ships."

❖ It is a donor's right to be listed "anonymously," or not at all, in publications and donor listings. Use the "anonymous" check box on the database system.

❖ Use the shredder for sensitive information not securely filed or currently in use.

❖ Do not leave sensitive information on the computer screen when you walk out of your office; log out of the program.

❖ Use passwords to protect data if you use volunteers who have no need to know certain information.

❖ The donor has the right to be excluded from any mailing list exchanges between organizations and should be advised of that right and given the opportunity to exercise that right if you sell or exchange mailing lists. Code these doors appropriately in the database.

The donor database system can help tremendously with donor acknowledgment and recognition. Some hints:

✎ Acknowledgments—thank them seven times before asking for the next gift.

✎ Know and follow IRS requirements.

✎ For top-level donors, in addition to thank-you letters, you might want to plan phone calls by a board member, volunteer, executive director, or development director. These steps can be coded in the database system.

✎ All donors should receive thank-you letters in a timely fashion—twenty-four hours from receiving the gift is ideal.

Budget Considerations

Although donor software might be one the largest investments your development office requires, you will need a budget that includes other items in addition to software. The old saying that "it costs money to raise money" is true. Some things that need to be budgeted for in the development office are:

Equipment

✎ Computer

✎ Hardware

✎ Software

✎ Maintenance

- ✎ Contracted services
- ✎ Photocopier
- ✎ Postage machine
- ✎ Letter folder
- ✎ Furniture
- ✎ Phones—office/fax/cell

Salaries & benefits

Publications/mailings

- ✎ Annual report
- ✎ Brochures
- ✎ Letters
- ✎ Postage
- ✎ Stationery

Resource library expenses

- ✎ Newspapers
- ✎ Journals
- ✎ Books
- ✎ Directories

Events

- ✎ Meetings
- ✎ Recognition events/gifts
- ✎ Special events "seed money"

Professional development for staff

✎ Professional association memberships for staff members

✎ Workshops/conferences/seminars

✎ Training

To Summarize

✎ You must have the infrastructure in place before you can be successful in fundraising. Infrastructure includes things such as policies and procedures and donor software.

✎ Policies must be approved by your board and should include both investment strategies and gift-acceptance policies. Procedures, on the other hand, are internal things that will make the operation of the development office flow smoother. Procedures guide on issues such as who receives donations, who records them, who signs thank-you letters, and other procedural issues. Staff members develop procedures, which are generally not approved by the board.

✎ A good donor software system cannot only help you save time, but will make your donor relationships more personal. You need a system that allows you to check for duplicate records, track donor history and donor preferences, and accurately record, report, and acknowledge gifts and pledges.

✎ Be sure to plan an adequate budget for fundraising. It takes money to make money. I provide a sample budgeting form in **Appendix Q.**

Chapter 17

Community Awareness of Your Programs

The foundation of the donor pyramid is creating awareness of your organization. There are numerous ways to create this awareness, which is the first step in building donor relationships. One way to begin the process of building awareness in others is to make sure your own "family"— your board and staff—understands the mission and is able to explain it to others.

One good way to communicate with your donors and potential donors is through a monthly or quarterly newsletter. The newsletter can be either

"News" for your newsletter should include:

- ✎ Program updates

- ✎ Staff and board appointments

- ✎ Personal stories from program participants

- ✎ Personal stories about donors

- ✎ News about expanded programs and facilities

All these are newsworthy items that can inspire and motivate donors. Most donors love to see their name in print, so list donors to your organization unless they have requested anonymity.

Perspiration!

in hard copy, electronic, or both. Most people today prefer the electronic "eNewsletter" because they are less expensive to produce and can contain more timely news. You can also track the readership of your newsletter, how many times it has been forwarded, and on which links people most often click. If you have email addresses of your donors and constituents, do consider an electronic version of your newsletter. If you do not have email addresses, you can start to gather them by explaining in a hardcopy newsletter that you are moving to an electronic version for those reasons—you can get them the information they need on a more timely business, and the cost savings will allow you to put more of their dollars to work directly in funding programs. Be sure your newsletter actually contains "news," not the monthly lunch menu in the cafeteria.

Your staff, board and other volunteers should be willing and able to speak passionately about your organization.

You should always use good quality photos in your newsletter, but make sure they are photos of no more than three or four people. Large group shots do not work well, because the people in the photo will not stand out when sized for your newsletter. Leave enough white space. Use fonts that are easy to read, especially considering whether it is electronic or hard copy, and keep in mind that many readers will be older people, so use a large enough font size. You should have your newsletter designed by a professional graphic designer who will be familiar with type styles to select the one that is appropriate for your organization and your readers.

Your newsletter should always prominently feature your organization's mission and vision statements and a list of your board of directors and administrative staff. You should also include a response envelope with hardcopy newsletters to make it easy for your readers to make a donation.

Your Annual Report

One of the most effective tools for creating awareness of your organization is your annual report. In fact, if your budget for printed materials is limited, the annual report should be your top priority. Your annual report does not have to look like the type of expensive publication General Motors or IBM sends its stockholders, but it must look professional. An interesting and well-written annual report can be a great donor cultivation tool. Be sure your annual report includes an accurate list of your donors for the year. This can help inspire others to donate.

You are most likely required to submit your financial information annually in the form of your 990 report (in the U.S.). This information is available to your donors and the general public through http://www.guidestar.com, so it needs to be accurate and transparent. But it also needs to tell a compelling story about your organization. Since you need to compile this information anyway, why not use this opportunity for another communication, and send the annual report to your donors and

---

An Exercise for Your Board and Staff

Your Elevator Speech

You get on the elevator in the lobby of the largest bank in your community. You push Floor 10, and the CEO of the bank gets in just as the door closes. The bank CEO pushes number 16, the top floor. She notices your briefcase and the organization brochure you are holding in your hand. "Oh, you must be with XYZ organization. My charitable contribution committee just mentioned that we received a funding proposal from you; tell me about your organization." You have about thirty seconds before you get off the elevator to tell her about your organization. What do you say?

Perspiration!

prospective donors or, better yet, post it on your website?

You need to make sure that the financial information included in your annual report is understandable. Pie charts and graphs make this sometimes dull information seem more lively and attractive. Speaking of financial reports, your Form 990 is a good public relations tool, as well. Besides all the financial information that is in the Form 990, there is space to describe your program and this is the place where you can "sell" you organization to prospective donors.

Be sure to include photos of your programs in action, stories about program successes, and your plans for

Surprising But True!

One organization was ready to publish its first annual report, but several board members were concerned that the financial statements might cause some concern for donors; its accounting method changed midyear, and the numbers looked worse than they really were. The finance committee was so concerned about this issue that it prepared a written statement and provided it to every person who answered phones in this organization so they could read the prepared statement and refer people to the finance committee for any questions. Approximately 10,000 annual reports were mailed out, and only three phone calls came into the organization about the annual report. One was from a donor whose name was misspelled (a mistake you don't want to make); one was from a donor who wondered why her name was not listed even though her gift was made after the end of the June 30 fiscal year (there was a notation with the donor list stating that gifts received by June 30 were listed); and the final response was from someone who thought he had contributed to this organization and wondered why his name was not listed (it turned out he had given to another organization with a similar name).

Lesson learned: Financial reports might not be as important to donors as being recognized publicly for their donation.

Pure Genius!

the future. Posting the annual report to your website can save you a lot of money on printing costs, and you can remind donors in your newsletter or through a post card that the annual report is online. This will also help drive people to your website.

Other Awareness-Creating Ideas

There are many other ways you can create community awareness of your organization, including:

- Participating in health fairs or other expos in your area of expertise
- Speaking at various professional and service clubs
- Writing letters to the editor about a cause that effects the people you serve
- Giving testimony at public hearings
- Using billboards and public service announcements

Your Website

Perhaps the most important tool for creating awareness of your organization is having a professional, interactive website.

Having a web presence is an important asset that you cannot do without. Your website is a key—perhaps the most important tool in your toolbox—to creating awareness about your programs and services, your mission and vision, and your goals.

Having a website is not enough. If you're not going to have an effective website, you might as well not have a website at all. An effective website is attractive and communicates to visitors immediately what your organization is all about. Its purpose is not only to provide information about your organization, but also to attract visitors to join in your work.

Your website needs to be interactive. You can provide options for visitors to volunteer, sign up for events, and donate with one click. You also need to provide fresh information on a regular basis to keep them coming back.

It is also critical that the website be kept up-to-date. There is nothing worse than a visitor to your website checking the "upcoming events" section and finding an event or activity that happened last year. And this happens more than you might think. Just check out some nonprofit websites for yourself and see! Also critical is that you don't forget the basic information. I can't tell you how many websites I have researched only to find that the organization does not include pertinent information such as a list of board and key staff members, an address and phone number, and a mission statement. You get the idea. Make sure you include everything on your website that you would include in a printed brochure.

Who should create and maintain your website? Even if you have a staff member possessing basic knowledge of HTML, hiring professional web designers is still a better option since, initially, the professional will be able to work not only on the web design, but also the website's usability and search engine optimization (an awesome design does not necessarily translate to user- and search engine-friendliness). You're paying web designers for their knowledge of coding, graphic design, web design trends, and visual communication; thus it might be best to leave your website's design to the experts (at least at first).

Once the designer has created your website, the next step is maintaining it. With the right website software/provider, you can still have the capacity to update your website, whether or not you are Internet savvy. Maintaining a website basically involves updating the content regularly, posting pictures and updates, and quality assurance — making sure that all the pages of your website are active and do not have broken links or images. So, you need to make sure you appoint someone internally to work on the website on a regular basis.

Some tips for your website:

- ✎ Always update your website's content regularly.

- ✎ Keep your website's content short, simple, legible, and plain. As with an effective case statement, do not use jargon or technical words your readers might not understand.

- ✎ Don't forget the basics.

- ✎ Provide information. Some examples might be:
    - ❖ A list of the warning signs of a disease with which your organization deals.

❖ Ten things you can do to reduce your carbon footprint (for an environmental agency).

❖ How to help your child excel in school (if yours is an educational group).

One final idea to help stimulate thinking about what can help your website attract visitors: Do some research on your competitors' websites, as well as those of other nonprofits. Make a list of the things you like and don't like about these websites. Share these ideas with your designer and the person who will be responsible for updating your website.

To Summarize

✎ Before donors will contribute to your organization, they first need to know your organization exists, what you do, and how well you do it. There are numerous tools to help create awareness of your organization. Among these are your website, newsletters, and your annual report. These are the most critical pieces of your public relations plan. Cultivation activities are also designed to help you in "friend raising," the first step in fundraising.

✎ A top-notch website is critical and needs to be professionally designed and kept up to date. Your annual report and even your 990 form can be a great way to boost awareness of your organization and show donors that you are using their money effectively.

Chapter 18

The Case for Support

In This Chapter...

- What is the case for support, and how do you use it to reach donors?

- Who should be involved in writing the case?

- What kind of materials do you need to develop that will help donors see the value in donating to your organization?

The case for support is the foundation from which all your fundraising materials will be developed. The starting point is your organizational case for support. From this organizational case, case statements can be developed for the various appeals and campaigns, and for different constituencies.

The case for support shows people why they should support your organization. The case is based on the mission and vision of your organization and outlines its history, the needs of your organization—although it should focus on how these match the needs of the community—and the solutions your organization offers to meet these community needs. It also lists the qualifications for operating the programs your organization is proposing to fund. It tells prospective donors about those who manage your organization, staff the program areas, and govern your organization.

You should tell readers about any endorsements that have already been received from the community. A good case for support is both rational and emotional. People give because they believe in the mission of the organization, and they must be shown, through the case for support, why your mission is important to them and to the community. The case statement checklist in the sidebar on the next page is a good way to evaluate the strength of your case for support. It is crucial to develop the case for support before launching any fundraising programs.

Many organizations do not have a written case for support and often don't even think about the need for one until they are ready for a capital campaign. Your organization, however, does need a written case for support from which you will develop the materials for *all* your fundraising appeals. There are several areas you need to address in order to make sure your case is compelling.

Always write your case from the viewpoint of the donor, not from the organization's perspective. What would motivate a donor to give to your organization? Understanding the psychology of philanthropy discussed previously is one good way to understand what will make a donor give to your organization. People often mistake what will entice a donor to give.

Explain the need, not just from your organization's standpoint. People don't give because *"we need more space, we need to hire staff, and we need to pay our bills."* They give because your organization is filling a need in the community. Use statements such as, *"This campaign will allow us to expand our services to 500 more families each month."* Or, *"Your gift will enable us to feed twenty-five hungry families each week."* Include personal stories of

Case for Support: The combination of reasons advanced by an institution or agency in justification of its appeals for support, with emphasis on its services, past, present, and potential.

Case Statement: A carefully prepared document that sets forth in detail the reasons why an institution or agency merits support, in the context of the "case bigger than the institution," with substantial documentation of its services, its human resources, its potential for greater service, its needs, and its future plans.

Checklist for Case Statement Evaluation

✎ Does it elicit emotional as well as rational "reasons" to give?

✎ Does it tell the potential donors how their gift will make a difference?

✎ Does it evoke a sense of the history and long-term importance of your organization and its work?

✎ Does it offer proof that your plan will work?

✎ Are the benefits to the donor clearly stated?

✎ If you include graphs or charts, are they striking?

✎ Is it concise?

✎ Is it reader-oriented rather than organization-oriented?

✎ Does it emphasize "opportunity" for the donor, rather than "need" of your organization?

✎ Is the information presented in a logical order?

✎ Is it readable with short sentences and paragraphs?

✎ Is the typeface appropriate to your organization's appeal?

✎ Is there enough blank space to make it easy to read?

✎ Is the type large enough for older prospects to read?

✎ Is the cover "striking?"

✎ Is the paper stock attractive without looking expensive?

✎ If you include photographs, are they effective and cropped to maximize their impact? (Photos should not include more than two to three people. Large group shots lose dramatic impact.)

practical
tip

A Teachable Moment for a Board Member: Why People Give

One board member of a nonprofit was misguided by what motivates donors. The director of development pointed out to this board member one day that there was a huge hole in the carpet in her office and suggested that the organization purchase a new carpet so no one would trip and fall on this carpet. The board member said, "Oh no, we don't want people to think we can afford a new carpet; they won't want to give unless they see that we need the money." The development director, however, pointed out to this board member that his *alma mater*, a prestigious Ivy League university, did not raise money because it "needed" it, but because it was known for providing a superior education, was well respected, and had influential alumni and trustees.

P.S. A new carpet was installed shortly after this discussion.

Pure Genius!

the people your organization is helping. People give to people.

Make sure your mission, vision, and values are included in the case. If you don't have these in place, start developing them. When explaining to prospective donors who you are and what you do, you also need to answer the question, "Why do you exist?" What would happen if your organization did not exist in your community? What is distinctive about you? Develop an interesting history of your organization that answers these questions: Why did your organization get started in the first place? What has been your track record of success?

Demonstrate credibility. What credentials does your staff possess? Are your board members known and well respected in the community? All of these help make your case.

Don't forget to make the "ask!" Tell people how much money you are trying to raise and what this money will allow your organization to accomplish. There must be a plan that demonstrates that your organization can do what it says it will do. A table of gifts will help show the need for leadership gifts. You should also offer opportunities to participate. Show donors how they can be part of the success. Give them options such as an outright cash gift, a pledge, gifts in kind, planned gifts, etc.

One of the important steps you can't afford to skip over is testing your case. Ask some of your top donors if they find the written case compelling— would they give to this cause after reading the case? If not, ask what they would suggest to improve it. Or, hold a focus group of donors and prospective donors to review your case. In a capital campaign your case will be tested during the planning/feasibility study. (More about this in **Chapter 25,** Capital Campaigns.)

Remember that a compelling case must have both emotional and rational appeal. Using photos and personal stories will draw people in emotionally. But before they write the check, they want to make sure your plan will work.

Who Should Write the Case?

In some organizations, the case is written by program people or marketing people. This is a huge mistake! Not that these people cannot write well; they usually can. But to develop a case that resonates with donors, there needs to be a fundraising person involved. Usually, the chief development officer has the main responsibility for developing the case for support. Do not attempt to have a team of people write the case. Although a lot of input from staff, board, volunteers, and donors can be valuable, you must have one person as the primary author of the case so it flows well and is consistent. The development staff person will also have the understanding of how to present the "ask," how to explain giving levels, and opportunities for participation. Sometimes, a consultant is engaged to write the case for support, especially for a capital campaign or planned giving program.

Your case should have a recurring theme. Once the case is written, decide what materials you will develop from the case. The reason it is so critical to have the case completed before developing any materials is so all the materials you develop follow this recurring theme and have a uniform look and feel. Typically these materials include:

- Grant proposals
- Fundraising brochures
- Fact sheets
- Pledge cards

- ✎ Letters of intent

- ✎ PowerPoint presentations

- ✎ DVD's

- ✎ Video

- ✎ Website

- ✎ Speeches

- ✎ Other special campaign materials such as bookmarks

- ✎ Volunteer training materials

How much should you spend on fundraising materials? This is always a tricky question. Some organizations, such as universities, hospitals, and museums, often have a constituency that expects attractive and well-done materials. Other groups, such as a local homeless shelter or a human service agency that serves the working poor, might have donors who would be outraged if the organization spent a lot of money on materials that the donors feel could be better used on programs to address the needs of the people they serve. There are ways you can save money on materials. For example, instead of a video, you might want to consider a PowerPoint presentation which is far less expensive and can be easily changed as things change within your organization or your campaign. You might also be able to get a sponsor to underwrite the costs of printed materials or a video. Regardless of what materials you need to develop and how you decide to allocate your budget among these items, remember that everything you do to present your case must be professional looking without looking too expensive.

Remember that there are some common mistakes made when developing your case for support—having an undefined purpose for your appeal, overstated emotionalism, being too factual and not emotional enough, making claims you cannot support, and misunderstanding what motivates donors.

To Summarize

✎ Your case for support is one of the most important documents in your development office toolbox. The case is the source document from which all your fundraising materials will be developed, including grant proposals, brochures, website, and speeches, to name a few. It is critical that you develop your case first, before developing any fundraising materials, in order that every piece of communication from your organization has a uniform look and feel to it. This helps establish your brand and assures that donors and prospective donors are not hearing mixed messages.

✎ The case must be both emotional and rational. Emotion helps draw people into your organization and causes them to want to be a part of your mission and vision. But before they take out their checkbook and write a check, they want to know that you have the capability to deliver what you promise, that you will use their money wisely, and that you are serving a real community need.

✎ Your case will be translated differently for different audiences; however, the themes and the message remain the same.

Part 5

What Methods Are Used in Fundraising?

Okay, now we are ready to actually raise the money. Bet you thought I would say we still have more to do, didn't you? In the following chapters, I talk about the various methods of fundraising and which of these are the most effective. As mentioned previously, it is important to have a diverse number of tools in your tool box. You can't use a hammer to screw in a screw, and a screwdriver probably wouldn't work well to saw a piece of wood. So knowing how and why donors like to give, knowing the costs and the return on investment of each of these types of funding, and knowing that you have a limited number of resources available, both human and financial resources, should help you decide how much time and effort to spend on each of these. But do try all of them. Don't rely on one type of fundraising to "do it all."

Chapter 19

Direct Mail

In This Chapter...

✎ Is direct mail effective in reaching out to donors, or is it perceived as junk mail?

✎ What exactly is an "acquisition mailing"?

✎ To whom should you be mailing, and how often should you mail them?

While direct mail usually does not generate major gifts, it is one form of fundraising that almost any organization can accomplish with relative ease. It is the type of fundraising that allows your organization to reach the most people in the shortest amount of time.

In an age of electronic media, social networking and instant communication you might wonder if direct mail is still viable for your nonprofit. Certainly "snail mail" is slower, more costly and usually less personal than other forms of communication. However, there are still lots of advantages to direct mail. When done correctly, direct mail can be very effective for many organizations. If you look at the number of pieces of direct mail you receive in your mailbox every day, you can well imagine that it must be effective or there wouldn't be so many organizations using it.

As a general rule of thumb, organizations that succeed with direct mail are those that have a "universal appeal," those that have a large number of constituents living in widely-dispersed areas, those whose constituency is older, and those that can segment their constituency base for various personal appeals. My best advice to those who are considering direct mail is to learn about the pros and cons, consider it as part of your overall development strategy, and then test, test, test with your constituents to see what works and what doesn't.

There are two types of direct mail that can be used in your fundraising program: acquisition mailings and renewal mailings.

Acquisition Mailings

The term "acquisition mailing" is used to describe a mailing made by an organization that does not already have a built-in base of constituents who could be likely supporters of their fundraising efforts. Your organization might never use acquisition mailings. If you work for a college or university, for example, you will probably not do acquisition mailing because you have a donor base of alumni. Hospitals, likewise, usually have a significant number of "grateful patients" to solicit, so if you work for a hospital you might not need to conduct acquisition mailings. Religious organizations are also unlikely to use acquisition mailings unless they are attempting to reach out to their community for more members.

On the other hand, if you work for a local homeless shelter, domestic violence group, or other human service organization, you might want to consider acquisition mailing because you do not have a large alumni or another natural constituency that could become donors to your organization. If you work for a national disease-related group, you might rely heavily on acquisition mailings, based on the premise that your organization has a universal appeal. Almost everyone has a friend or family member who has had cancer, heart disease or diabetes. If you are with one of these groups that reaches out to the general public for donations, you are likely to be fairly successful because readers can identify with your cause.

So how do you determine whether acquisition mailing is right for you? Some questions to ask yourself:

✎ Do we have a compelling need to acquire new donors?

✎ Can we easily obtain names of individuals who would be potential supporters of our organization?

✎ Can we afford acquisition mailings?

Do You Need to Acquire New Donors?

If your organization does not have a database of names and addresses, acquisition mailings might be the way to go. They will identify those who have an interest in your organization. In most cases it will also provide unrestricted money. If your organization is currently dependent solely on grant fundraising, you might find yourself in the position of being able to get specific programs funded through grants, but unable to raise operating funds. Direct mail can help solve this problem, because direct-mail donors are typically low-end givers who are not expecting that their gift will be directed to a specific program.

How to Build Your Mailing List

Effective ways to build your mailing list include gathering names of individuals who:

✎ Attend your special events

✎ Visit your website

✎ Attend programs sponsored by your organization

This method is more effective than relying on staff and board members to provide lists, because there is some level of certainty that these individuals have an interest in the programs of the organization.

Perspiration!

Acquiring Names for Direct Mail

There are several ways you can acquire names for direct mail:

- ✎ Building your own list

- ✎ List sharing

- ✎ List rental

Building Your Own List

Building your own list is one strategy to consider. You can ask your board members, staff or volunteers for names of their friends, relatives or others they think might be interested in supporting your organization. This option will have its limitations, because board members and others often do not want to "bug their friends" for money, so they might be reluctant to pass along names. If they do provide names, they will not supply you with large numbers of potential donors, and these friends and relatives might have little interest in your organization's mission.

On the other hand, relatives or friends of board members and volunteers sometimes will contribute just because they are asked by someone they know.

List Sharing

Some organizations might be willing to share lists with your organization if you have a similar mission but they do not consider you a direct competitor. Of course, if your organization has no list to share in return, it will be hard to convince even a friendly organization to provide its list. Also, the *Donor Bill of Rights,* reproduced in **Appendix C,**

Have a Strategy to Renew and Upgrade Donors

The most important thing to remember is that you must have a strategy to renew and upgrade donors acquired through acquisition mailings. Be aware that the average response rate on acquisition mailings is .5 to 1.5 percent. On the other hand, sending direct mail to individuals who already know and support your organization usually yields a response rate of 15 to 20 percent.

Inspiration!

and some state laws require that the organization planning to share its list give donors the opportunity to "opt out" of having their name given to other organizations.

List Rental

Renting lists of addresses is the most effective method of acquiring names. A list broker can provide names and addresses of individuals who have an affinity to your organization. When deciding on potential list brokers, ask for several names of similar groups that have used this company previously. Call these organizations and ask specific questions about their experience with the referred company. Remember, though, that every organization is different, and results will vary. Also, companies will be likely to give you the names of references that had outstanding results. Rather than asking about specific percentages of return, ask the organization if the company's lists were accurate, did it respond in a timely manner to questions and concerns, and did it deliver what was expected.

Make certain to obtain in writing the restrictions on the use of the names and addresses before you agree on a fee. List brokers will rent names usually for a one-time use or a time-limited use, say, one year, meaning that you can mail to these individuals as many times as you want within that specified time period.

The advantage of renting a list from a reputable list broker is that you can identify individuals with an interest in your cause. For example, if you work for an environmental group, you can rent lists of subscribers to

How One Organization Got the Envelope Opened!

One environmental group was sending its first direct-mail appeal. In order to assure that its donors would open the mail, since it had not tried this approach before, it secured Robert Kennedy Jr. as chair of the annual appeal and enlisted him to sign the letter. On the outside of the envelope it used a photo of Mr. Kennedy along with the tagline: "Inside...an important message from Robert Kennedy Jr." The appeal was successful in great part because people opened their mail!

Pure Genius!

outdoor magazines whose readers will likely be interested in protecting the environment. In addition, the names to be rented can be qualified in a number of ways, including household income, age, ethnicity, zip code, or owners of property. Be aware, however, that the more qualifiers you put on the list, the higher the rental charge.

Should You Consider Acquisition Mailings?

When considering acquisition mailings, be aware that the income generated from these mailings often does not exceed expenditures. However, the long-term benefit of acquisition mailings often outweighs this initial cost because, once individuals make a gift, they become *your* donors, and you can solicit them in any way you choose, forever. Direct mail offers a tremendous opportunity to build a strong relationship with the donor that can result in renewed and increased gifts. Many major-donor relationships, even with those who make planned gifts, begin through an acquisition mailing.

The Direct-Mail Package

Direct mail consists of more than just writing a letter. The whole package needs to be considered:

- What will your outside envelope look like?

- Who will write the letter, who will sign the letter, and how lengthy should it be?

- What type of response form will you use?

- What other information will you include in the mailing?

- Are the mailing lists accurate?

The Outside Envelope

The outside envelope, known in the trade as the "carrier envelope," is important because, if your package is not inviting, chances are your letter will not even be opened. Studies show that live stamps typically get a better response than metered mail, because the letter looks more personal. For small mailings, first class stamps can be very effective. For large mailings and acquisition mail, nonprofit bulk rate stamps are often just as effective. A message or a photo on the outside envelope can also persuade individuals to open your mail.

Most organizations use a "mail house" when sending a large mailing. Often, your organization can save time and money by working with a mail house, because it will handle every aspect of the mailing, from helping you with list rental selection to designing the mail package. If you decide to handle your mailing "in house," you might be able to find a group, such as at a senior center, that will stuff, stamp, and mail envelopes as a volunteer service. When planning your first direct mail, if you choose not to use a mail house, you should meet with the bulk mail staff members of your local post office. They can help you with getting a bulk rate mailing permit, envelope size requirements, setting up your indicia, how to address the mailing accurately, and other aspects of direct mail. If you work with a mail house, it will handle this for you.

Personalization is Critical

Because there is amazing technology available today, you do not need to use labels on your outside envelope. A personalized printing that looks like a hand-typed envelope or even a handwritten envelope is much more effective. In order to make your appeal more personal you should also ask key community leaders to be a letter signer, and they might even be willing to send the letter on their letterhead and to use their personal envelopes.

Inspiration!

The Letter

Staff members should not sign your appeal letter. It is much more effective to have a high profile community leader, preferably a board member or someone else who is very visible in your community, sign the letter. This immediately gives credibility to your organization and lets the reader know that the community supports your organization. If you can secure the signer's personal letterhead and outside envelope, it can be even more effective, especially if your organization is not well known in your community. You should, however, make sure the letter is professionally written and tells the story of your organization. The volunteer can add personal touches, subject to your approval.

In many states, mail solicitation appeals are also required to carry a statement that the organization is registered within the state to conduct fundraising. Be sure to check the requirements not only in the state in which your organization is located but in any other states to which you might be mailing.

The length of the letter varies depending on the audience. Many direct-mail experts say a three- or four-page letter is the most effective. Some individuals, however, will not read more than a one-page letter. You should test a few approaches to see what *your* prospective donors respond to best. A good rule of thumb to follow is that the letter should be as long as it takes to tell your story. The story is drawn from your case for support.

Always use a personalized inside address to the prospective donor. The first paragraph should be a "grabber" that will keep the reader interested in reading more. The letter must contain a call to action, or the ask. It is always best to ask for a specific amount of money, to ask higher rather than lower, and to tell donors how their money will be used. A P.S. is often used to reiterate important concepts or to stress the urgency of the appeal.

Enclosures

Many organizations enclose brochures, photos, or token giveaways such as labels or bookmarks, with the direct-mail piece. Again, knowing your audience is critical to a successful mail appeal. Some people like the giveaways. Others have so many labels, etc., that they get annoyed when they receive these items or would rather see their money spent on the programs of your organization. It is important to test your audience and see which approach gets the best response.

The Response Piece

The response piece is the most important part of a direct-mail package. The outside envelope, while important, is usually the first thing to get thrown away, followed by the letter and then the enclosures. The one piece that people generally save the longest is the response envelope. It makes sense, therefore, to spend a lot of thought to what the response envelope and pledge card should look like.

Various options should be provided for people to check off the amount of their gift, starting with the highest amounts first.

Giving clubs, which are various levels of giving each with a name conveying the size of the gift, can be effective in encouraging individuals to consider moving up to a higher gift. These can also be listed with the amounts. Examples of giving clubs might include generic names such as the Founder's Circle, the President's Club, the Century Club, or could be specific to your organization such as the Blue and Gold Club (school colors), or the Harris Society (founder of your organization). These names should be carefully thought out. Avoid things such as naming giving clubs in a museum after specific artists, as some individuals might think the Picasso Circle is not as prestigious as the Degas Circle even though the contribution size is larger. This can result in losing a gift because the donor happens not to like Picasso's work.

Use a Larger Response Envelope!

A larger response envelope (#9) stands out more than a smaller one (#6) and gives the opportunity for individuals to enclose larger size checks—in inches, and sometimes in dollars.

practical tip

The Most Important Factor in a Successful Direct-Mail Appeal

No matter how you obtain your mailing list, accuracy is of primary importance. Nothing turns off a potential donor more than being addressed improperly. A misspelled name, a Mr. and Mrs. salutation to individuals no longer married, or a Mrs. if the woman prefers to be addressed as Ms., can make the difference between a gift or having the letter tossed in the trash without even being opened. If your mailing list is internal, be sure it is kept up to date and reviewed before each mailing. If the list is being obtained from an outside source such as a list broker, ask the broker how accurate the list is and ask this question to representatives of other organizations that have previously hired the company. You will also want to review the list to make sure none of your major donors is on the list—those you might be planning to call or visit.

Renewal Mailings

Direct mail can also be used to renew and upgrade donors. You should have a plan for how you will deal with first-time donors in order to build a relationship that leads to renewed and increased gifts. Some options might be:

> ✎ Send a special welcome packet to first-time donors, acknowledging that this is their first gift, providing them with additional information about your organization, and outlining your need for continued support.

> ✎ Have your staff, board members, or program participants call new donors, thanking them for their gifts.

> ✎ Send thank you letters within twenty-four hours of receiving donors' gifts.

Renewal mailings should always include the amount of the donor's last gift and request a specific increased gift amount. Be certain to let your donors know that their previous gifts were appreciated and how the money was used to further your mission. The giving club concept can be very effective by asking the donor who, for example, has given $50 a year for the past three years to consider stepping up to the "Century Club" with a $100 gift. Donors who are considered likely prospects for a larger gift can often be motivated to join a giving club to which their peers belong.

How often should direct mail be sent to the same donor? This should be tested with your donors. Do they respond better to more frequent or less frequent mailings? Your budget might dictate how frequently you will use direct mail. Most direct-mail experts suggest mailing several times a year, as often as seven or more times seems to be very successful for organizations whose donors are responsive to direct mail. For many small organizations, once a year is sufficient for a direct-mail appeal. Many organizations find that direct mail is effective at year-end (November or early December) when people are considering tax consequences of their charitable giving and are often in a more generous mood. Renewal mailings can also be used to encourage monthly giving with an option to contribute using a credit card or through PayPal.

You should also consider mailing for purposes other than fundraising, for example letting donors know how you used their money after they've made a contribution, letting them know about new programs and services you are offering, or to update them on special project they have been asked to support.

To Summarize

✎ Direct mail is not the most effective form of fundraising, but it can work well for many organizations, particularly those that do not have a built-in base of "alumni."

✎ Direct mail is more than just writing a letter. You need to develop a whole "package," including the letter, the outside envelope, the response envelope, and any enclosures you would like to include.

✎ The most important part of your direct-mail program, however is the list you are working with. There are a number of ways to build your mailing list but, for large mailings, renting a list from a broker is usually the best method. Whether you are using your own internal list or renting a list, make sure it is "clean," meaning that all names and addresses are correct.

Chapter 20

Telephone Fundraising

In This Chapter...

- Do people become annoyed by telephone fundraising programs?

- If you approach donors by phone, should you use volunteers or professional callers?

- Which of your constituents should be approached by phone?

Perhaps your organization is one of those that dreads the "T" word, thinking that callers hate it and that those being called hate it even more. However, studies have proven that telephone fundraising is always more effective than direct-mail campaigns.

The secret is in how the telephone is used to create the relationships that will lead to major gifts. Statistics also show that most people do not complain to authorities about calls from individuals in their community raising funds for local nonprofits. They do complain about the storm window salespeople, the credit card telemarketers, political and other "robo-calls," and other similar calls. Nonprofits are also exempt from the "Do Not Call" lists. However in many states nonprofits are required to register to conduct telephone fundraising, as well as other types of fundraising. If a professional firm is used, it is also required to register in most states that require nonprofit registration.

Should You Try Telephone Fundraising?

Once you've established an effective mail program, the next logical step is using a phone campaign to renew and upgrade donors.

Who Should You Call?

The reason many organizations do not use the phone in their fundraising program is they think of telephone fundraisers as being the typical "telemarketers" who call names from the phone book, call during dinner, read a prepared script, and will not take "no" for an answer. The first rule of using the phone effectively for your fundraising is that the people receiving the call know your organization. They could be members, donors, or users of your services. You should never make cold calls to those who do not know your organization or who have any affiliation with its mission. How many prospects should be in the database to start a phone campaign? Phone appeals can be made to a few dozen, several hundred, or tens of thousands of individuals. The method you use depends on the number of people to be called.

The Phone is Your Friend!

In addition to using the phone to solicit gifts, the phone may also be used for a number of other purposes:

- To invite your previous donors to upgrade their gifts

- To ask for pledges in the community phase of your capital campaign

- To identify prospects for planned gifts

- To survey donors about your case for support

- To thank your donors for their contributions

- To update your database

Perspiration!

Who Makes the Calls?

Before deciding who should make the calls, you need to determine the number of people to be called. If, for example, you are planning to call a few dozen major donors to thank them for their gifts, the calls can be made by board members or other volunteers who gather for an evening to hold a "thank-a-thon."

If you have several hundred members to call for pledges or to renew or upgrade their membership, you can enlist a team of a few dozen volunteers to staff a phonathon. For a phonathon, all the callers are in the same room, usually in a set-up with cubicles. They can use a "phone bank" or bring their cell phones and make the calls. Many volunteers feel that it is much easier to make a large number of calls when they are in a room with other friends who are also making calls. It is not a good idea to just give volunteers a long list of names to call from home when they have time. You will lose control of the process and most volunteers, although they have good intentions, never get around to making all of their calls.

However, if you have thousands of names to be called, you will want to engage a professional telephone fundraising firm to handle the calling program. Or, if you are calling for a specialized purpose such as a capital campaign or planned giving, a professional firm will be your best choice.

Volunteer Phonathons

Volunteers you can invite to work on your phonathon:

✎ Current users of your organization's services

✎ Previous users of your organization's services

✎ Current members or donors

✎ Students

✎ Alumni

✎ Board members

✎ Volunteers from local businesses or service clubs

Each of these groups has something to offer to your organization. Students or individuals who benefit from the services provided by your organization or institution can be excellent volunteers because they can effectively thank donors for their support and ask for continued support. Who can resist

A Few Incentives for Volunteers!

A few incentives can make volunteers feel appreciated. A low-cost item, such as a T-shirt or coffee mug given to each caller at the end of the night, is a good idea. Most volunteers are motivated by a little "friendly competition," so prizes for the caller procuring the most pledges, the largest pledge of the evening, or completing the most calls are always a good incentive. You can ask popular local restaurants, spas, golf courses, movie theaters, etc. for gift certificates that can help motivate volunteers.

Inspiration!

the call from a student who has received a scholarship, someone who has been a patient of the free clinic, or a person who attends the art classes at the local community center?

Alumni, likewise, have a great deal of affection for their benefactors and can relate well to other alumni. Do not think of alumni only as graduates of a school. Most organizations have groups of individuals they can call alumni. Board members and users of your services know your programs well and can be very effective at translating the case into an ask. Similarly, current members of your museum or zoo will have an affinity with other members, or attendees at the local orchestra's concert can also relate well to other concertgoers.

Do not forget to encourage the participation of local business persons such as bankers, real estate agents, insurance salespeople, and stock brokers. These people often make a lot of phone calls in their business, so they are not afraid to pick up the phone and "dial for dollars." Local service and professional clubs will often take on a project such as this to benefit a local charity as part of their community service work.

Preparing for Your Phonathon

Your volunteers might not always be comfortable or skilled at asking for phone pledges. You need to plan a training session for volunteers before they start calling. First, they should be totally familiar with your organization and its programs, especially the particular project or program for which they are seeking funding. You can treat them to a light meal while you show a video or PowerPoint presentation about your organization and

How One Organization Helped a Volunteer to Overcome Reluctance to Phone!

We planned a first-ever phonathon for a small nonprofit and were successful in recruiting a good team of volunteers. However, the first volunteer to arrive on the night of the phonathon was obviously not comfortable with the whole process of making calls for donations. Her negative attitude concerned me, since I was managing the phonathon. I pulled the executive director aside and expressed my concern about this volunteer. I suggested that I ask her to help me with paperwork that evening rather than have her on the phone with a less-than-positive attitude. The executive director had a brainstorm though. She rifled through the phonathon forms and pulled one out with a name unfamiliar to me. "This is my mother's phonathon form; however, the volunteer does not know this is my mother. I know, though, that no matter who calls my mother tonight, and no matter what they say to her, she is planning to pledge $500. Let's give this reluctant volunteer my mother's form and maybe she will see how easy it is." So we "stacked the deck," putting the ED's mother's form on the top of the pile. I tactfully said to the volunteer, "I know you aren't really comfortable with this process, but how about making two or three calls, and if you don't feel comfortable with making calls, maybe you could help me with some paperwork." "That would be great," she said, I really want to help this organization but I just don't know if I want to make phone calls." A few minutes later, we heard an audible scream from her cubicle, and she came bouncing into the area where the ED and I were sorting phonathon forms. "Guess what, I just got a $500 pledge! Isn't that wonderful!" After we congratulated her enthusiastically, I then asked her, "Do you want to try a few more calls?" "Sure! Give me some more forms." At the end of the night she had raised more money than any of the other volunteers, and we almost had to drag her away from the phones.

Pure Genius!

review the case statement with them. Do not plan a huge meal, or they will spend the whole night eating and socializing instead of making calls. Serving pizza, sandwiches, or salads during the orientation period, so they can eat while being trained, works well. Be sure to have lots of water and other beverages available during the evening. During the orientation period, you will also want to review all the forms they will be using and especially go over the talking points for them to share with the donors they call.

A list of talking points will be critical. It is best for volunteers to not read directly from a "canned script" but rather to take the talking points and put them into their own words. They will sound more sincere and less like a telemarketer. They might want to use a script for the first few calls until they get into a rhythm and practice by first calling a few good friends or relatives.

Some tips on handling customary objections will also help them feel more at ease on the phone. Of course, be sure to instruct them to not use high pressure techniques to obtain pledges. They also need to be instructed how to handle reluctant callers and how to complete the phonathon forms and tally their totals.

Using Professional Callers

There are many times when it will make sense for you to use a professional firm for your telephone fundraising program. If you work for a larger organization, or have a large volume of names to call, or you are seeking major gifts or planned giving prospects, I recommend that you hire professionals to make the calls. You should hire a professional telephone fundraising firm that works exclusively with nonprofits and that will work on a flat-fee basis. The fee may be based on the number of calls completed or a flat hourly fee. According to the AFP, percentage-based fundraising of any kind is unethical. Callers working on a percentage basis are often too aggressive. You should avoid any firms that use high pressure tactics and unethical practices.

If you haven't had any experience with professional telephone fundraising firms, you can start by calling other nonprofits that have worked with such firms. Ask about their experience with the firms they have used. You can also find reputable firms listed in the AFP Consultant Directory or the CharityChannel Consultants Registry.

You might want to interview several firms. If there is a regulatory authority in the state, ask if the firm is registered before engaging it for the phone campaign. Most professional firms will offer full service consulting, such as writing and mailing the pre-call letter, sending out the pledge forms and follow-up letters, and assisting with the selection of prospects to be called. These firms will also prepare management reports showing the results of calls and make recommendations for future calling programs. Most firms will allow you to listen in on the calls they are making on behalf of your organization and will usually offer to change the script if it isn't working. Many firms will also come into your organization and train your callers if you have available volunteers or callers, such as paid student callers in a university setting.

Preparing Your Constituents for the Call

Whether you are planning a volunteer phonathon or using a professional firm, having an accurate list will be a critical part of your success. Be sure you have correct names and phone numbers. Many individuals tend to be mobile. They get married and divorced, change their phone numbers, and some people have even eliminated their landline and use a cell phone exclusively. If you feel the list is not accurate, spend some time "cleaning it up." You can contract with a service to make sure your addresses and phone numbers are accurate. Using a professional telephone calling firm can save you a lot of time, money, and volunteer frustration.

No matter which approach you take to your telephone program, you should always plan to send a pre-call letter. This provides legitimacy to the call and can lay the groundwork for successful calls. Finding the right letter signer is an important part of the process. Letters should be signed by a volunteer— preferably one with a high community profile who the recipient will warmly receive.

Do not give people the option in the letter to send a donation "so they won't be called." It gives the donor the idea that the phone call is "punishment" for not sending in a donation. Your letter should state the case with sufficient urgency that explains why you want to talk to the donor personally about it. The letter and any supporting material will be based on your case for support.

The Calls

Volunteers should begin every call by introducing themselves as a volunteer with your organization. They should state whether they are board members, past or present users of your services, or involved in another volunteer role. They should next ask if the person they are calling has received the previously-sent letter and if they have any questions about the information they received. Some people will not have received the letter, perhaps because of an incorrect address. Some will say they received it but have not had a chance to review it. Others will have read all the materials and are well prepared to make a pledge. For those who have not yet read the materials, the volunteers can either review the case briefly with them or ask if they would like a call back after they have an opportunity to review the materials. The caller should then ask the prospective donor about any present involvement with your organization or interest in any particular programs, especially if the donor has supported certain programs in the past.

Phonathon forms should contain the giving history of each person to be called. If the prospective donor has contributed in the past, the caller should be sure to tell the prospect how much this past support of your organization is appreciated and stress what the gifts have allowed your organization to accomplish.

How to Determine the Amount of Your 'Ask'

Both professional callers and volunteers should always ask for a specific pledge amount based on the donor's history with your organization and the caller's sense of the phone call. A phone appeal can be a very effective way to encourage your donors to upgrade to a higher level. For smaller donors, the callers can start by asking for double the amount of their previous gift. With larger donations, do not increase the ask amount too much; a 10 or 20 percent increase is usually appropriate. If you are using a professional firm, the consultant will guide you through the process of setting ask amounts. If you are using volunteers, a fundraising consultant might help with the letter, the process of setting the amount to request, and the volunteer training.

practical tip

Follow-up

Even though volunteers are well trained, your prospective donors might have questions the caller cannot answer. If this is the case, be sure a process is in place to get back to the donor, either by phone or mail, with the information requested. Some donors might prefer not to be called. If a donor requests to be removed from future phonathon lists, be sure to honor this request and make note of the donor's preference in your database so that this donor is not called in the future. Be sure that your callers thank donors for their past support, whether they make a contribution at this time or not. The caller should always graciously thank donors for their time, whether or not they have made a pledge. It is important to lay the groundwork for a future ask. Remember, "no" is not always "no forever."

Collecting pledges after a phonathon is obviously an important step. One practice that helps collection rates tremendously is sending out the pledge forms the very next day. Include a return envelope so donors can easily write a check and drop it in the mail. You can prepare the envelopes prior to the night of the phonathon and use a two-part form so that one part can be sent to the donor and one part retained by you. If you are using a professional firm, the company will handle this for you. For a volunteer phonathon, consider asking some volunteers who do not like to make phone calls to help with tallying results and preparing the pledge confirmations for mailing. Or you can bring along a clerical person from your office to handle all the mailing and pledge recording.

Integrating Phone Results into Your Development Plan

Phone appeals are important because they allow your organization to build relationships with your donors—relationships that will help move them up the donor pyramid. Using information from the phone program in the overall development program is critical. First, be sure to record any address or name changes, those who wish to be removed from future phone lists, donors who want to remain anonymous, or any other pertinent information gained during the call. A good caller will often elicit valuable insights that can help in future solicitations with donors, such as the donor's interest in a particular program. All this information needs to be entered into your donor database along with the amount of the pledge.

Other approaches to consider are telethons and radiothons, in which volunteers staff a phone bank and take incoming calls from people who are tuning in on the television or radio. These programs can work well if you can get a local radio or TV station to donate their phone bank and air time. The station will usually help you plan the programming for the event. This is a far more reactive program than a proactive telephone program, so you need to plan a program that encourages people to call in. The advantage of such programs is that you are often raising money from first-time donors who you can then cultivate and approach for future gifts.

To Summarize

✎ Do not be afraid to try telephone fundraising. It is always more effective than direct mail, because it is a more personal approach. You should, however, always call donors who have a relationship with your organization—not total strangers.

✎ You can invite volunteers to run a phonathon or hire a professional telephone fundraising firm. When involving volunteers, be sure they are well trained and provided with the needed tools, including your case for support, a script or talking points, and the donor history of the people they will be calling.

✎ Be sure to send a pre-call letter to the people on the call list to legitimize your phone call, and set the stage for a successful call.

Chapter 21

Internet/Social Media

In This Chapter...

✎ What is all the buzz about social media—is it a passing fad or a legitimate way to raise funds?

✎ How do you start a program to raise money on the Internet?

✎ How do you approach your donors for support through these methods?

One of the fastest growing forms of fundraising is raising money through electronic media. If you are not already engaged in some form of Internet or social media fundraising, you should develop a strategy for Internet fundraising that is designed to grow with your organization.

Although electronic forms of fundraising are a fairly recent phenomenon and the full measure of their impact has not been fully analyzed, there is one thing that is certain. If you haven't added these forms of fundraising to your "toolbox," you are missing something critical. One day, you will wake up and find yourself trying to build a house without a hammer.

A statistic that you might have heard about is that during Hurricane Katrina more than $5 million was raised in a single day using text-messaging. The number of people world-wide using all forms of electronic media is staggering. If you are over thirty and don't believe some of what you are hearing, ask a thirteen-year-old (or even a twenty-five-year-old) child, grandchild, or neighbor. Of course, to ask them you will have to text them. Because they don't answer email or their cell phone! Okay, so maybe the thirteen-year-old grandchild and the twenty-five-year-old neighbor are not donors to your organization, so why should you care? Well, in a few short years, they could be donors! Whether or not the youth of today become our donors is up to us. We have to be ready for them!

There are several ways you can use the Internet effectively in your fundraising efforts:

- ✎ Your website

- ✎ Email fundraising

- ✎ Social networking sites

You need to understand that it is not just young people who are using the Internet. The number of individuals of all ages using the Internet is growing. The uses of the Internet for fundraising are also growing. Internet fundraising is used for capital campaigns, endowment campaigns, special project campaigns, planned giving campaigns, as well as

Some Questions to ask about your website

- ✎ Is your website appealing?

- ✎ Is it interactive?

- ✎ Does it provide visitors with useful information?

- ✎ Is it up to date?

- ✎ Is there a way for visitors to easily make a donation?

- ✎ Does it contain the basic information about your organization (location, phone number, email addresses)?

- ✎ Is it easy to navigate?

Perspiration!

the annual fund. In general, larger, nationally known organizations are more successful at online fundraising simply because they have awareness among larger numbers of individuals. But even small organizations can benefit from having an up-to-date website that encourages online donations.

Your Website

Your organization's website is probably the easiest place to start and has the most potential to raise money. Take a look at your current website or, better still, have an outside party review it and provide an honest assessment of its effectiveness.

After reviewing hundreds of nonprofit websites, I have been amazed to see the poor quality of so many of them. I hope yours is not one of those that is not effective. If you are not happy with your website, think about how it was developed initially and what you can do to make it better. Perhaps a well-meaning volunteer has offered to "do a website" for your organization. But, you must ask yourself, does this volunteer have the background and experience in designing a website to make it work effectively? It will be worth the cost to have your website designed by an expert designer but, at the same time, someone who has experience in nonprofit fundraising will be knowledgeable about what motivates donors, so it might be a team effort to build the perfect website for your organization.

Making Your Website Appealing

Photographs of people being served by your programs or good stock photos that represent the types of clients you serve will instantly make your mission clear to visitors. Just as with your newsletter, do not use large group photos that are hard to see. Use good close-up face shots or action shots of the type of services you provide. Tell some personal stories about the people you help. Look at websites of similar organizations. Note their positive and negative qualities. Share these with your website design team.

Building an Interactive Website

Interactive websites get far more return visits than those that are static. Some things you can do to make your website more interactive include:

- Invite people to answer a quick poll about a subject that relates to your organization. For example, ask visitors to your site about a local or national issue that affects your clients.

- Invite visitors to take a survey.

- Allow visitors to sign up for events online.

- Provide visitors with information they can download, for example, the *Seven Warning Signs of Cancer* for a health-related organization or *Ten Things You Can Do to Stop Global Warming* for an environmental group.

Some guidelines for your online fundraising:

- Your appeal must demonstrate a compelling need.
- Your website must be attractive and functional.
- You must provide information your visitors find valuable.
- You must have the ability to accept donations.
- You must have the ability to collect email addresses and determine how you will use them.

Inspiration!

Keeping Your Website Up to Date

Keeping the website up to date is critical. If individuals visit your website in October and see an event listed that was held in February of the previous year, they will likely not come back again. You need to constantly monitor and update the events and activities that are time-related. Adding fresh information on a regular basis will keep visitors coming back to your website to see what is new, and they will refer others to your website.

Inviting Donations on Your Website

You should always invite donors to contribute through your website. However, donors will not contribute online unless it is a simple process.

Statistics prove that individuals might only click two or three times. If they do not find what they are looking for on your website, they will move on quickly to another site. You need to add a "Donate Now" button on your home page that allows visitors to easily donate online, using a credit card or a service such as PayPal. Of course Internet fundraising should be just one strategy in your overall fundraising plan. And remember, this is a fairly new way to fundraise, and for most organizations results will not be extremely high until your website reaches optimum usage. If you are not offering online contribution capability, your donors might seek out a similar organization that does offer this quick and easy way to make a donation.

Don't Forget the Basics

Don't forget to put basic information on your website. I am stunned by how many nonprofit organizations do not list their address, phone number, and an email address for people to contact the organization. Think about your organization's brochures, and be sure to include on your website the same information that is on your printed materials. Your address and phone number should be on the home page as well as a "Contact Us" button that points to staff email addresses and multiple locations, with maps if needed. The development office, too, should be on this list. A roster of your board members also adds credibility to your organization. Your mission, vision, and values statements should be on the home page. Your annual report should be prominently featured. You might also want to consider adding your case for support, your strategic plan, and any other documents that would be of interest to donors.

Making Your Website Easy to Navigate

Remember what we said about website donations—that people only want to click once or twice to get the information they need. You should have a directory of website features and a site map to help people easily find what they are looking for. If you've ever tried to find something on a website and gotten stymied by the search feature, you know how frustrating that can be. Visit your own website frequently, and search for different topics. If you find it is not an easy process, talk to your web design team to see what can be done to facilitate navigation on your website. Using keywords to code the different features of your website might take some time and some added expense, but will provide worthwhile in the end.

Email Campaigns

Email fundraising is much less expensive than direct mail. Donors are likely to give a larger amount than they will with direct mail. The first email gift received from a donor might be only $10, but subsequent gifts will generally be larger, just as with direct mail. Use mail and email to direct individuals to the website. Ask them to make a gift after visiting the site, reviewing the information presented and clicking the "Donate Now" button.

Email fundraising will get better results if your organization can:

- Keep the email short.
- Make it graphically appealing.
- Give people an opportunity to "opt out" of future email solicitations.
- Send the email with a personalized address.
- Have someone the recipient knows sign the email.

Perspiration!

Giving via website and email is the one type of fundraising that grew in recent years when fundraising results were declining. As high as 44 percent of nonprofits report having successful Internet fundraising programs. Although Internet giving accounts for just about 4.8 percent of total donations, this figure will likely grow in coming years. Internet donors give more on average than direct-mail donors. Network for Good reports an average online gift of $155. Often direct-mail averages are closer to $15 to $25. Likewise, the costs of Internet fundraising can be as low as five cents for every dollar raised, where costs of direct-mail acquisition can be as high as $1.25 to $1.50 for every dollar raised.

Some ways to gather email addresses include:

- Ask website visitors to register in order to obtain information.

✎ Publish an eNewsletter, and ask hard copy newsletter subscribers to provide their email addresses, explaining that an eNewsletter will save your organization money and provide them with more timely information.

✎ Ask for email addresses when people attend your events.

While Internet fundraising is important, it might take several years for you to develop an online fundraising program that pays off. As with all fundraising, building relationships with donors that result in major gifts requires an investment of time and money.

Social Networking Sites

Many of your donors (and not just young people) are using social networking sites to connect with other like-minded people. The statistics on the growth of social networking are impressive. Reports state that well over 500 million unique monthly users are on Facebook alone. LinkedIn reports having 600 million users, many of whom being in various subgroups within LinkedIn. Social media is becoming an increasingly important way to reach a young and often elusive audience.

You should consider increasing your web presence on social networking sites such as Facebook in order to increase your exposure to donors and potential givers. You can link these sites to your organization's website.

The use of Twitter and YouTube can also spread the word about your organization, your programs, and events. Millions of people hook into these sites daily, so you should be sure you're noticed there.

To Summarize

✎ Internet fundraising, while in its infancy, is the fastest growing type of fundraising. You need to plan now for building a strategy for fundraising using technologies such as text messaging, Twitter, YouTube, and Facebook.

✎ Start collecting emails and cell numbers of your donors. You can put a notice in your newsletter that you will be able to use donors' money more wisely and communicate on a more timely basis if donors provide you with this information.

✎ Be sure that your website is user friendly, and that donors can easily contribute online with one click.

Chapter 22

Special Events

Special events are one way you can raise both funds and friends for your organization. Events can be both fun and profitable and can help solidify relationships with potential donors. However there are some things you need to watch out for with special events. And you should think about running one or two events a year, not ten or twelve.

It is difficult for many organizations to avoid "special event fever." Sometimes board members, volunteers and even staff can put pressure on to hold events. After all, "everyone else is doing it," "but the Boy Scouts raised $200,000 from their golf tournament, so we should do one," and "events are great, we love parties, and we don't have to go meet with someone face-to-face and ask for money." These are just a few of the reasons why some organizations never get past event-based fundraising.

Don't get me wrong, I've been part of some very successful events, and have seen a lot of good relationships built during the process of growing an event. But, as with all the methods of fundraising mentioned in this book, special events should be *part of* your fundraising strategy, not *be* your strategy for raising money.

Some of the reasons you might want to consider special event fundraisers:

- ✎ Almost any organization can run a special event, since there are usually no specialized skill sets or education required, other than being very well organized.

- ✎ The money raised from your events can generally be used for unrestricted operating costs of your organization, since most event attendees do not expect that their event money will fund a particular program.

- ✎ Events are an excellent way to raise awareness of your organization.

On the other hand, there are some important negatives you need to consider:

- ✎ Events are very labor intensive for your staff, and might keep staff from other fundraising duties that could be more profitable.

- ✎ Events usually require a large number of volunteers and these volunteers need staff support. Volunteers can get burned out by attending *and* working at events.

- ✎ Your donors might feel there are too many events in your community, and this can cause donor fatigue.

- ✎ Special events can actually lose money if not run properly.

There are many types of events you can consider. There are all types of "thons," including walkathons, marathons and other runs, dance-a-thons, bike-a-thons, and bowl-a-thons, to name a few. There also various types of dinners, such as galas which usually involve dancing and dinner, award dinners, testimonial dinners, and roasts. Then there are sporting events that you might find appealing, such as golf tournaments, tennis tournaments, and polo games. Many dinner events also include live or silent auctions. And some organizations are getting involved in online auctions. Races are popular, including horse, pig, balloon, hospital bed, and mini Grand Prix or auto races.

Many types of events are not meant to be fundraisers. Some of these were discussed in **Chapter 17,** Community Awareness of Your Programs. Others are discussed when we talk about building strong donor relationships.

The Keys to Successful Special Events

There are a number of questions you should ask yourself when planning a special event:

- ✎ Do you have enough volunteers who are willing to work at this event?

- ✎ Is your board willing to support this event?

- ✎ Does your staff have time, skill, and experience to manage all the details?

- ✎ Are other organizations in your community holding similar events?

- ✎ Is this an event your constituents will support?

- ✎ How much seed money is needed to fund the start-up costs?

- ✎ How much can you reasonably expect to net from this event?

- ✎ What are the total costs to run the event, including staff time?

- ✎ Is there enough time to plan this event?

- ✎ Is this event consistent with your mission?

The Event Committee

Your fundraising events should always involve a volunteer committee to help plan and implement the event. The size of your committee will vary depending on the event. Events could involve a committee of ten or a planning committee plus a hundred or more volunteers. A golf tournament, for example, generally has a chair and a few committee members who will secure prizes for the tournament, a publicity chair, a facilities chair who will work on the arrangements for the golf course, a refreshment chair, a subcommittee to recruit foursomes to play in the tournament and a sponsorship subcommittee. A week-long arts festival might have hundreds of volunteers working at various venues in two- or three-hour shifts managed by a planning committee of a dozen or more people.

No matter what type of event you choose, there are a few things you need to consider before recruiting volunteers to work on this event:

- ✎ Make sure your board, staff, and volunteers are aware of the goals of the events. That is, is this a fundraising event or a friend-raising event? If it is a fundraising event, what are the dollar goals? If a friend-raiser, what is the goal for the number of individuals you want to attend, and what information do you want the participants to receive?

- ✎ Every volunteer must have a job description outlining the expectations and the timeframe involved.

- ✎ You must provide the volunteers with the tools they need to do their job. They might need special training, staff support such as handling the event registrations, or special technology to make their job easier.

- ✎ Volunteers should be carefully matched to the skill set required for this event. For example, if the event requires a master of ceremonies, do you have a volunteer who is experienced and comfortable with public speaking?

Before embarking on an event, you need to know how many volunteers will be needed, what type of volunteers, and whether you can reasonably expect to recruit a sufficient number of volunteers with the skills needed to implement this event.

Board Support

Another critical factor in deciding which events to run is the level of support that can be expected from your board. For example, if you are planning a black tie gala dinner dance in a posh hotel, can your board members afford to attend, and will they sell tickets to their friends? Events such as award dinners or dinners with a silent auction can be very effective, but people who attend your event will notice if your board members are not there. Board members should be willing to host a table, get a foursome to play golf, or sponsor a bowling team. If they are not "on board" with the event, then you need to find an event that board members are more likely to support.

Staff Time

No matter how dedicated and enthusiastic your volunteers and board are about the event, your staff must be both willing and able to devote a great deal of time to managing the event and the volunteers. Staff will be needed to assist volunteers with things such as handling registration for the event, mailing out invitations, and sorting and storing prizes. You need to assess how much time this event will take away from other tasks that your staff could or should be doing. Be sure to have adequate staff support before launching your special event.

Everyone Showed Up—Except Most of the Board Members

One organization held an annual awards dinner attended by members of the business and philanthropic communities. Unfortunately, this organization's board did not understand its responsibilities and the importance of board involvement at events. During the CEO's presentation at the dinner, he mentioned that he would like to thank his board members and asked them to stand as he read their names. Out of a board of eighteen people, guess how many were in attendance—four! After the dinner, several community people came up to me and questioned why there were not more board members in attendance. I attended the event the following year and noted that the attendance was about 60 percent of the number that had attended the previous year. The following year, I skipped the event myself, but noticed that the quality of the invitations had seriously deteriorated and, after that year, it dropped the whole event.

Uninspired

Competition

Many communities have dinner dances and golf tournaments every week, and your constituents can get burned out by too many of the same types of events. Even if you come up with a novel idea for an event, after a few years, staff, volunteers, and attendees might get burned out with the event. Before planning an event, investigate who else in your community is running similar functions, for how many years they have run the event, how long it took before they were raising the money they currently net from this event, and if they are planning to continue this event?

Events: Count the Cost of Staff Time

I worked at an organization that decided to hold a gala dinner dance. We recruited a top notch volunteer committee and the event was successful in raising $37,000; not bad for a first effort. However, during the six- to eight-months planning period, one of my part-time staff members had practically no time to do anything except support this committee's efforts. At the same time, we were running a corporate appeal that raised over $200,000 and were getting ready for a major campaign. Imagine how much more we could have raised in our other efforts if I had been able to better utilize the staff member's time instead of having her work on this event.

Uninspired

Community Support

You need to determine whether your community will support this event. If people feel there are already too many galas, golf tournaments, and runs, they might not support one more. Some companies have established guidelines that prohibit sponsorship of all events or certain types of events or they are simply bombarded with too many requests and eliminate all sponsorships. Ask some of your donors and board members if their employers would sponsor this event. Some people might limit the number of events they will attend annually. An informal survey of your constituents can be helpful when deciding whether you want to hold this event.

Planning Time

It is also critical to make sure you allow enough time to plan the event. Most functions take about a year to plan. Some facilities, entertainment, or guest speakers might need to be booked far in advance. Usually, the planning for next year's event starts with the debriefing after the current year's activity. It is wise to have a co-chair of the event who will take over the chair position the following year so event planning will be seamless.

Mission Related Events

The most successful events are those that are closely related to your mission. For example, the local 4H Club could be very successful with a "Kiss a Pig" contest or cow chip bingo. However the local art museum's patrons will likely not relate to such an occasion, but would probably rather attend a gala dinner in the art galleries of the museum.

Before deciding on an event, think about how well it relates to your mission. Will it help attract the individuals who are likely to become donors to your organization? Will it inform attendees of the value of your mission? Will it solidify relationships with your existing donors?

Choosing the Right Event for Your Organization

So, how do you find the right event for your organization? Answering the following questions will help you decide on an appropriate event:

- ✎ Does this event fit with and promote our mission?

- ✎ How much are we likely to raise at this event?

A Disastrous Event

I actually heard once about an organization whose mission was to end hunger, and it planned a special event that went against its mission: a bowl-a-thon where it drilled holes in frozen turkeys and people used the turkeys to bowl. Not a good choice for someone who is trying to feed the hungry to waste good food on such a silly event.

Uninspired

✎ How much do we need to spend to run this event?

✎ Do we have volunteers who know anything about running this type of event?

✎ Will our board members attend, sell tickets, and sponsor the event?

✎ How much staff time is involved, and do we have staff persons with the skills to manage this type of event?

✎ Will this type of event help raise community awareness of our organization?

✎ Will our donors and friends support this event?

Pitfalls to Avoid

Some questions to consider before deciding what type of event you want to hold:

✎ Is this event likely to be adversely affected by bad weather (an outdoor concert for instance)?

✎ Is it possible to insure against losses at the event (i.e. hole-in-one insurance for a golf tournament)?

✎ Are there risks inherent with celebrity involvement (hidden expenses in the contract, or a celebrity who "falls from grace")?

✎ Will this event risk fallout with your donors (e.g., a politically incorrect comedian)?

✎ Does the event require seed money you cannot afford?

✎ Is there a chance this event could lose money and, if so, is your organization prepared to assume that loss?

Perspiration!

What risks does this event have, and are we prepared to handle them?

A Word about Collaborative and Third-Party Events

If you do not have the capability to run a major event, several other options are available. Collaboration with another organization is a possibility you might want to consider, especially with organizations that have a similar but not directly competing mission. One word of caution when embarking on collaborative events: Make sure that both organizations are willing to sign an agreement outlining how expenses and income will be shared and how the workload will be divided.

Another option is a third-party event, in which another group holds an event and gives the proceeds to your organization. Again, a written agreement should be in place outlining exactly how income and expenses will be shared. The event organizers should clearly tell you how your organization's name, logo, and other information will be used promoting this event. With the proper written agreement, both third-party events and collaborative events can

Joint Event? These Organizations Failed to Agree in Writing

Two agencies decided to pool their resources and run a joint event, agreeing verbally to split the proceeds 50/50. The event was fairly successful but on the evening of the event it became apparent that one organization had only sold a few tickets while the other accounted for about 80 percent of the attendees. It turned out that the organization that sold most of the tickets had also obtained most of the door prizes and had done most of the legwork to make the event succeed. When the proceeds were split, the organization that didn't do much work was happy, but the other group felt, justifiably, that it was not receiving much return for all its work. Lesson learned: Always have an agreement in writing outlining who is doing what and how the proceeds will be shared.

Uninspired

be very successful, especially if you do not have the staff, time, volunteers, or expertise to run an event on your own.

Avoiding Special Event Overload

Perhaps your organization is already conducting multiple events and needs to decide which ones to continue and which ones to drop. Using the forms in **Appendixes X** and **Y**, which are discussed in **Chapter 27**, can help you decide which events are the most appropriate and most effective for your organization.

If your staff is bombarded with requests from board members and volunteers to add yet another special event to your bag of fundraising tricks, take heed! Many organizations get caught up in "special event fever" when a board member or other well-meaning volunteer hears about a successful event run by another organization and decides that your organization should hold a similar event. The first thing you need to do is help the board understand that each proposed event must be closely examined to be sure that the benefits outweigh the costs, *including lost opportunity costs*. Unless staff members are hired exclusively to run special events, development staff members who should be focusing their energy on building relationships with major donors find themselves instead using all their time and energy to run events. Board members and volunteers need to understand that if you are busy with events, it might keep you from visiting major donors, meeting grant deadlines, and raising money in other ways.

To Summarize

✎ Special events are just one way of raising money for your organization and might not be the most productive or cost effective way. Board members often opt for events because they relieve them of the burden of directly asking others to support the organization. When it comes to the various types of fundraising and the average costs of each method, special events rank low on the ladder of effectiveness.

✎ You should consider holding one signature event each year. Events should, whenever possible, tie into the mission of your organization. The goal of the event must be clear to all involved. Is it a friend-raiser, or a fundraiser, or both? There should always be a careful analysis *before* undertaking an event to set specific objectives and *after* the event to see if the objectives have been met.

✎ Perhaps the best way to avoid over-dependence on special events is to have a well-thought-out development plan that encompasses all types of fundraising activities. Your board members should have input into the development of your plan. If they buy into the plan, they are less likely to want to deviate from it. Having a solid plan has enabled many organizations to avoid the temptation to add one more event to their list and encourages a focus on more productive ways to raise money.

Chapter 23

Grant Proposals

You will most likely be writing grant proposals to different types of funders—government (federal, state, or local), private foundations, family foundations, and community foundations. Grants often fund programs, but some foundations will fund operating expenses, capital needs or endowments.

Although the proposals for each of these types of funders and each purpose might vary greatly, there are some basic questions that most funders will ask. So you should begin by preparing your case for support, which will provide answers to these questions. It will be much easier to develop your grant proposals once you have your case for support in place, so that document should be written before you start writing grant proposals.

You can add any additional information that funders request and store it all in one file on your computer. For example, copies of your organization's IRS recognition letter as a 501(c)(3) tax-exempt organization will almost always be requested. This file of information can be thought of as your "grants vault." When preparing to write a grant proposal, ask for the funder's instructions, and select the information from the "vault" needed to prepare the grant application. Sometimes the funder will issue a request for proposal, or RFP. When the request for proposal is obtained from the funding source, you need to read very carefully. Follow the instructions to the letter. If you have questions, contact a representative of the funder. Meet with that representative, if possible. Before this meeting, write as much of the grant proposal as possible so your questions can be as specific as possible.

Sometimes the funding source asks for a letter outlining your request, called a letter of inquiry. If the funder is interested in your project, you will then be invited to submit a formal grant proposal.

Checklist for Identifying the Problem or Need

✎ Clearly and compellingly state the need for the proposed project or program.

✎ Demonstrate understanding of the problem to be addressed—cite examples, use statistics.

✎ Avoid going beyond the problem stated in the proposal.

✎ Provide data that support the claims made in the proposal and demonstrate the need; be sure the data are current and accurate.

✎ Document sources, being sure to use reliable references.

✎ Create collaborations to solve the problem.

✎ Use quantitative documentation:

❖ Statistical information,

❖ Specific statements of fact, and

❖ Graphs, charts, maps, and tables.

Perspiration!

Most often, the funding source will request specific forms to be attached to the grant request and the information to complete these forms will also be available from your "vault." Some information you should begin to gather will be discussed on the following pages.

Statement of Need

You need to think of the statement of need not in terms of what your organization needs. You need to understand that funders do not care about the fact that your staff is stumbling over each other, that your building is falling apart or that you don't have enough staff to run the programs you want to provide. You should identify the needs of your community, and then determine how those needs would be met by this grant. Some requests for proposal will call this a statement of the problem. As we discussed in **Chapter 18,** The Case for Support, remember that you are being asked for the need of your potential clients for the service—not your organization's need for the funds. You should also be able to cite statistics that show the community need, including demographic and psychographic information.

Here are some ways you can quantify the need for your services:

> *Survey:* If you do not have the expertise to conduct surveys internally, you can ask someone with expertise in this field, perhaps a statistics expert or a college intern, to help you conduct a survey to find out the need for a particular program or service. Once the survey instrument is developed, staff members or volunteers might be able to ask the necessary questions and tabulate the data. A college statistics class could undertake the survey as a class project. There are also online tools available, such as *Survey Monkey,* which can facilitate the process of completing the questionnaires and tabulating results.

> *Talk to your clients:* Sit down with some of the people who receive your services, and discuss with them the need for the particular service for which you will be requesting funds. If 80 percent of the people you serve say they would use this new service, this could address your statement of need. This can be accomplished in a

focus group setting or one-on-one, which will obviously take longer than a survey, but will give you some personal stories you can incorporate into the proposal narrative.

✎ *Compile a waiting list:* If you have a waiting list or letters requesting a service, this could also affirm the need for these services. Your program staff should maintain records of individuals requesting services not currently offered.

✎ *Hold public meetings:* Many organizations have been successful in calling a public meeting and taking testimony on the need for a particular service. This could be done in collaboration with other nonprofits, with which you might also collaborate on the grant proposal.

✎ *Gather available data:* Information from the census can provide statistical data about the need for a particular program. For example, housing and homelessness data are available through the census. State departments of health could be approached to obtain health data. The Office of Employment Security will provide the latest employment information. Local police departments are an excellent source of crime statistics.

Objectives

Remember what I said in **Chapter 14** about objectives having five characteristics that make objectives SMART? These also pertain to how you can measure your service delivery objectives:

✎ *Specific:* The objectives should list specific tasks to be accomplished, such as, "We will feed 2,000 children a nutritious meal each month."

✎ *Measurable:* Estimate in specific numbers how many clients will be served, how many jobs will be obtained or any other objective. Before listing an objective in the proposal, you should determine if it can be measured. "We will evaluate the results of this program by means of surveying our clients, reviewing test scores, etc."

✎ *Action-oriented:* The objective must outline specific steps to be taken. For example: "Print and distribute 2,500 copies of an informational piece about the dangers of smoking in fifteen high schools," rather than a nebulous idea such as increasing awareness among teens of the dangers of smoking.

Examples of SMART objectives might be:

✎ We will obtain full-time employment for one-hundred unemployed youth by July 2013.

✎ We will provide a training program on diabetes treatment for 250 Native Americans each month from January through December 2014.

✎ We anticipate a reduction in drug use by 20 percent of the program participants within three months of participating in the program.

Perspiration!

✎ *Realistic:* You must be realistic about the services you can provide. Do not seek funds for program results that cannot be achieved. Remember that if your proposal gets funded, you need to assure the funder that you can achieve the goals you've outlined.

✎ *Time-defined:* Set objectives for a specific time period, such as year, a quarter, or a month: "We will complete our building project by December 20XX."

Your Services or Project

The proposal should always provide a description of the services or the project that will be accomplished through the grant funds. Always be as clear as possible, since often the individual reading the proposal is not familiar with the services you provide. Try to avoid industry jargon. When using an abbreviation or acronym, indicate what the formal name implied with this abbreviation the first time you use it. For example: Advanced Certified Fund Raising Executive (ACFRE). Subsequent uses of this terminology can then be stated as ACFRE, without explanation. It is always helpful to have someone who does not work for your organization or industry read a draft of your proposal. This is often called the "Grandma Review." It assures that the proposal will be understood by a layperson.

The Five "W" Questions, Plus One More

No matter what the length of the proposal or who the potential funder is, the answers to these questions should always be part of your proposal.

- ✎ *Who?* Who are the people who will benefit from this grant, and how are they selected for participation in the program? What populations are most affected by this program, e.g., senior citizens, Hispanic females, person is living below the poverty level? Who will be administering this program, and what are their credentials? If the proposal is for a capital project, who will benefit from the services provided in this place?

- ✎ *What?* Exactly what services will be provided? Your program staff should be able to provide accurate descriptions of the programs you are seeking to have funded by this grant. If this grant is for a building, for example, your facilities manager will be able to provide you with specifications on square footage, costs per square foot, and building designs.

- ✎ *Where?* Where will the services be provided? In your facility? In schools? In the home of the recipients? At a senior center? If you have multiple facilities, you should describe how many people will be served at each location. If the grant will fund a capital project, list the building site and why this particular site was selected.

- ✎ *When?* When will you begin providing these services, and what hours will the programs be offered? How long will the program run? If you are seeking funds for a building, when will ground be broken, when will construction start, and what is the anticipated move-in date?

- ✎ *Why?* What is unique about your program? Why are you the best organization to provide these services? What are your unique capabilities and history of success? If a capital grant, why is this building needed, and what difference will this facility make to your constituents?

There might be one additional "W" to address if you are collaborating with other organizations on this proposal:

✎ *With whom?* If appropriate, list the other organizations with whom you will collaborate. Explain the services each one provides the clients and how this relates to the services being funded by this proposal.

And the Other Question: "How?"

How qualified are you to offer this service?

You should always outline the credentials of the staff members who will provide the services outlined in the proposal. List a salary for each individual that is consistent with the salary figure in the budget. Do not forget fringe benefits and taxes when preparing a budget.

How will you know you're successful?

Most funding sources will ask how the results of the program will be evaluated. Just as in the development plan, each proposal must have its own evaluation method:

✎ Who will participate in the evaluation process? Outline how staff members and clients will participate in the evaluation.

✎ What will be the evaluation tools? Will there be surveys, interviews with program participants, forms to track results? You will need to show that you can evaluate success and report back to the funder. For example, a client satisfaction survey could be helpful. You can check attendance figures to see if attendance objectives were met. If there was a waiting list for a particular program, you can determine if those on the list are now participating in the program. Measurable outcomes are a critical requirement for most funders.

How Will You Fund This Program Once the Grant Funding Ends?

Will this program be self-funding after the grant ends? If you ask for capital funding, how will the new facility affect your budget? It will be critical that you can show that buildings, programs and services are sustainable once they have been funded initially. It is important that you can provide the funder with an accurate estimate of budget expenditures. If you request a grant to purchase equipment, you should obtain cost estimates for that equipment before submitting the proposal. If you request funds to hire staff, you will need to work with your human resource and finance departments to determine the salary for the staff member and compute the fringe benefits before submitting the proposal. If you can show salary comparisons, that would also be helpful, so the salaries you request are in line with acceptable industry standards.

Capital campaign budgets should show all expenses including purchase of land, site preparation, moving expenses, architect, and other fees as well as construction costs. Endowment budgets should show what programs the fund will endow and what other sources of funding are available for these programs.

The budget should accurately reflect the true costs of the project. Budgets are typically divided into two parts—personnel and non-personnel.

Personnel costs include:

- Salaries
- Fringe benefits
- Consultant fees
- Contracted services
- Volunteer time

Non-Personnel costs include:

- Rent or cost of program space
- Utilities
- Rental, lease of purchase of equipment
- Supplies
- Travel/transportation
- Telephones, cell phones, pagers

✎ Fax

✎ Internet

✎ Postage

✎ Printing

Reviewing Your Proposal

The Four-Step Review Process

Initial Review

✎ Make sure you have met all guidelines

✎ Make sure you've answered any questions the funder might have

✎ Look for unsupported assumptions

Grandma Review

✎ Ask colleagues and friends outside the organization to read proposal

✎ Do they understand it as you do?

✎ Is it free from jargon?

Teacher Review

✎ Check for spelling, grammar, punctuation, dates, address, addition, order of the proposal, and attachments

Final Review

✎ A comprehensive reading by a board member or program volunteer

✎ Does the idea come across?

✎ Does it flow?

✎ Does it make sense?

Perspiration!

Follow Guidelines

Read the instructions carefully. You might lose out on a grant simply because you didn't get the proposal in on time, you didn't include letters of support that were requested, you didn't follow the guidelines regarding the maximum number of pages, you didn't follow the required formatting, or you didn't include information requested by the funder. Read the instructions before you start working on the proposal and again when the proposal is completed to make sure you've caught everything.

Letters of Support

Often, letters of support from key community individuals as well as clients can be helpful in securing the grant. Sometimes the funder will specify a maximum number of letters of support to include. If letters of support will be included, you should have them addressed to your organization, and include them in the proposal rather than asking the writer to send letters directly to the funding source.

There are several types of letters of support:

✎ Letters from potential or existing clients: A letter from a client outlining the need for the specific service for which the request is made can be very powerful. When seeking funds to expand an existing service, letters from present clients stating specifically how they have been helped by the service should be included with the proposal.

✎ Letters from cooperating or collaborating agencies: Include letters from the executive director or board chair of organizations with which your organization is collaborating on this proposal or from which you receive referrals on a regular basis. These organizations should include examples of how funding this program will help them serve their constituents.

✎ Letters from political leaders: Letters from your U.S. Senators and your Congress person, your state senator or representative, county officials, and the mayor of your town or city can be helpful. These people should be as specific as possible about how the grant would help their constituents. It is helpful if you provide these political leaders with "talking points," outlining suggestions of what to include in the letter.

Some Questions about the Proposal

✎ How long should the application be? Most foundations tell how many pages the proposal should be, and some will be very specific about the type size and font you should use. Also, be aware that more and more proposals, especially from government agencies, require online submission. In this case, there are usually strict guidelines about how lengthy the application can be. Online applications force you to write succinctly and get your point across, using a minimum of words.

✎ Who makes the funding decisions, and what are their backgrounds? If those making the funding decisions are experts in the field, the application will be written much differently than if they have no knowledge of the industry. If you are applying to a small family foundation, the decision makers are often family members who serve as trustees for the foundation. If a larger foundation, there will be program officers making decisions who might be more familiar with the terminology used in the proposal.

To Summarize

✎ Providing grant funders with the information they need is easy if you store all this information in one place and update it as needed.

✎ Each funder will have different requirements, but some basic things you should expect to be part of most grant proposals are the project budget, qualifications of the staff who will be providing services, outcomes measurement methods, and a statement of need.

✎ Be sure to carefully review your grant proposal several times before submitting; proof it for grammatical accuracy, to make sure the text is free of jargon, and to assure that it makes a compelling statement of why your organization is the best one to provide the services your community needs.

Chapter 24

Personal Solicitation

In This Chapter...

✎ How do you find time to visit donors personally?

✎ Who should participate in major-gift calls?

✎ How do you know how much to ask for and when to make the ask?

Personal solicitation is always the most effective way to raise money. However, you can't see all your donors in person, so the logical approach is to personally visit those with the most potential, remembering the 95/5 Rule.

You need to identify your best prospects for individual solicitation. These might be foundations, individuals, or businesses. Individuals in this prospect pool are usually categorized as major donor prospects and most large organizations will have major gift officers to manage the process of soliciting these donors. You can refer back to **Chapter 9** for more information on identifying and cultivating potential major donors. Once you have a pool of donors ready for solicitation, the next step is deciding who will solicit these people, and how.

Building Your Solicitation Team

Major gifts should not be the responsibility of any one individual in your organization, but rather a team effort. Your chief executive officer (executive director, pastor, president) plays a key role in the major gift process. Visionary and ethical leadership is one of the primary elements a donor will consider before making a major investment in the organization.

Your development officer will usually play a pivotal role in planning and organizing the major gift program and managing the time of staff and volunteers. You will need to allow sufficient time and training available for your staff and volunteers to build those critical relationships with major donors.

The Key to a Successful Gift

It has been said that the key to a successful gift is having the right person ask the right person, at the right time, in the right way, for the right amount and for the right reason. Finding the right person to make the ask is critical. During the screening and rating sessions, it will be essential to find the best "asker." While several individuals might know your prospective donor, you must identify the person with the best connection to your prospect.

Inspiration!

Most major gifts programs rely very heavily on the involvement of board members and other volunteers. These people, because they are volunteers, bring a special ability to open doors and to speak peer-to-peer to potential major donors. They can talk with the enthusiasm of a donor who invites a friend or colleague to join them to invest in an organization for which they have a shared passion. While a staff member should be on the solicitation team, the volunteer's special connection with the prospective donor is so important that the volunteer, too, should be included.

Prospect Research

The ability of your prospect to make a large gift must also be considered in order to make sure the ask amount is right. Researching the prospect's giving history with your organization and with other organizations, and estimating your prospect's assets, will help determine the right amount to ask for. There are many ways to conduct research online, and there are companies that can help with wealth screening so you can determine the ability of the prospect to give. Determining linkages and interest usually takes the personal touch, and much of this information is gathered through screening and rating sessions.

Suspect: A possible funder/donor about whom you know very little other than the existence of this person.

Prospect: A possible funder/donor you have researched and identified as having an interest in your organization, a potential linkage, and the ability to give.

Expect: A possible funder/donor you anticipate will fund your organization because you have prepared the potential donor for the ask.

Starting with a list of those identified as potential major donors, bring together your board and development committee members who have identified those people and carefully review each name. Do this in a series of meetings if the list is large. Discuss each name to determine the ability (how much *could* they give if properly motivated and approached by the right person); the interest (are they known to give to causes similar to your organization's mission, have they given to your organization in the past, do they have any connection to your organization, is there a particular program of your organization in which this person might be interested?) and the linkage (who is the best person to contact this person? how strong is the connection? if there are several people who have a connection, which relationship is the strongest? is there a "team" of people from your organization who should approach this prospect?). As we've already discussed, it is crucial to understand that screening is a very sensitive issue, and participants in this process must be carefully selected. Information that is sensitive should not be openly discussed. Participants can suggest giving amounts of areas of interest without discussing the prospect's private details. And, of course, no information about a donor's giving history should be given out unless that information is public information (for example listed on your organization's annual reports with the donor's permission).

In addition to information on prior giving, it is helpful to have additional information about your prospective donors before setting up the appointment for the visit. Your major gifts committee should try to obtain the following information about each major gift prospect, remembering that if the prospect is a couple, the information should be collected about both individuals:

The LAI Principle

The keys to getting major gifts are known as the LAI Principle:

✎ Linkage

✎ Ability

✎ Interest

Inspiration!

✎ *What is the prospect's profession?* You might be able to research typical salaries for various professions or make links to others in this profession who might know the prospect.

✎ *What is the prospect's religious affiliation?* A connection to this prospect might be found through a member of the same church, synagogue, mosque, temple, etc.

✎ *From what schools was the prospect graduated?* Most major donors give significantly to their *alma mater*, so you will want to obtain the annual reports of schools the prospect attended and check for donations this prospect has made.

✎ *Is there a spouse or partner?* This information will be needed in order to schedule an appointment with all decision makers. You will want to know if there is a divorce in process that could affect the donor's ability to give.

✎ *What are the number and ages of the prospect's children and grandchildren?* Often a prospect with a high income might not be as capable of making a gift because of a child with special needs, several children in college, or some other circumstance that might be draining funds.

✎ *What hobbies and activities is the prospect involved in?* This information can be helpful in finding a linkage to the prospect and also provide an indication of assets, e.g. does the prospect own a boat or a private plane?

✎ *What awards has the prospect received?* If the prospective donor has received awards for community service or philanthropic giving, this will shed some light on the prospect's community involvement and ability to give.

✎ *What about business holdings, board positions held, etc.?* Again, this can help determine linkages and ability.

✎ *How open is the prospect to being approached?* Some donors are reclusive, and it might take a special effort to find a linkage with someone who can get the appointment.

✎ *Is there an interest in a particular program or aspect of your organization?* If there is a particular program this prospect is

---

One Private School Heeded Advice to Wait. It Paid Off!

One private school was conducting a screening and rating session, and a prominent physician's name was on the list of prospective donors because he was a parent of a student at the school. Another physician who was part of the screening committee mentioned that this was not a good time to approach this prospect for a gift. He did not want to elaborate but suggested that the committee wait a while to approach his colleague. The committee deferred to the physician's suggestion and placed this prospect's name on a list of people to be approached at a later time. It turned out that the prospect in question was having some personal problems that later resulted in a divorce. By waiting until the right time to approach this prospect, the school was able to secure a significant gift when the prospect had sorted out his personal and financial status.

Pure Genius!

interest in supporting, the approach to the prospect should be connected to this area of interest.

 Does the prospect have a giving history with your organization? The team that will make the call needs as much information as possible about this prospect's history with your organization in order to determine the right ask amount and also to be sure the donor is recognized for past support.

The interest of the prospect should always be considered, particularly when the individual is a leadership-donor prospect. Is there a named gift opportunity that fits this prospect's interest? Named gifts are opportunities for major donors to name a building, a room, or a piece of equipment after themselves, their family, their company, or a loved one. Named gifts are almost always used in a capital campaign, but might also be invited during an approach to a major donor prospect.

Training the Team

During the screening process, you need to determine whether the prospect is ready to be solicited or if more cultivation is needed. This enables the prospective donor to be approached by the right team at the right time. You should train the volunteers who will be directly involved in soliciting donors in how best to make the ask. Staff, volunteers, or a consultant can lead the training session. Keep in mind that the trainer must be skilled at helping volunteers develop an approach that uses their own unique style to present the case. If your staff is experienced with major gift calls, you might be able to provide the training internally. Sometimes a volunteer who has a great deal of experience with major gift fundraising is willing to donate time in order to help your organization launch a major gifts program. Many organizations work with a consultant to conduct this training because volunteers might respond better to an outside expert.

If you don't have the experience or expertise in-house, you should consider bringing someone in to train your volunteers and staff in how to make the ask. Your training should include having them always ask for a specific amount for a specific project. And remember that people are very seldom, if ever, insulted by being asked for too much, but they can be insulted by being asked for too little. Role-playing is often a successful and fun way to help your volunteers feel at ease before they have to ask for the "real thing." A consultant or development professional with experience in major gift fundraising is usually needed to provide training on the techniques and the psychology of asking for money.

Regardless of who does the training, some of the key points the trainer should cover with volunteers during the training sessions are:

- All solicitors must make their own gift first; volunteers who are not willing to make their own contribution should be asked to step aside.

- Knowing your organization's case and being able to talk passionately about it is critical. This is the reason it is important that the volunteers are involved enough with your organization to make their own gift first.

- A solicitation team of at least two people is usually the best approach for major gifts. The best team is usually the CEO of your organization and a volunteer who has a close relationship with the prospective donor. A donor or another staff member who has a relationship with the prospect might also be effective members of the team.

- The team needs to rehearse the approach beforehand, including determining which one will make the ask. This is where role-playing can be helpful.

- Getting the appointment is usually the hardest part of the call, so the person who has the best relationship with the prospect should schedule the appointment.

- When scheduling an appointment with a couple, make sure both are available for the meeting. Most people, especially when considering a major gift, make contributions as a joint decision. You want to make sure both partners hear the same message so they can discuss their contribution together.

- After a period of small talk, the solicitation team should talk about the mission of your organization and the project you are there to talk to the prospect about.

- Small talk can include asking the prospects to talk about anything in which the prospect is interested, e.g., children, grandchildren, hobbies, etc.

🖋 You can also ask prospects to talk about their involvement with your organization if they are involved in any way. Ask them to elaborate on what drew them to your organization.

🖋 If prospects are already donors, this is a good time to thank them for their past support of your organization.

🖋 The team should present the case using the materials that you have developed, and should be able to speak with enthusiasm about your organization and its case, especially emphasizing how this project meets the prospect's interests.

🖋 All solicitors must be prepared to demonstrate their own financial commitment. Although they do not need to share the amount of their gift or pledge, sometimes this can be an effective tool to persuade peers that they should give at the same level as the volunteer who is soliciting them.

> ### The Golden Rule
>
> Although sometimes people think the golden rule means, "Those who have the gold make the rules." But to a good fundraiser it is, "Silence is Golden."
>
>
>
> Inspiration!

🖋 Experienced solicitors will be able to determine when the time is right, so that the predetermined solicitor will make the ask.

🖋 The solicitors should always ask for a specific amount (the amount that has been determined in advance of the call). Not being specific in your ask makes it very difficult for the prospective donor to make a suggested commitment.

🖋 The amount of the request is the largest amount you think the prospect might give. You can always negotiate the gift amount, but you will never be able to raise it once an amount is on the table.

✎ The way you phrase the ask is important. Use words or phrases such as "investment" or "joining us in the vision" rather than asking for a donation or contribution. One effective way to phrase your ask is to suggest that the prospect consider an investment *in the range of* $10,000 (or whatever amount has been determined). In this way, you state an amount but leave the door open for negotiation.

✎ The most difficult part of the call for most solicitors is probably remembering that, once the ask is made, the solicitors should remain silent and wait for the prospect to react. Do not answer for your donors; leave it up to them to say the amount is too high, this is not a good time, etc.

✎ Your solicitors should be prepared to answer any questions the prospect has or be willing to get the answers to those questions. This can be a good way to lay the groundwork for future meetings. Remember that most major gifts will not be received in a single meeting. The donors will usually need time to discuss the project, to talk to financial advisors, to pray and/or think about the amount of their commitment.

✎ If the prospect says "no," your solicitors should probe for the reasons—is it "no, not that amount,"

Things your team needs to know to be successful askers:

✎ Make your own gift first.

✎ Ask people you know.

✎ Know your organization's case for support.

✎ Know your donor's capacity and needs.

✎ Ask for a specific amount.

✎ Ask high.

✎ Analyze what went wrong or right during the meeting.

✎ Plan the next step.

Perspiration!

"no, not now," or "no, not for that project." In most cases, "no" is not "no, forever."

✎ Once the prospect has indicated readiness to make a gift, your solicitors should ask the prospect to fill out a pledge card or letter of intent. They should not leave the pledge card or letter of intent for the prospect to return by mail, since this usually results in a lower gift or no gift at all. If a prospect does not wish to make a pledge on the spot, but wishes to think about it or discuss the pledge with a spouse/partner and/or financial advisors, to solidify the pledge the solicitors should set a specific time to make a return visit or phone call.

The Five-Call Rule

It is important not to ask too much of your volunteers, especially the first time around. No team member should be asked to make more than five personal visits. That is usually a manageable number for most solicitors.

Inspiration!

✎ All visits should end with the solicitor thanking the prospect for time and interest shared. Remember that this is about more than just getting a gift—it is about building relationships. Follow-up is vital to success, so a thank-you note should be sent along with any information the prospect has requested. This will help lay the groundwork for future asks.

Making the Ask

Your volunteers must realize that they are not "begging for money," but are giving individuals an opportunity to be a part of the exciting work of your organization! Major gift team members need to understand that giving really does feel good and that being generous even helps people live longer. Team members need to experience the joy of giving themselves. One of the keys to a successful solicitation is that all askers must make their own gift first. It is a proven fact that those who have made a gift will always be more successful at asking others to give, because they can ask the prospect to "join me in investing in this great project." Of course the team members also need to be convinced that what they are asking for is a worthy project—your organization must have a compelling case for support.

Through the screening process, your team members will have identified individuals with whom they have a relationship and feel comfortable asking. In most cases, the asker should be giving at a level equal to the amount the prospect is being asked to give. It is usually easier for individuals to ask someone they know than a total stranger. It all goes back to the compelling case. If volunteers really believe in the mission of your organization and know others who share their values and beliefs, it is very likely that their friends will also be interested in supporting this organization. Always have volunteers start with a visit that is likely to be successful. Nothing builds enthusiasm like success. A volunteer who has made that first successful call will be far more motivated to continue making calls.

Give your volunteer fundraisers any information that you think can be helpful in making solicitation calls. Include the donor's past giving history to your organization, if any. Research will also allow you to provide a list of other gifts that this individual might have made in the community and any connection this prospective donor has to your organization.

Never send out team members to make a call without having established the amount they will be asking each prospect to consider. And remember that individuals are usually not insulted by being asked for too much, but they can be insulted by being asked for too little!

Report Meetings

Make sure you schedule regular reporting meetings so your team can share successes and challenges they have faced. Knowing that others are sharing their experiences helps build team spirit and helps solve some of the challenges that solicitors might be having. And, of course, everyone likes to report success. Often team members have a healthy sense of competition and having an opportunity to report their success to others is a strong motivator. Report meetings will help build enthusiasm and help plan for the next approach to each prospective donor. A few large gifts will be the motivator needed to make all the other parts of the fundraising campaign successful.

Your leadership must always be encouraging. Remember that not all calls will be successful, especially if this is a first effort for your organization. Encourage solicitors to continue by stressing that they are building relationships and not just raising money. After all, the three keys to successful fundraising are Relationships, Relationships, Relationships.

To Summarize

✎ Major gifts should always be solicited through personal, face-to-face visits with the prospective donors. After doing your research and identifying the linkages, ability, and interest of the prospective donors, you need to put together the best solicitation team for each individual prospect. This team is usually led by a board member or other volunteer, along with a staff person—most often the CEO of your organization.

✎ The solicitation-team member will need training and must prepare for the meeting with the prospective donor. They need to know the case, how to get the appointment, and how and when to make the ask.

✎ Volunteers and staff should not become discouraged if every visit does not result in an immediate gift. In fact, if they receive the gift on the first call, they probably have not asked for enough. Although none of us likes to hear "no," you need to remember that "no" is not necessarily "no forever." It could be, "no, not now," "no, not for that amount," "no, not for this project," or "no, not until...."

Chapter 25

Capital Campaigns

At some point in time, your organization will probably face the need to expand facilities and will either plan to build a new building, renovate your current facilities, or purchase an existing building and expand or renovate it to suit your needs. A capital campaign can be demanding but very rewarding, not only because it enables your organization to grow to meet increased community demands, but because the campaign process can help strengthen your organization and strengthen your position for future fundraising efforts.

First, your organization should decide whether a campaign is needed, how much money must be raised, and whether you are ready for a campaign. Any discussion of a capital campaign should start with the strategic

Capital Campaign

A campaign to raise substantial funds for a nonprofit organization to finance major building projects, to supplement endowment funds, and to meet other needs demanding extensive outlays of capital.

Definition

planning process. Your board and staff must evaluate your organization's needs for programs and services.

You should consider planning a day-long retreat for your board and staff members to discuss these issues at the culmination of the planning process. The retreat should be facilitated by an independent party who will lead you through this process. Once your organization reaches consensus that a campaign is in order, a steering committee is then appointed to begin the next step. Members of this steering committee for a building campaign might include the following individuals:

- ✎ Key board members, including your board chair, chair of the development committee, chair of the facilities committee, and the treasurer.

- ✎ Staff members, including your CEO, the CFO, and the Director of Development.

- ✎ One or two donors who have the capability to make a lead gift to the campaign.

- ✎ Individuals with experience in construction (this could be your facilities chair or facilities director). If you have no one with this knowledge, you might want to engage a construction manager who will serve on the steering committee.

- ✎ Your campaign consultant should also be part of this committee.

- ✎ If you do not have a CFO or finance chair on the board, you might want to identify someone with financial experience to serve on this committee.

It could be that your campaign's focus will be on building a permanent fund for maintaining or expanding your programs. You do this by establishing an endowment fund. Whether your campaign is for building or endowment, it is important to remember that the focus of the campaign should not be on the building or amassing a large endowment fund, but on the benefits to your community that this facility or endowment will provide through expanded, increased, or more efficient programming.

In the capital campaign planning process, you should ask:

✎ What is the potential for growth in our organization?

✎ How are the demographics of our constituents changing?

✎ Is our organization prepared to meet the needs of our community?

✎ Are our facilities adequate to handle growing needs?

✎ If not, what must be done to improve our facilities?

Perspiration!

If a capital campaign is in your organization's future, you will want to do everything you can to assure success. There are several key ingredients to every successful campaign. Three of these surface as most crucial.

The following items will help assure success:

✎ Strong annual fund history

✎ Realistic goal

✎ Sufficient pool of qualified prospects

✎ Strong staff support

✎ Gift acceptance policies

✎ Campaign organizational structure

✎ Adequate donor software system

The three *key* ingredients:

✎ Compelling case for support

✎ Committed board of directors

✎ Strong volunteer leadership

Annual Fund History

During a campaign, many organizations think they need to find new donors, seeking to solicit major gifts from foundations and corporations from which they have previously been unsuccessful in raising money. Don't make this mistake! You need to remember that most donors, whether individuals, companies, or foundations, will be reluctant to support your campaign with a major gift unless they already have a track record with your organization. Although you might not have a cadre of major donors, it is always best to start with those who have a relationship with your organization. Look at the top 10 percent of your annual donors to see if there might be some prospective lead donors for your campaign. Another group you should review is your list of "loyal donors," those people who support your organization, year after year. Even if their gifts have been modest, it is possible that among them will be a few major donor prospects who were simply never asked for a large gift before.

Realistic Goal

To determine the goal of your capital campaign, first start with the architectural study. An architect will develop renderings to aid in presenting the case for support to potential donors. Donors will be motivated to give if the vision is inspiring. A building that looks too extravagant might turn off donors to a human service agency if they feel money will be spent on buildings that could be better spent on programs. On the other hand, your project should inspire people to see how your clients and the community will be better served by this building. Once these plans are in place, they should be tested in the community, usually by means of a planning study. The planning study will also determine the interviewee's thoughts regarding the proposed goal. It is important to realize that the case that will be presented is a preliminary case for support, and that the feedback from interviewees might alter your plans in order to arrive at a realistic, attainable campaign goal.

Qualified Prospects

A prospect becomes a qualified prospect when adequate research is done to determine the Linkage, Ability, and Interest (the LAI Principle) of the prospect. Without the three qualifications listed above, it is unlikely a major gift will be forthcoming from a prospect. Screening sessions during the early phase of your campaign can help determine the ability of a prospect to give, and at what level; who is the best team to make the ask; and which possible named giving opportunities might appeal to this prospect.

Staff Support

A capital campaign tends to disrupt the overall operations of your development office. The campaign, because it is runs on a tight timeline, requires intensive periods of concentration on developing prospect lists, working with volunteers, developing campaign materials, and scheduling solicitation visits. The CEO of your organization will need to be involved in identifying, cultivating, and soliciting donors. As much as 50 percent of your CEO's time might need to be devoted to the campaign. Support staff is also crucial during a campaign. A lot of paperwork will be generated during the campaign, including volunteer training packets, letters of solicitation and acknowledgement, recording of gifts and pledges, and grant proposals. Often, additional staff support is hired for the duration of your campaign.

Gift Acceptance Policies

Before launching a campaign, you will need to have clear policies in place regarding what type of gifts you will accept, how those gifts will be disposed of, and how they will be recognized. It is important that both your volunteers and staff are aware of policies before they are assigned to solicit prospective donors. More about gift acceptance policies can be found in **Chapter 16,** Infrastructure.

Organizations That (Rightly) Looked a Gift Horse in the Mouth!

Some organizations have been offered gifts they turned away during a campaign:

✎ An organization desperately seeking land on which to build was elated when it was offered a gift of land…until it found it would have to pay $500,000 to remediate the soil on this land! It turned down the offer.

✎ An organization was offered a $1 million gift on the condition that the building was named after the donor's mother. The building project total was $17 million. It turned down the $1 million!

✎ Still another group was offered a gift from a person who wanted the building named after him. It turned the gift away because the prospective donor was a convicted felon.

Pure Genius!

Campaign Organizational Structure

You will need to develop your campaign plan before recruiting the campaign cabinet. This plan will include position descriptions for all members of the campaign cabinet, timelines, campaign budget, and a scale of gifts, along with suggested goals for each division of the campaign. The campaign organization chart in **Appendix R** showing how many volunteers you will need in each division is crucial before recruiting volunteers to head up each campaign division. If you do not plan to hire a consultant to manage your campaign, you might want to consider engaging the services of a consultant to develop the campaign plan and show you how you can implement the plan on your own.

Planning Your Campaign Materials

Typical capital campaign materials developed from your campaign case statement include:

✎ Grant applications

✎ Individual donor proposals

✎ Solicitation letters

✎ Campaign brochures

✎ Pledge cards

✎ Letters of intent

✎ Campaign letterhead and envelopes

✎ Response envelopes

✎ Website (you should always plan a campaign web page as part of your website)

✎ Press releases

✎ Campaign newsletters

✎ Speeches to be made by staff and campaign volunteers

✎ Fact sheets

✎ Question-and-answer sheets

✎ Volunteer training materials

✎ Scripts/talking points for phonathons

✎ Named-gift opportunities form

Perspiration!

Donor Software

An adequate donor software system needs to be in place during a campaign. Your capital campaign might be the first time you have found the need to record pledges. Most campaigns will have a three-year pledge period, and often donors will want to make quarterly or semi-annual payments on their pledges. Therefore, it is important for you to have a software system that can manage all this, in addition to being able to record which solicitors are assigned to which prospects, so you can track results of each solicitor. If you are financing the building project during the pledge payment period, it will also be crucial to have a system that can generate a cash-flow projection report to show your bank when pledges are expected to be paid.

The Three Key Ingredients

While most of the qualifications discussed above can be developed during the early phase of your campaign, there are three key ingredients you should have in place before you decide to go forward with your campaign:

Case for Support

You must have a clear, compelling case for support that inspires and motivate donors. The case is often referred to as "bigger than the organization." Your case talks about the people this building will serve, the importance of this project to the community, and the difference the donor can make in the people's lives by supporting this campaign. Once the preliminary case is tested during the planning study, it should be reviewed again in light of the input received from community leaders. If you find that your case is not strong enough, it might not be the right time for you to launch a campaign, at least not for this project. Or, there might be ways you can strengthen your case.

The case forms the basis from which all your campaign materials will be developed; therefore, it needs to be written early in the campaign. Your case will be used to inspire volunteers and donors.

Remember that different constituents will be attracted to different aspects of your campaign. Although the way the message is presented will vary according to donor needs and expectations, the message must be consistent in all your campaign materials.

How One Organization Listened to Its Donors, Revised Its Case for Support, and Succeeded

One organization, a fraternity chapter, had what seemed to be a compelling case for support. Its plan was to raise money through a capital campaign that would fund three areas: renovations to its chapter house, a building endowment fund for future facility needs, and a scholarship endowment that would enable it to attract serious students as members of the fraternity. The preliminary case presented this plan and how much would be raised for each segment of the plan. However, when conducting interviews, I found that none of those interviewed felt that scholarship endowments should be a priority of this campaign. To a person, they felt that scholarships were not the responsibility of the local chapter. We revised the final case for support, eliminating the scholarship fund, and were successful with raising the money to complete the project. All because we listened to our donors!

Pure Genius!

Commitment of Your Board of Directors

Board commitment must be present before making a decision to proceed with a campaign. Your board should pass a resolution approving the campaign once the planning study report is received and discussed. Board commitment means that the board is committed to this campaign in every respect—emotionally, mentally, spiritually, and financially. At least five or six board members should be willing to serve on your campaign cabinet. Every board member must make a financial commitment before any other gifts are solicited for your campaign. It will be crucial to show other funders that the "family" of your organization has made its commitment first, and at the highest level possible for each board member. This is the time to ask board members to stretch their giving to a truly visionary level.

Volunteer Leadership

Good leadership can make or break your campaign. It is essential to select a campaign chair or chairs who can inspire others to become involved and to support your campaign. Selecting the campaign chair might take several months in order to identify, cultivate and recruit the right person(s). You will need to prepare a recruitment package that includes your case for support, the campaign timeline, and position descriptions for each member of the campaign cabinet along with an organization chart. I provide a sample job description for the campaign chair in **Appendix S.** Whenever possible, your campaign chair should be someone who has been involved with your organization, preferably a major donor. The chair should always be someone who believes in your organization's mission and supports it wholeheartedly. The campaign chair should also be someone who is known and respected in your community and has the ability to both give a leadership gift themselves, and solicit leadership gifts from others. Once your campaign chair is in place, other key positions should be filled on the cabinet. These volunteers will, in turn, recruit others to serve on the campaign as needed.

Your campaign cabinet needs to meet regularly. Whether it meets monthly, bimonthly, or quarterly depends on the size and scope of your campaign. The various subcommittees that are responsible for each division of the campaign should meet individually between meetings of the campaign cabinet. It is very important that you have regularly-scheduled meetings for subcommittees to report on progress and to discuss developments within the organization, the project, and the campaign. These meetings also help motivate volunteers.

With effective volunteer leadership, full board commitment and a compelling case for support, your campaign will succeed.

If you are considering a capital campaign, you will probably want to work with an outside consultant since this might be the largest amount of money you have ever raised, and you will probably be dealing with a tight timeline. You might not have the expertise to deal with a capital campaign on your own, and often you need the support of a consultant to guide your leadership and board members in the right path, so your campaign does not falter.

The Campaign Planning Study

You might have heard different terms to explain the process of evaluating the chances for a successful campaign. This process in years past was usually referred to as the campaign feasibility study, and you might still hear that term used. In recent years, the term "planning study" has been used more often, partly because, for many organizations, it is not a case of "is it feasible for us to do a campaign?" but rather a case of "how do we best plan for a successful campaign?" Some people also prefer the term "planning study" to avoid confusion between the campaign fundraising study

How An Organization Listened to Its Supporters

One organization performed a planning study for a capital campaign. Although it did not have land or final drawings, it had a rendering of a building drawn by an architectural student. The building featured a rounded entrance and some other rather extravagant features, including a large office for the executive director. As the consultant conducting the interviews, I was intrigued by the comments of one interviewee, the president of a local bank. The banker studied the sketch and then looked around his office and said, "The executive director's office is bigger than mine! Why does a nonprofit need such an extravagant building?" His comment and other similar remarks led the organization to go back to the drawing board and come up with a new plan that was more palatable to community leaders who they were asking to support this campaign.

Pure Genius!

and the architectural feasibility study. In this discussion, I will use the term planning study.

The planning study is an important step in your campaign process. It should be a planning tool for your organization. Most organizations need to conduct such a study before launching a campaign. The study provides your organization with the means to assess both internal readiness to launch a campaign and the community's willingness to support your project. The study should be done by outside consultants, for several reasons:

✎ An objective viewpoint will be needed to analyze the internal readiness of your organization.

Some categories of people who should be interviewed during the planning study:

✎ Major donors to your organization.

✎ Potential major donors you think would be likely to support this campaign

✎ Key board members. Sometimes all board members are interviewed; other times the consultant will talk to key board leadership including the board chair, the development committee chair, board members who are known to have good community contacts and/or the ability to give a major gift, and possibly board members whose support you feel needs to be confirmed.

✎ Key staff people. The executive director and key administrators may also be interviewed.

✎ Community leaders, especially those who have the ability to make a significant gift and/or those who have access to major donors. The consultant will also likely suggest people who might not have the ability to make a significant gift themselves, but who have their finger on the pulse of the community, such as the head of your local chamber of commerce.

✎ Key volunteers, especially if your organization has an auxiliary, an alumni association, or some other group that can be influential during the campaign.

✎ Political leaders, especially if you anticipate seeking government support of your project. However, political leaders are often interviewed because of their community influence and ability to identify potential donors for the campaign.

Inspiration!

✎ Interviewees will generally be reluctant to speak frankly to a representative of your organization about its leadership and its case.

✎ You will need a professional experienced in conducting studies to analyze the data, based on the consultant's expertise, and provide you with objective recommendations.

During planning study interviews, the consultant asks interviewees about:

✎ Their opinion of your organization

✎ Their perception of the strength of your case

✎ Their propensity to make a major gift to the campaign

✎ Their willingness to serve in a leadership role in the campaign

✎ Suggestions for others who might contribute to your campaign

✎ Suggestions for campaign volunteers

Inspiration!

Assessing Internal Readiness for a Campaign

You will find a capital campaign will be challenging if your organization does not have its internal house in order. An internal assessment should be conducted by an individual who can look objectively at the infrastructure of your organization to prepare for a capital campaign.

Infrastructure areas that need to be assessed:

✎ Staffing of your organization

✎ Office systems, including donor database software

✎ Gift acceptance policies and office procedures

✎ The level of involvement and commitment of the board and volunteers

Staffing for your campaign is critical. No matter what the size of your organization, you need to think about the amount of time the campaign will take from your existing staff's time. This is an especially sensitive area for organizations that do not have a formal development office. Often a campaign director will be hired, or a staff person will be pulled from current duties to manage the campaign. You need to make sure that there is someone on your staff who can dedicate sufficient time to campaign coordination. This is not a task that can be handled by a staff member "when there is time."

One of the elements that will make your campaign management, reporting, and stewardship flow more efficiently is a good donor database software package. You will need to access giving history of your donors and be able to use this donor history, combined with additional research, to qualify prospective donors and assign them to an appropriate solicitor. Donor history is an invaluable resource in the preparation for your capital campaign, since in most cases the major gifts will come from those already supporting your organization. Even if your organization is new to fundraising, there are probably donor prospects with a history of involvement with your organization that should be tracked. A good donor database software package will also be used to track all information about your campaign, including donors, prospects, volunteers, pledge amounts, and restricted gifts.

In addition to staffing and software, you must assess your internal policies and procedures. You should have gift acceptance policies that will provide your staff and volunteers with guidelines on what types of gifts you will accept during the campaign, how these gifts will be recognized and, in some cases, how you will dispose of gifts. Gift acceptance policies, discussed in **Chapter 16,** are even more important in a capital campaign in which gifts of land or buildings are more likely to be offered.

As I mentioned previously, transparency is critical, especially in a capital campaign, which is generally the most public type of fundraising you will ever do. There might be individuals or companies from whom you would not want to accept a gift. For example, some organizations have policies that prohibit them from taking gifts from an alcohol or tobacco company or from companies that are not considered socially responsible.

It is also important to have policies about accepting and handling gifts of real property or other non-cash gifts. These will be more likely to be offered during a capital campaign, so even if you have policies in place, this is a good time to review and possibly update them. You need to have internal procedures in place for accepting, recording, and acknowledging pledges and gifts received. For instance, who opens mail, photocopies checks, makes the bank deposit, and signs the acknowledgment letters? These procedures should be in place for all fundraising, but will be especially important in the capital campaign since this might be the first time the organization has accepted multi-year pledges in addition to one-time gifts.

Community Assessment

Once you have determined you are internally ready to run a capital campaign, the next step is an external assessment of whether your community is willing and able to support this project. Interviews with community leaders should always be done by an outside consultant, because people might be reluctant to talk with internal staff about their views of your organization and the campaign. Your consultant will work with you to determine the key players who will be interviewed during the study. Generally, anywhere from thirty-five to fifty individuals will be interviewed. Sometimes, it will be

How an Organization Offended a Volunteer

While researching for a book on volunteers in fundraising, I held a number of focus groups with volunteers, asking them questions about their volunteer experiences. One of the questions I asked was whether volunteers were offended by being asked to contribute financially to the organizations for which they volunteered. Not one of the participants in the four focus groups was offended by this practice, although one gentleman said he was very offended when approached through a general direct mail to support an organization for which he had been volunteering for twenty years. The thing that upset him was not that he was asked for a donation, but that, by approaching him as it would any member of the general public, the organization did not recognize his volunteer work.

Uninspired

necessary to meet with more individuals due to the size or scope of your campaign. Occasionally, a study will involve fewer interviews if there is a very small goal or you are certain that you have several donors who will make leadership level gifts. Interviewing the *right* individuals is more important than the number of interviews.

The Interview Process

Interviews will be held one-on-one with the consultant and the person or couple to be interviewed. Most consultants will attempt to do the interviews at the interviewee's home or place of business in order to gain more knowledge about the interviewee's interests and capability. Sometimes interviews will be held at your organization's facility.

The consultant will prepare a report and deliver it to your leadership. This report will outline the qualitative and quantitative responses to the questions asked during the interviews. The consultant will recommend whether to move forward with a campaign, along with a proposed time schedule. If the consultant recommends that your organization is not ready for a campaign, you should expect to receive suggestions on what you need to do to better prepare for a campaign.

Structuring Your Campaign

Once your planning study is complete and you have decided to proceed with your campaign, the first step is to develop a campaign plan outlining the entire structure of the campaign. If you are working with a consultant, generally the consultant will draft the plan. If there is no consultant involved, you must allow sufficient time to develop the plan, and your leadership must have confidence in the staff member's ability to complete this task.

The campaign plan is the foundation for a successful campaign and will help you get off to a good start. The plan should include a brief overview of the process you've been through that led to the decision to move forward with a campaign. A key ingredient is your campaign organization chart showing all the various divisions and the number of volunteers that will be needed to participate in each division. Position descriptions for all volunteers should be included along with a timeline for each committee and an overall time schedule. Your campaign budget is also part of the campaign plan. The campaign will be implemented by a group of volunteers known as the campaign cabinet, which includes chairs of all the various subcommittees that will be involved in the campaign, led by a chair and vice chair, or co-chairs. Once the members of the campaign cabinet are in place, the campaign cabinet will review the plan and make suggestions for possible changes. It will be critical to show volunteers a well-thought-out plan and the time and monetary expectations that will be asked of them.

Having the plan in place and assuring that it is followed will make your campaign flow smoother. As with the planning study, it is one of the essential building blocks of a successful campaign. If your organization is on a tight budget, it might be wise to pay a consultant to develop the plan and then you can implement the plan on your own or with limited guidance from the consultant.

Premature Announcement

One organization not only hurt its own reputation but affected future fundraising campaigns in its entire community. I was making a presentation to the board of an arts organization in a small town about its possible $1.5 million capital campaign. Because of another organization's failure, the board members were not persuaded that they could achieve success. A youth-serving group in their community had also planned a $1.5 million campaign the year before and made the fatal mistake of holding a public kickoff announcing that it had raised $16,000 to date. Not only did its campaign fail because of its premature announcement, but it affected other organizations in its community who felt that if this group could not raise more than $16,000, no other organization in its community could be successful.

Uninspired

Identifying and Cultivating Donors

You should not make the mistake of thinking that you must find a whole new group of donors for your capital campaign, because you feel that you do not want to ask your loyal donors to help again. A basic principle of fundraising is that the most likely donors to the capital campaign will be those who are already supporting your organization. Another mistake that some people make is thinking they can raise all the money they need for their capital project through grants. While grants might play an important part in your campaign process, it is important to remember that more than 80 percent of all contributions to charitable organizations come from individuals.

The first people you should solicit are members of your organization's "family"—board, staff, and others close to your organization. It is crucial to have 100 percent board commitment before asking others to support your project. You should also conduct a staff appeal early in the campaign to show the public that the family of your organization has given its full support to the campaign.

Ready, Fire, Aim...Oops

One organization ruined its chances for success by being too eager to market its campaign. While the consultants were in the process of conducting a planning study using the preliminary case for support, the marketing consultants engaged by the organization convinced it that "glitzy" materials were needed to present to potential donors. The organization produced an expensive video and glossy brochures. The consultants doing the study told the organization's leaders they could not present a final case to prospective donors, and then asked them for their input about the campaign goals and plans. Leadership donors need to be "in on the ground floor" and see the insider's view of the plan so they can feel that their input will be valued. Since this organization had prematurely produced campaign materials, the consultants could not complete the study, and the project never came to fruition.

Uninspired

If your organization has a strong annual giving history, the best place to start is by searching your donor records. Even if you think you do not have alumni or a built-in constituent base, you probably do have a pool of prospects who are close to your organization. Many organizations have "alumni," individuals who have received services or have given service to the organization. Those who have given blood, adopted animals, or used a library card are likely donors when your organization launches the capital campaign.

Volunteers are another good source of campaign donations. Many organizations hesitate to ask their volunteers for money, knowing they are giving of their time. However, remember that volunteers' time is often as precious to them as their money. If they are giving of their time, they are likely to support your organization financially, as well.

Companies from which your organization buys goods and services are another likely pool of prospective donors.

Campaign Events

While you should not depend on special events to raise the needed money for the capital campaign, events are an important step in the campaign process. Volunteers and donors need to be cultivated, inspired, and recognized. Some typical events you will be conducting in the campaign are:

✎ Cultivation breakfasts, luncheons, dinners, cocktail parties

✎ The campaign kickoff event

✎ A groundbreaking event

✎ The dedication and open house

Cultivation will often be one-on-one and will be handled through the various divisions. However, it might be wise to plan a series of cultivation events designed to bring in small groups of individuals, usually with a common interest, during the early stages of the campaign. Some examples of cultivation events are open-house type events, house parties in a board member is or volunteer's home, or information meetings held at your facility or at a local restaurant or country club.

The key event of your campaign will be the kickoff. The primary focus of the kickoff event is to announce your campaign. Other things you should accomplish at your kickoff event are to recognize donors who have already made a contribution to the campaign and inspire new donors to the campaign. Your kickoff event can be anything from a formal black tie dinner or a cocktail party to a series of luncheons in different regions, if your organization is state-wide or national in scope.

Regardless of the type and location, it is important to remember that your kickoff event should not be held until approximately 60 to 80 percent of the goal has been raised. Announcing a campaign prematurely can be the "kiss of death" for the campaign. The costs of the kickoff event should be included in your campaign budget, as there is usually no charge for attending. Your goal should be to get as many current and prospective donors to attend the event as possible. Whatever type of event you choose, it should always be upbeat and inspirational.

The groundbreaking is another campaign milestone you can celebrate with an event. Depending on your building schedule, you might not be breaking ground until your campaign has been completed. If this is the case, your groundbreaking and victory celebration can be one and the same. However, if you will be breaking ground during the campaign, your dedication and open house become your victory celebration. The timing of the project and the events should be carefully coordinated in your overall campaign calendar. You will need an event committee to coordinate all

One Organization Failed to Train the Staff Person in Charge of the Donor Software

One organization not only did not build on the success of its campaign to keep donors active in future annual funds, but it didn't even collect on all the pledges made during the campaign. The reason? Although it purchased a donor database system to track campaign pledges, it did not send the responsible staff person for training on this system, so pledges were entered but no reminder notices were sent out. The result was that it had a much lower pledge fulfillment rate than the average of 90 to 95 percent.

Uninspired

your campaign events, and this committee is usually divided into different committees for each event.

Campaign Publicity

The public relations subcommittee of your campaign cabinet is responsible for all the public relations efforts of the campaign. These might include:

- Developing the campaign theme and logo

- Arranging for the development and printing of campaign printed materials, including brochures, letterhead and envelopes, response envelopes, letters of intent, fact sheets and question-and-answer sheets

- Developing a campaign CD, video, DVD, and/or PowerPoint presentation

- Preparing and distributing media releases

- Developing the campaign website, which might include a webcam tracking construction progress

- Planning and coordinating media conferences

- Preparing and presenting campaign speeches for various audiences

- Planning for promotional items used to generate publicity for the campaign

The public relations subcommittee usually works with your campaign consultant, a marketing firm, and/or a graphic designer to create the theme and design a logo. The brochures and other campaign materials are developed based on the case for support and need to be completed early enough in your campaign so the various committees can use them in their work. As with your campaign events, it is important to not release information about your campaign too early in the process. Your pre-campaign publicity should be planned to focus on your organization's programs and services without mentioning the campaign. The reason for this is so that, when your campaign is publicly launched, there will be sufficient public interest in the project to ensure a successful campaign.

Donor Recognition

Recognition is an important facet of your capital campaign, and it can come in many forms. Listing donors in your campaign newsletter and annual report, issuing a press release about a major gift, or donor walls, bricks, and plaques are all effective ways of providing recognition for your donors. Special recognition events at which donors are publicly recognized for their contributions can also be effective. Many donors will want to have a building, a room, or area of the building named after them, their family, their company or in memory of a loved one. Named giving opportunities can play a significant role in a capital campaign and should be decided early in the campaign in order to fully utilize this effort in the leadership gifts phase of the campaign where you are approaching donors who could be motivated by a named giving opportunity. Remember, however, that some of your donors might wish to remain anonymous, and their anonymity must always be ensured. Providing a place on your pledge card or letter of intent for donors to print their name exactly the way they wish to be recognized and a box where they can check if they want to remain anonymous are simple ways of ensuring that donors are recognized according to their wishes.

Life After the Campaign

Once the campaign is over, the first thing you will probably want to do is to kick back and relax after the final celebration. A well-deserved vacation, or at least a few days off, is probably a good idea. However, before the glow of a successful campaign fades, you should think about how you can "capitalize" on your success to build a stronger development program and stronger organization for the future.

Many times when I meet with an organization to discuss its capital campaign, I ask about previous capital campaigns and what information is available from these previous campaigns. "Oh, we had a campaign a couple of years ago, and all that stuff is in a box somewhere in storage," is a common reply. What a shame that this information has not been assimilated into the organization's ongoing fundraising activities. One of the major benefits of a successful campaign is that it leaves your organization much stronger than it was prior to the campaign. The reasons for this are several:

✎ Your campaign starts with an internal assessment and, if the recommendations to strengthen the infrastructure of your organization are followed, this will result in a more effective development office.

✎ Your increased public relations efforts during a campaign will result in a heightened awareness of your organization in the community.

✎ The involvement of volunteers in your campaign will provide future volunteer fundraisers for your ongoing fundraising efforts.

✎ You will benefit from working with a consultant and will gain knowledge and experience that will be an asset to you and the organization.

As soon as possible after the end of your campaign, a debriefing should be held with your board, staff, and campaign volunteers to discuss what went right, what went wrong, what should be done differently next time, and how to build on the campaign's success to enhance your development program.

The database system developed for the campaign must be maintained on an ongoing basis. Pledge reminders need to be sent out on a timely basis to ensure a good collection rate. Donor pledges should be tracked and, when the pledge is paid, it might be time to invite donors to increase their annual giving. You might even do this while pledges are being fulfilled. Don't be afraid of asking donors for additional funds. Once donors have supported a major project such as your capital campaign, their level of interest in your organization as well as their level of commitment generally increases dramatically. Donors are then more likely to support your organization on an ongoing basis, so they should be included in your annual fund appeals as soon as they become part of your database system.

Staying in touch with donors on a regular basis and keeping them updated on the progress of the campaign and the project are important. Inviting all donors to the dedication and open house when the new facility is completed are steps that sometimes get overlooked. But remember, the key to successful fundraising is relationships, relationships, relationships. In order to build these good relationships, the organization needs to maintain good donor communications.

Similar to donors, campaign volunteers will have developed more awareness and commitment to the organization. Keeping campaign volunteers involved in the organization's ongoing development efforts can be a real boost to fundraising. Volunteers can help in the annual fund, major gifts programs, and planned giving campaigns, especially those who have been involved in making personal solicitations. They will have the training to be effective fundraisers because of their involvement in the campaign. Some of these volunteers might also be invited to serve on your board or your development committee.

Your board's involvement in the campaign might have been the first exposure they have had to the importance of their own giving. Build upon this commitment in future annual appeals by starting each year's fundraising program with an annual board appeal. Through their involvement in the campaign, board members will have more experience and knowledge about fundraising, so they should now be invited to get more involved in your ongoing development program.

Increased public awareness of your organization during the campaign can help your future fundraising efforts tremendously. You should continue to cultivate the media contacts made during the campaign. Getting stories in the newspaper about the increased services your organization is able to provide due to the successful campaign will help your future fundraising appeals.

To Summarize

✎ If you are with a smaller organization, a capital campaign might be a once-in-a-lifetime occurrence for you. If you are working for a hospital or university or other large institution, you might be ready for another campaign within a few years after the current one ends. Regardless of your situation, do not miss out on the opportunity to build a stronger organization after the campaign ends.

✎ Careful planning and excellent leadership from staff, board, and volunteers is critical to the success of your capital campaign. The campaign will depend on strong infrastructure, a compelling case for support, and volunteers with contacts to major donors.

✎ Once you have completed a successful capital campaign, every other part of your fundraising effort becomes easier and more effective.

Chapter 26

Planned Giving

There are many definitions of planned giving, but the one I will use is the simplest: It is any gift in which the donor makes a decision to support your organization with a larger gift than would normally be given annually. Most often, this is done in the form of a "deferred gift," or one that your organization will not immediately realize. Many different instruments may be used in your planned giving program, including charitable trusts, annuities, gifts of appreciated stock, and gifts of real estate, life insurance, and many more.

For most organizations, planned giving is primarily received in the form of estate gifts through the donor's will or living trust. In fact, estate gifts for all organizations usually account for about 90 percent of all the organization's planned gifts.

How can you take advantage of the large generational transfer of wealth that will account for many charitable bequests? A good way to start is by establishing a planned giving committee. Include an estate planning attorney, CPA, financial planners or consultants with expertise in this area. Remember that not all attorneys are well-versed in planned giving. A litigator, for example, might not have extensive knowledge of planned giving vehicles, so look for the experts who work in the field of estate planning. With the guidance of these professionals, review the many instruments and select a few that are appropriate for your organization. You do not have to be an expert in all the details of planned giving to have a successful program. Having the right volunteers involved that do have the knowledge of detailed planned giving vehicles and having staff and volunteers who are not afraid to broach the subject of planned giving with your donors is the first step in setting up a planned giving program.

I've asked Frank Vidin, CFP®, an experienced planned giving officer and financial professional, to describe the various instruments used in planned giving:

Charitable Gift Fund

A charitable gift fund is an account with a "supporting organization" (often a community foundation, a mutual fund company, or a trust company). Contributions are invested by the supporting organization, and distributions are made to nonprofit organizations as requested by the donor. Because contributions to the fund receive an income tax deduction (subject to IRS limitations) when made, there is no deduction when distributions are actually made to the charities.

Each sponsor sets the rules (within IRS guidelines) regarding contribution limits, frequency, and minimum amounts of distributions, etc. All programs are managed by trustees who approve distributions to approved charitable organizations based on the donor's recommendations.

Gifts of Securities

Gifts of securities involve gifts of stocks, and mutual funds. Stocks might be closely held (private companies) or publicly traded. Due to a variety of issues, including valuation and marketability, closely held stock should be accepted only after thorough and careful evaluation. However, publicly traded stock or mutual fund shares can be an excellent gift. The shares of stock are transferred in-kind from the account of the donor to a brokerage (or mutual fund) account of the charitable organization. If the stock or mutual fund has appreciated in value, it is important that the actual shares of stock are transferred, and not sold with the cash distributed. An income tax deduction is available for the fair market value of the stock, which in effect eliminates the tax on the appreciation of the security. If the stock or mutual fund has lost value, there is greater tax advantage if the donor sells the security and makes a gift of cash.

Gifts of Real Estate

Although it requires more processing than most other gifts, real estate can be a very valuable gift. The real estate is typically sold shortly after transfer to the charity but, if the nonprofit can use the property (for campus expansion, a campground, etc.), it might be held for many years. Unlike other outright gifts, real estate often comes with holding costs, such as insurance and property management during the holding period.

Bargain Sale

Bargain sales typically involve real estate, but might involve other assets, as well. A bargain sale has two components—a gift and a sale. Put simply, an asset is sold to the charity for a price much less than its value. The proceeds received are subject to income tax, while a charitable deduction is available for the gift portion. A bargain installment sale follows the same principle, but payments are received over more than one year and are subject to income tax in the year that the payment is received.

Gifts of Life Insurance Policies

Gifts of unneeded life insurance policies can provide significant benefit to a charity at a low cost to the donor. Older donors often discover that they no longer need as much life insurance as they did at earlier stages of life. Often the policy dividends or cash value growth offsets any premium due, so there is little to no ongoing cost of holding the policy. When the policy is received, the charity may either cash in the policy and use the current cash values or hold the policy and receive a much larger benefit when the donor dies. Because life insurance is governed by state law, make sure that the laws of the state where the charity is located are satisfied. In some states the charity must be named both the owner and the irrevocable beneficiary of the policy. If both requirements are not met, the charitable deduction might be jeopardized. The gift value of a cash value life insurance policy is its replacement value, or interpolated terminal reserve. This value needs to be obtained from the insurance company, and is roughly equal to the policy's cash value. The gift value of a term life insurance policy is minimal—the unused premium. If a charity is the beneficiary of an employer-provided group term policy, the premium amount that would be taxable to the employee is tax-free, but no additional deduction is available. *Example:* Jennifer purchased dividend-paying whole life insurance to protect the family financially if she died before her children were raised. Now that the children are on their own and successful, she feels the policy is no longer needed. On the last annual statement she noticed that the dividend was more than the annual premium. Rather than cash in the policy, she contacts the insurance company and has her local church named the policy owner and irrevocable beneficiary. Jennifer receives a charitable deduction for the gift, and at her death the church uses the policy proceeds to build an education unit named after her.

Will/Living Trust Citations

Most people choose to distribute their assets at their death by means of a will or a living trust. Differentiating between wills and living trusts is beyond the scope of this writing, but the process for including charitable bequests is similar enough that they can be covered together. In both cases the individual uses the appropriate legal form to designate in writing that certain assets or a portion of the estate be distributed to charitable organizations.

The amount of the bequest can be determined in dollar amounts, as a percentage of the estate, or by designating specific assets. For smaller bequests (perhaps $10,000 or less), a specific dollar amount might be the most appropriate type. For larger bequests, a percentage of the estate is usually fairer, since the other recipients will benefit proportionately if the estate either grows or diminishes prior to death. Of course, if a specific item is to be left to charity, that item should be specified in the will or living trust.

It is very important that each charity ensure that the legal name of the organization is included in the bequest. This is particularly important for affiliates of national organizations because the policy of many national organizations is that, unless the local affiliate is specifically named, all bequests go to the national organization. It is also important if the name of an organization can be confused with that of other organizations. Many attorneys routinely check with nonprofit organizations for the preferred wording when drafting estate planning documents, but that is not always the case. To facilitate such inquiries, it is suggested that you prepare specific language that can be emailed to the attorney or provided directly to your donors on request. Such language should include the legal name of the organization (including differentiation from national organizations) as well as the city and state in which the organization is located. Since charities might merge or change their names, it is always safe to add: "or its successors" to the description.

If the donor wants the proceeds used for a specific project, that project should also be named with a disclaimer like: "In the event that fulfilling this specific request is not possible, the Board of Trustees shall apply the proceeds in a way that shall fulfill the donor's intent as closely as possible." For example, if a bequest of funds to find a cure for breast cancer is received after a cure for breast cancer has been discovered, the Board of Trustees might choose to use the funds to make that cure available to more individuals, or for research to discover a cure for another cancer that predominately impacts women.

Retirement Plan/IRA Beneficiary Designations

Naming a nonprofit organization beneficiary of an IRA, 401(k), or other retirement plan can be a tax-effective, efficient way to contribute to charitable organizations at the donor's death. It is efficient because these assets are distributed to the beneficiary immediately upon proof of death, so there are no delays as in probate. Its tax-effectiveness comes from the fact that pre-tax money is usually contributed, and the account grows tax-deferred. Therefore, the beneficiaries will owe income taxes on most, if not all, of the account as it is distributed. However, no income tax will be owed on the portion that is distributed to a tax-exempt charity. If multiple beneficiaries are named, separating the charitable beneficiaries' portion of an IRA into a separate account might allow the other beneficiaries more flexibility over the timing of distributions.

It is very important for each charity to ensure that the legal name of the organization is used in the beneficiary designation.

Pooled Income Funds

A pooled income fund is similar to a "charitable mutual fund." The gifts of multiple donors are pooled in a managed portfolio. Any interest or dividends from the assets in the pool are distributed directly to the donor. At the donor's death, his or her shares are retired, and the share value is distributed to the charity.

Charitable Gift Annuity

A charitable gift annuity is an agreement between a donor and a charity whereby the charity agrees to make periodic (typically quarterly) payments for life in exchange for a gift. The gift becomes the outright property of the charity when received, and the periodic payments are supported by the total assets of the nonprofit. The dollar amount of the payment is set and is not adjusted for inflation or investment performance.

Charitable gift annuities are subject to a variety of state regulations. Some states have complex rules that must be followed, while other states have no rules at all. The American Council on Gift Annuities recommends payout rates, which most charitable gift annuity issuers follow, based on actuarial calculations and the assumptions that 1 percent of the value will be used to cover expenses, and that 50 percent of the gift will remain for the charity at the death of the income beneficiary.

Charitable Remainder Trust

A charitable remainder trust is an irrevocable trust that provides income payments to the donor or persons they designate in the trust document, with any remaining balance distributed to the named charity on termination of the trust—usually at the donor's death. All distributions are collateralized by the assets in the trust. Should the trust assets be depleted before the end of the distribution period, distributions will cease.

There are two types of charitable remainder trust allowed by law—the charitable remainder annuity trust (CRAT) and the charitable remainder unitrust (CRUT). Charitable remainder annuity trusts cannot accept additional contributions, and because they make distributions based on the initial amount placed into the trust, the dollar amount never changes. Charitable remainder unitrusts may accept additional contributions and make distributions based on the value of the trust assets at the close of the previous year, resulting in an annual adjustment, depending on the earnings of the trust assets.

By law, the minimum stated payout for a charitable remainder trust is 5 percent per year, and the trust must exist for either the lifetimes of the income beneficiaries or for a term of years not to exceed twenty. The amount of the charitable deduction is determined by prevailing interest rates, the percentage paid out, and the number of years that the payout is expected to last.

Most charitable remainder unitrusts begin payments immediately upon funding, and are called standard CRUTs (SCRUT). However, if the trust is funded with illiquid assets and time is needed to sell those assets before money is available for distribution, the trust may be set up as a net income CRUT (NICRUT), or a net income with makeup CRUT (NIMCRUT)

Charitable remainder trusts are complex legal entities and should be set up only in close consultation with attorneys experienced in this type of transaction. Ongoing remainder trust issues include determining who will serve as trustee and administrator, and trust investment issues.

Charitable Lead Trusts

A charitable lead trust allows the income from the irrevocable trust to be paid to a charity for a set period of time, with the remaining principal returned to the donor at the end of the distribution period.

There are two types of charitable lead trust allowed by law, the charitable lead annuity trust (CLAT) and the charitable lead unitrust (CLUT). Charitable lead annuity trusts cannot accept additional contributions and make distributions based on the initial amount placed into the trust. Charitable lead unitrusts may accept additional contributions and make distributions based on the value of the trust assets at the close of the previous year. The amount of the charitable deduction is determined by prevailing interest rates, the percentage paid out to the charity, and the number of years that the payout will last.

Charitable lead trusts may be used to help meet limited-term charitable needs, such as bridge-funding a project for a few years until permanent funds are available. They are also used for sophisticated income, gift, and estate tax planning.

Charitable lead trusts are complex legal entities and should be set up only in close consultation with legal and tax advisors experienced in this type of transaction.

Getting Started in Planned Giving

Once you have decided which instruments you want to offer, you can develop a brochure that explains the options in simple terms. Clearly outline the benefits and risks of each type of giving opportunity. Show the benefit to your service to recipients as well as to the donor. Several companies have planned giving materials available that can be customized for your organization.

The planned giving committee should develop a plan to publicize the different planned giving opportunities. As with any type of fundraising, your planned giving program should start by asking the board to make a planned gift, so the first audience for your planned giving presentation should be your board. You should also plan to make a presentation to your staff about the options for making a planned gift to your organization.

Bequest Program

You might feel that you do not have the expertise to solicit and accept all of the types of planned gifts mentioned. So, start simple. A so-called "bequest program" is the most successful planned giving program for most organizations, since it is simple to administer. Many times, your donors who would like to give a significant gift to your organization find

Why "Bequest Program" is a Bit of Misnomer

Although it is commonly used, the name "Bequest Program" is something of a misnomer. A "bequest," strictly speaking, is a gift made via a person's will. But gifts at death may also be made via a living trust, though such gifts are not called "bequests." Broadly speaking, gifts at death are called "testamentary gifts," and include gifts made by will and by living trusts. So a more accurate name for such a program is "Testamentary Gift Program." Yuck. Only a lawyer would like that name. So it's okay to call it a "Bequest Program," but just know that your program is not limited to just gifts by will. Gifts by trusts are just as welcome!

themselves unable, because of financial reasons, to do so in their lifetimes. However, they are willing to make a testamentary gift (a gift at death). People who are philanthropic during their lifetimes are generally inclined to want their philanthropic support to continue after their demise.

A bequest program is fairly easy to establish. For donors who do not have a will or living trust, you can start by having an estate planning attorney on your planned giving committee offer a seminar on the advantages of having wills or living trusts. Donors who do have a will or living trust can be encouraged to amend their will or trust to include a testamentary gift to your organization. Many attorneys will ask about their clients' intentions to support the organizations they care about when they are preparing their wills or living trusts.

Testamentary gifts can be made in the form of a specific dollar amount, a percentage of the donor's estate, or the residual (the amount left over after final expenses and other testamentary gifts have been taken care of). Often donors will not advise you that they have remembered your organization in their wills or trusts, and you will not find out about the gift until they die and the estate is settled. Or, you might be notified of the testamentary gift while the donor is still alive, but often not the specific amount. When the individual dies, the executor of the estate, in the case of a will, or the trustee, in the case of a living trust, makes arrangements to send the funds to your organization in accordance with the instructions in the will or trust. You can encourage donors to let you know what the gift amount is likely to be by establishing a special planned giving society that requires members to notify you that they have made provision in their will or trust for a contribution. You can even encourage the donor to let you know what amount you might expect.

You should publicize the bequest program in your newsletters, on mail response envelopes, on your website, and through other media.

To Summarize

✎ Planned giving might seem like a complex form of fundraising and many organizations feel they do not have the expertise to start a planned giving program. However, there is a huge potential for the transfer of trillions of dollars of wealth into the hands of beneficiaries. Your organization should start planning how to best take advantage of this opportunity.

✎ You can start simple. A so-called bequest program is the easiest type of planned giving to implement, and almost any organization can start one. Once you get this down, you can look at some of the more complex planned giving vehicles and decide which ones are appropriate for your organization.

✎ You should start by recruiting a planned giving committee comprised of experts in the field, such as estate planning attorneys, financial planners, CPAs, and other with expertise that can help you get your program started.

Taking it to the Next Level

Once you have a well-established development program, the next step is to make sure you evaluate results on a regular basis and strive to continually improve results. In this section, I will describe some helpful evaluation tools and how to take your development program to the next level.

Continuous improvement starts with evaluating your development program on an ongoing basis and developing ways to improve the areas that need improvement. Next, think about new initiatives that might improve your development program. And, finally, always be thinking about ways to move your donors up the donor pyramid toward the ultimate gift.

The first chapter in this section, **Chapter 27,** deals with evaluation methods. In **Chapter 28,** we will discuss initiatives you might want to utilize to increase the results of your development program.

Chapter 27

Evaluating Your Development Program

In This Chapter...

- ✎ How do you know if you are doing a good job?

- ✎ What is a development audit, and when do you need one?

- ✎ What tools are available to evaluate your development program?

O nce you've been working at the business of fundraising for a year or more, you should think about the ways you can evaluate your development program in order to assure continuous improvement. Often, this is approached through a development audit.

What is a development audit, and when does your organization need one? A development audit is an internal assessment of your fundraising program and your readiness to embark on new development ventures. The development audit looks at involvement of board, staff, and volunteers in the fundraising process and offers recommendations on how to best use the human resources available to your organization. It further evaluates the strengths and weaknesses of your development systems, including fundraising software. The audit also offers suggestions to help improve donor communication and stewardship.

Many organizations consider a development audit when they are:

Development Audit

An objective evaluation of internal development procedures as practiced by a nonprofit organization and as conducted by professional fundraising counsel.

- Preparing to embark on a major gifts, capital, or endowment campaign.

- Not satisfied with the results of the annual giving program.

- Seeking to increase board participation in fundraising efforts.

- Attempting to compare results with similar organizations.

- Looking for an objective evaluation of their development program.

- Trying to diversify funding streams.

- Engaged in the strategic planning process.

- Looking at restructuring the development office.

- Seeking to take the development program to a higher level of professionalism.

In most cases, the audit is conducted by a consultant in order to gain both objectivity and utilize the knowledge and years of experience the consultant will bring to the table. The staff, while not involved directly in the evaluation process, will need to devote time to the audit process. Typical staff roles during the audit include:

✎ Completing development audit questionnaires.

✎ Providing supporting documentation.

✎ Meeting with the consultant to clarify information and set goals for the audit.

The board is also involved with the process, usually completing questionnaires and participating in interviews with the consultant. Typically the board chair, chair of the development committee, and other selected board members will be involved in interviews. The consultant generally makes several visits to the organization to meet with key staff, board, and other volunteers.

An audit looks at these areas:

1. The Organization's Readiness for Fundraising

✎ Legal structure—does your organization have 501(c)(3) status or some other nonprofit status that allows you to accept donations that are tax deductible by the donor?

✎ Organizational structure—to whom does your chief development officer report?

✎ Strategic planning—does the organization have a long range plan?

✎ Fundraising guidelines—are there gift acceptance policies in place?

✎ Case for support—is there a written organizational case for support and case statements to support various fundraising needs?

2. The Board's Role in Fundraising

✎ Board composition—is the board diverse, and does it have the appropriate mix of skills and talents?

✎ Board performance—is the board actively involved in fundraising, and do board members support the organization financially?

✎ The development committee—is there a development committee or other volunteers involved in the fundraising program?

3. The Role of Staff

- ✎ Departmental structure—is there adequate staff, doing the right jobs with the right tools?

- ✎ Functions of the development office—does the development staff have the time and skill to perform all development functions?

- ✎ Training and educating staff—is there a commitment to professionalism in the development office?

- ✎ Evaluating the role of the CEO in fundraising—is the CEO involved in fundraising and regularly communicating with the development office?

4. Systems and Procedures

- ✎ Donor Database Software—is there an adequate donor software program in place, and is staff trained to use the program?

- ✎ Are there gift acceptance policies, recognition policies, and investment policies in place?

- ✎ Procedure Manual—are there procedures in place to receive, record, and acknowledge gifts?

- ✎ Hardware—is there adequate hardware to support development systems and programs?

- ✎ Internet usage and website—does staff use technology to improve donor relations?

5. Cultivation and Stewardship

- ✎ Does the organization regularly hold cultivation events and activities?

- ✎ Are gifts properly recorded, acknowledged, and recognized?

- ✎ Are gifts used as the donor intends?

- ✎ Does the staff subscribe to a code of ethics?

✎ Does the organization promote the *Donor Bill of Rights*? (See **Appendix C.**)

6. The Integrated Development Program—does the organization rely too heavily on one source of funding, or is there a plan in place to develop funding from various sources including:

✎ Grants

✎ Special events

✎ Direct mail

✎ Internet

✎ Telephone fundraising

✎ Major gifts

✎ Corporate gifts

✎ Planned gifts

Once the development audit is complete, the report should be used to develop a strategic plan for development, addressing the areas raised as issues needing improvement. A comprehensive development audit can help an organization build on its strengths, overcome its weaknesses, and address opportunities for future growth.

Self-Evaluation

There are many things you can do to evaluate your development program on your own. If your budget does not permit a full-blown development audit, you can use some of the tools included in this book to perform some self-evaluation. Remember that the main purpose of evaluation, whether through an outside audit or an internal self-evaluation, is not to find fault with people or with systems but to learn how to build on your strengths, improve in areas in which you are weak, take advantage of new opportunities, and develop strategies to deal with threats to your success.

One way to begin the self-evaluation process is to compare your results with accepted industry guidelines. If your costs or results are out of line in some areas, you might want to look deeper into that aspect of our program.

To calculate true net proceeds from a benefit event, calculate the estimated value of these elements, plus internal and overhead support costs, and subtract them from the revenue sum after direct costs.

All performance measurements must include assessment of added value in the areas of marketing, media relations, community relations, major gift cultivation, donor relations, image building, and influence on other external affairs constituents.

Evaluating Your Direct Response Program

Renewal and upgraded gifts through direct mail, Internet and telephone should be analyzed on an annual basis. Some questions to ask:

✎ How many donors renewed?

✎ How many donors upgraded?

Reasonable Fund-Raising Cost Guidelines

Fund-Raising Method	Cost Guideline
Direct-mail acquisition	$1.25 to $1.50 per $1 raised
Direct-mail renewal	20¢ to 25¢ per $1 raised
Special & benefit events	50¢ per $1 raised (direct costs only)
Corporations & foundations	20¢ per $1 raised
Planned giving	20¢ to 30¢ per $1 raised (plus lots of patience)
Capital campaigns	10¢ to 20¢ per $1 raised

Inspiration!

✎ How many donors lapsed?

✎ What was the dollar increase in gifts?

✎ What were the costs of each program?

✎ What was the average gift size and did it increase or decrease from previous years?

✎ Are individuals who gave more than a specific amount moved into the next level of personalized approach, e.g. direct-mail donors who give over $100 are moved into the telephone program?

Special Event Analysis

Using the special event analysis forms provided in Appendixes X and Y, you should analyze every event after all the records are completed, as well as evaluate the potential of any events you are considering. Once you have given yourself points in each category of the event analysis, see how it stacks up:

✎ 35 Points—The perfect event (don't we all wish)!

✎ 30-34 Points—An excellent event, definitely worth keeping.

✎ 25-29 Points—A good event. Probably worth keeping, but you might need some minor changes.

✎ 20-24 Points—A reasonably good event. Might be worth keeping, but you should evaluate ways to improve this event.

✎ Fewer than 20 Points—You should consider dropping this event or making serious changes.

Please keep in mind that this evaluation is subjective. For example, if an event raises $1 million dollars but requires a lot of staff and volunteer time, it is probably worth keeping, despite a lower rating.

Perspiration!

Evaluating Your Special Events

For events, accurate record-keeping and evaluation are essential. Track not only how many individuals bought tickets to your events, but who volunteered for which tasks and how reliable they were. After each event, when it is fresh in everyone's mind, hold an evaluation meeting involving all the committee people to review what went right and what went wrong. Make sure to ask some participants to rank the event, not just the organizers. Keep information in written form to pass on to next year's event committee. I've provided tools in **Appendixes X** and **Y** to evaluate your special events.

Evaluating Your Board

Evaluating your board of directors should include an evaluation of the board make-up and performance, the board's role in fundraising, and the effectiveness of board meetings. Board evaluation must be done on several levels. First, your governance committee, or board resource committee, should evaluate the performance of the board in order to determine the need for various skills and talents when recruiting new board members. The board should also evaluate themselves, both as individual board members and the board as a whole, on a regular basis so they feel they have true ownership of their success. The board should also evaluate board meetings to assure they are productive. I've provided several tools in **Appendixes T** through **W** to help you evaluate your board.

To Summarize

✎ It is critical to evaluate both board performance and performance of your development activities and programs. Using the forms in **Appendixes X** and **Y** will help you evaluate your success in order to better plan for the future.

Chapter 28

Expanding Into New Development Efforts

In This Chapter...

✎ How do you keep on top of new trends in fundraising?

✎ How do you increase donations from your loyal donors?

✎ What are some additional fundraising techniques you can try?

Once you've evaluated your results and have developed strategies to improve in the areas in which your fundraising is weak, you can develop strategies for improving in those areas. You should also look at adding new programs and new strategies to raise funds.

There are a number of strategies that you can use in an effort to strive for continuous improvement in your development program. First, take another look at all the fundraising methods we've discussed in this book—telephone fundraising, direct mail, Internet, corporate giving, etc. Some of these might be new to you so start by taking a fresh look at the pros and cons of each of these methods. Once you have an appropriate mix of these in place, you might want to look at some fresh ideas such as a monthly giving program, an increased effort toward individual giving through moves management, or any of other methods described in this chapter.

Here are some ideas on new programs you might want to implement:

Memorial Giving

Many people, when hearing of the death of a friend or family member, wish to make a contribution to a nonprofit organization instead of flowers. Often the family of the deceased will request this rather than receiving flowers or other memorial offerings.

You can start a memorial program by asking your board and staff to talk to their families about their desire to have contributions made in their memory to your organization. Once the program is established, you should notify donors, members, and the community that it exists.

Funeral directors can also be approached to place envelopes in their funeral homes for visitors at wakes and viewing to consider making a contribution to your organization in memory of their loved ones.

Another fundraising opportunity is the establishment of a memorial plaque in a prominent location in your facility. For a set fee, the family of the deceased can have the name of the deceased and the date of death included on a permanent memorial. Religious institutions often use this method very effectively.

Monthly Giving

Many people, especially in tough economic times, like to spread out their gifts to charities. Instead of making one larger payment, it might be easier for many people to make monthly pledge payments. So how can you start monthly giving program?

First, using your database, identify those donors who have supported your organization loyally over the past five to ten years. Also, review your LYBUNT and SYBUNT list to see if you have donors who have stopped giving. Then plan a telephone appeal to those people. First send them a letter letting them know that you appreciate their past support and that you want to re-engage them with your organization. Be sure to make your case for support—why your organization needs money and how many people will be helped by their contributions. Then organize a phonathon, and call

all these people, letting them know that instead of their usual $100 annual gift, for example, they could pay their pledges in twelve installments of $10 each. You've made their contribution easier to budget and, guess what, you've raised a $100 donor to a $120 donor. Next year, you can go back and ask them to increase their monthly pledge to $15 a month, just a $5 increase monthly. But again, you've increased their giving to $185 annually.

You can use this same approach with your major donors, using personal visits to encourage them to give on a monthly basis. Both major donors and your other donors can use a credit card to pay their pledge, assuring you a better fulfillment rate and giving them airline points, etc. A win-win situation, if I've ever seen one.

Giving Circles

A fairly recent phenomenon in fundraising is the use of "giving circles." These groups are formed mainly by groups of women who want to make a significant impact in an area about which the circle's members are concerned. Rather than give $1,000 a year which might be split between a number of organizations, twenty-five women who all care about the health of women and families might get together to pool their funds. The giving circle then has $25,000 to give to a charity of its choice. These pooled funds allow a group of friends who have mutual interests to accept proposals from various groups that deal with the issues they are concerned about, and make a strategic gift that has a real impact. If you don't know of any giving circles in your community, you might suggest to some of your donors that they start one.

> ### What's in a Name? Plenty!
>
> One organization has a giving club for monthly donors, called the "Alpha Society." This same organization calls its planned giving group the "Omega Society." These titles are appropriate for recognizing entry-level donors and those who have made the ultimate gift.
>
>
>
> **Pure Genius!**

These are just a few new initiatives you might want to try once your development program has been established. In order to increase donations from existing donors, you should also be an expert in building relationships with your donors in order to move them up the donor pyramid. One effective method of doing this is called "moves management."

Moves Management

While the philosophy of your organization should be to move all donors to a higher level, the moves management process is designed to focus on a select number of donors with the ability and interest to make significant gifts to your organization. Moves management is a process of carefully planned activities to advance the relationship of major donor prospects with your organization. Moves management involves a series of regular but often unexpected contacts with the prospect. The prospective donor eventually comes to feel that your organization is a meaningful part of the prospect's life.

Moves management is customized for every prospect. It must be based on genuine concern for your prospective donors and always puts the donors' best interests above anything else, including the interests of your organization. Furthermore, the moves management process always adheres to the strictest ethical codes and the Donor Bill of Rights. (See **Appendix C.**)

How Does Moves Management Work?

Moves management is based on the five principles of moving the donor up the donor pyramid, which we've examined in earlier chapters, towards making the ultimate gift. Those principles are:

- ✎ Identification
- ✎ Information
- ✎ Interest
- ✎ Involvement
- ✎ Investment

Moves management can occur through a variety of media:

✎ Group events to which selected donors are invited
✎ Smaller events with a more intimate setting
✎ One-on-one personal interaction

Have an individual moves management plan for each prospect, which will involve a mix of media and will be used to move the prospect through the process.

Who Is Involved in Moves Management?

The key individual responsible for moves management is the chief development officer. Other individuals involved in the moves management process include:

✎ Your CEO
✎ Your board members
✎ Development committee members or committee on philanthropy members
✎ Other staff members as appropriate
✎ Other volunteers as appropriate

It is crucial that the chief development officer manage the moves management process, and that all others involved with a particular prospect report any contacts with that prospect to the chief development officer. The moves management team should meet periodically to discuss the next steps planned for each prospect.

Furthermore, it is essential to gear all moves toward building a better relationship between the prospect and your organization, not any individual members of the moves management team.

The Moves Management Plan

1. Determine criteria for placing a prospect into the moves management system. Criteria should be determined by the moves management team and should be based on the LAI principle:

✎ **Linkages**—Does your organization have a relationship with this individual? Who is the best contact for this person? Who should be the primary cultivator/asker?

✎ **Ability**—What is this prospect's ability to give, if properly motivated? Has this prospect given to other charitable causes? What research is needed to determine financial ability?

✎ **Interest**—Is this person interested in your organization? Has this interest been demonstrated by giving history? Can this interest be further cultivated?

2. Determine a reasonable number of people who can be managed in your system:

✎ Goals need to be set so you can track progress of the moves management program.

✎ Start with a small number. Twenty-five top prospects is a good number if this process is new to your organization. Add prospects as the program grows and more people are involved.

3. Select those prospects to be placed in your moves management system based on the criteria that have been determined. Establish a ranking system based on the LAI Principle (Linkage, Ability & Interest), for example:

✎ Rate interest as A-E, with A being high and E being low.

✎ Rate ability as 1-5, with 1 being high and 5 being low.

✎ List the person who has the best relationship with this prospect as well as alternate contacts.

4. Insert in the tracking from current moves being used with each prospect, these moves might include:

✎ Newsletter mailings

✎ Invitations to events

✎ Personal visits already scheduled

5. Develop an annual plan of moves management for each prospect. These moves might involve:

- Personal visits

- Letters

- Phone calls

- Event invitations

- Contact by a board member, staff member, or volunteer

- Other cultivation activities

Major Gifts and Moves Management Tracking and Planning

As your number of major donor prospects identified and researched grows, prospect tracking becomes increasingly important. Since multiple contacts are usually required to close major gifts, tracking the assignment of contacts with prospects is crucial to the success of your fundraising program.

A prospect tracking system includes critical data elements and will be used to produce information needed for staff review of major prospect assignments. Some of the elements that must be tracked for effective prospect management are the following:

- Staff and volunteer assignment.

- Date of the last contact with the prospect.

- Step or status in the cultivation and solicitation process. This might include:
  - ❖ Additional research needed
  - ❖ Information ready for evaluation
  - ❖ Solicitor assignments made
  - ❖ Prospect under cultivation
  - ❖ Prospect solicited
  - ❖ Gift made

- ❖ Request declined
- ❖ Solicitation readiness
- ❖ Capability rating indicates financial capability
- ❖ Area of interest, related to the organization's needs
- ❖ Prospect assigned to fundraising division
- ❖ Strategy summary describing the overall approach

✎ The plan of action, including:

- ❖ Next step with a date for action
- ❖ Description of planned activity (letter, telephone call, personal visit, etc.)
- ❖ Person responsible for the action
- ❖ Date by which action is to be accomplished

✎ An action summary:

- ❖ Date the action occurred
- ❖ Summary of the contact

Categories of Donors/Prospects to be tracked:

✎ Prospect Type:

- ❖ Individual
- ❖ Company
- ❖ Foundation
- ❖ Organization

✎ Status:

- ❖ Current donor
- ❖ Donor prospect
- ❖ Volunteer
- ❖ Board member

Tracking to be done:

Possible Volunteer Involvement

✎ Volunteer type:

❖ Development committee prospect

❖ Council for philanthropy prospect

❖ Campaign committee prospect

❖ Board prospect

Asker:

✎ Name of person who will contact this potential volunteer

Response:

✎ Agreed to serve

✎ Was contacted—awaiting reply

✎ Declined

✎ To be contacted

✎ Assigned to committee—name of committee

Donors/Prospects:

✎ Type of prospect:

❖ Leadership gifts

❖ Major gifts

❖ Special gifts

❖ Foundation gifts

❖ Organization gifts

Solicitor:

✎ Name of person assigned to call this prospect

Giving history:

✎ Past giving to your organization

✎ Giving to other organizations

✎ Suggested ask amount

Next Step:

✎ Invited to cultivation event—date of event

✎ Assigned to solicitor: _____ (Name)

✎ Proposal, appeal letter prepared

✎ Solicitation call made

✎ Declined

✎ Pledge made

✎ Pending decision

Some of the tools you can use to help track results of your moves management program include:

✎ Research forms

✎ Contact report

✎ Call report

✎ Intake form

I provide samples of some of these forms in **Appendixes Z** and **AA.**

What If You Need Help Growing Your Program?

I've tried to fill this book with lots of tips and tools to help you plan an effective program, but there are a lot more resources available to you. Among these are:

- ✎ The list of Suggested Reading in **Appendix EE** offers some of my recommendations for further study.

- ✎ Your local AFP Chapter, which might have a mentoring program.

- ✎ The largest online network of nonprofit professionals is available through http://CharityChannel.com.

Sometimes the best tool to help you improve you development results is bringing in an outside consultant who might have new ideas or ideas on how you can better improve on your results. A consultant can also help train your board and staff in new or tried-and-true fundraising techniques.

When Do We Need a Consultant?

Many times a consultant is needed to help the organization get a development program off the ground or to help with taking your development program to the next level. Consultants can assist you in the search for the right CDO or other staff members. A consultant can also help you with the development plan and give your organization guidance in specific areas of need. Once a CDO candidate is identified, find out what that person's strengths and weaknesses are, and then determine if the organization needs additional staff and/or a consultant or outside contractor to help round out that person's skills and abilities.

Consultants are often brought in on the strategic planning phase to provide the outside objective viewpoint that is needed to help the organization set realistic goals and objectives. Sometimes, the best way to get started is hiring a well-rounded person who is a generalist in development and then hiring outside consultants to perform specific tasks, such as grant writing, special event management, board development, campaign management, database consulting, etc.

Board training can be more effective using a consultant; the old adage about a consultant being someone who "comes fifty miles and carries a briefcase" is often true. The consultant, while not only bringing some fresh ideas, will be seen as the expert by your board members. An all day training program or a special board meeting set aside for training by a consultant can often reenergize your board to get involved in fundraising. Staff training, as well, can benefit from the involvement of a consultant to help with specific areas, such as moves management, a capital campaign, or planned giving. Sometimes a consultant can be used to handle special events or grant proposal development. You should consider the costs of these outside consultants, and weigh them against what it would cost to have staff handle these tasks. The advantage of consultants is often that they don't get caught up in office politics or unnecessary activities that take them away from their real work, as tends to happen sometimes with staff. Also, consultants receive what might seem like a hefty fee, but you will not be paying benefits and payroll taxes on their fees, so it is often more economical in the long run. And, of course, the consultant will have special expertise in an area where you lack internal experts.

Remember, too, that development planning is an ongoing process. At least once a year, perhaps more often if any aspect of your development program is falling short, you should evaluate your goals to see if they still make sense, and think about the ways you might fast-track some programs that show promise. I've provided some planning tools in **Appendixes BB** through **DD** to help you with this.

To Summarize

✎ Once your development program has been evaluated, you should look at ways to build on your strengths, overcome your weaknesses, take advantage of opportunities, and be prepared to handle threats to your fundraising program. You should also stay in tune with new trends in fundraising and implement new techniques if they are appropriate for your organization.

✎ There are a few new techniques. But some techniques that have been around for a while are gaining new interest and have helped many organizations improve results. Some you might want to try are monthly giving, giving circles, and/or memorial giving.

✎ Moves management is a system that can help you grow existing intermediate donors into major donors.

✎ You should take advantage of all the resources available for fundraisers, and obtain training for your staff and board in both new and tried and true fundraising methods.

Chapter 29

Setting Goals

We've come to the end of our time together learning about fundraising, how important it is to your organization and to society, how rewarding it can be for staff and volunteers, and how to implement a successful fundraising program. The next step is setting goals to assure your success.

While fundraising *is* about raising money, and many of your goals will be monetary, don't forget that it is also about the act of building relationships—development—so some of your goals should be non-monetary ones. And remember that goals must be lofty enough to encompass the entire world of philanthropy.

It is critical that your development office be part of the leadership of the organization and that goals are set with some consideration to what resources are available to the development office. Go back to **Chapter 16,** Infrastructure, and make sure you have everything in place that you need to reach your goals. One final note about setting goals: You need to set goals for your organization, but you should also be setting goals for yourself and your development staff.

Might I suggest that you set goals in each of these areas—fundraising, development, and philanthropy? Some of these goals might include the following items that I've used in establishing goals for the organizations for which I've worked, the clients I've served, and my own career in fundraising.

Suggested Goals for Fundraising

If your organization has been raising money for any length of time, you should start by reviewing past fundraising history. How much have you raised from special events (remember to evaluate the true cost of these events), direct mail, telephone fundraising, corporate appeals, grants, major gifts, planned gifts. You can then establish goals in each of these areas; often adding 10 percent to past history will be a reasonable goal. If results have been slipping in some areas, you might want to establish a goal to raise the same amount of money you did two years ago. If there is an area that shows particular promise, you can easily increase your goals to 20 percent, 30 percent, or even more, depending on the circumstances. For example, if your community has been successful recruiting a lot of new businesses into your area, you might be able to double your corporate appeal results. If, on the other hand, businesses have been closing or moving to other communities, you might need to set goals lower than what you've raised in the past.

How NOT to Set a Goal

One way *not* to set goals: The CFO walks into your development office and says, "Okay, Ms. Development Officer, here is our budget for next year. Here are the income, the expenses, and the deficit. Go raise the money to cover the deficit."

Uninspired

For a new development office, monetary goals are harder to establish; however, you can begin by looking at the budget for your organization, seeing how much is needed to run your programs. Then take a serious look at the income from fees, services, and other areas, such as endowment income. Some organizations are also involved in for-profit endeavors, such as running a gift shop at their facility, operating a thrift store, a coffee house, or one of any number of social enterprises. Once you have an idea of how much the development office needs to raise and if it has the resources to raise that kind of money, you can set some realistic goals based on your organization and your community. Is your organization well-known in the community? Do you have the infrastructure in place? Are the CEO and board willing to get involved in fundraising? What is your competition? What is the economic climate in your community? What are other similar-sized organizations raising on an annual basis? All of these answers will help you set realistic goals.

Don't be afraid to aim high. Your goals should be lofty enough that it is a stretch to reach them, but not so high that you are setting yourself up for failure. You might look at what you raised last year and, unless there has been a major shake-up in the way you raise money, aim for a 10 percent or 20 percent increase. Or, if you have lost staff, your community is economically challenged, or there has been a major setback in your organization, you might want to consider maintaining the status quo and try to raise the same amount you raised last year. You might also rely on the help of a trusted advisor, a colleague, or fundraising consultant, to help you establish reasonable goals as part of your development plan.

Some typical fundraising goals might be:

✎ Raise $25,000 in our annual board appeal (an average of $1,000 per board member).

✎ Raise $100,000 in major gifts by securing four $25,000 gifts for our scholarship program.

✎ Increase our direct response fundraising results to $50,000.

✎ Implement a telephone fundraising program to raise $50,000 the first year from our alumni.

✎ Initiate a small-business appeal with a minimum of twelve volunteers to raise $50,000 from a pool of one-hundred small business prospects.

✎ Initiate a capital campaign to raise $3 million over a two-year period.

One note on capital campaign goals: You should work with your architects and fundraising consultant to develop a reasonable goal that includes things such as the purchase of land, site preparation, fees and licenses, construction costs, and contingency and campaign costs. And don't forget to include endowment funds.

Suggested Goals for Development

I've mentioned repeatedly that development is about more than raising money, and some of your goals

How One Organization Raised its Goal and Succeeded!

Think Big: One organization new to development had a board that was a bit timid about setting goals. The board thought that, for its first year, an annual fundraising goal of $150,000 was ambitious. However, the development director it hired had a lot of experience in growing programs and, based on her recommendations, it reluctantly agreed to a $250,000 goal, along with several non-monetary goals. Within the first year, this organization was able to grow its board from eight people to thirty-three, raise $375,000, and increase public awareness to the point where it had become the "cause célèbre" in its community. This is the exception to the rule, but the organization was able to accomplish this because it hired an experienced fundraiser, engaged a consultant to assist in the planning, and had several dynamic board members who were determined to make this development effort succeed.

Pure Genius!

should be non-monetary ones, aimed at strengthening or developing relationships with donors. When preparing your plan, you will be developing strategies designed to do this. So some of your goals for the development office might include things such as:

✎ Equipping your board members to become more involved in fundraising by providing a board education program.

✎ Forming a volunteer development committee to help implement your development plan.

✎ Increasing your planned giving results by recruiting a planned giving committee.

✎ Preparing for a capital campaign by developing architectural plans and conducting a planning study.

You will notice that many of the non-monetary goals have costs associated with them, and no immediate income, but the return on investment must be considered in the long term.

Suggested Goals for Philanthropy

The broader area of philanthropy should also have goals for your organization and for yourself. Some of these goals might include things such as:

✎ Provide stewardship to your donors through a planned program of personal visits, enhancing awareness of ethical standards and providing appropriate recognition.

✎ Enhance public awareness of philanthropy by preparing media releases and educational programs.

✎ Become certified as a CFRE or, as with your's truly, ACFRE.

✎ Write for the profession.

✎ Serve as a mentor to someone new to the profession.

No matter in which areas you set your goals, remember to evaluate them on a regular basis. One way to do this is to make certain you've established specific objectives and timelines for each goal. You might then want to prepare a Gantt chart or some similar benchmarking system and post it in a prominent location in your office so you see it on a daily basis. Or you can put reminders in your computer system to prompt you to work on your goals daily. Before long, you will be an expert fundraiser, a true development professional, and even a philanthropist.

To Summarize

✎ Setting goals is a critical part of the development process. Don't be too ambitious in the beginning, but do set your goals high enough that they are worth working towards and present an opportunity for board and staff to grow in their thinking.

✎ Be sure to set both monetary and non-monetary goals for your development program.

✎ I encourage you to take advantage of the resources that are available to you by reading more about fundraising, development, and philanthropy; joining a professional group and talking to experts in the field. One of the greatest things about the world of development is that its practitioners are not only willing but actually enthused about sharing their expertise with others in the field. Armed with this knowledge and expertise you will become a fundraising genius in no time!

Appendix A

Glossary

Acknowledgment—An expression of gratitude for a gift or service, often in letter form.

Annual fund (annual appeal, annual giving program)—Any organized effort by a nonprofit organization to obtain gifts on a yearly basis, usually to support in part or in total the general operations.

Audit (development audit)—An objective evaluation of internal development procedures as practiced by a nonprofit organization and as conducted by professional fundraising counsel.

Bequest (testamentary gift)—A transfer, upon the death of a donor, of personal property such as cash, securities, or other tangible property.

Board of directors—individuals selected in accordance with law (usually reflected in bylaws) to establish policy and oversee the management of an organization or institution.

Capital campaign—A campaign to raise substantial funds for a nonprofit organization to finance major building projects, to supplement endowment funds, and to meet other needs demanding extensive outlays of capital.

Case—The combination of reasons advanced by an institution or agency in justification of its appeals for support, with emphasis on its services, past, present, and potential.

Case statement—A carefully prepared document that sets forth in detail the reasons why an institution or agency merits support, in the context of the "case bigger than the institution," including substantial documentation of its services, human resources, potential for greater service, needs, and future plans.

CFRE—Certified Fund Raising Executive—A credential granted to a professional fundraiser by CFRE International, which is based on performance as a fundraising executive, knowledge of the fundraising field, tenure as a fundraiser (minimum of five years), education, and service to the profession. The ACFRE (Advanced Certified Fund Raising Executive) is a designation conferred by AFP that requires ten years experience in the field, rigorous testing, and preparation of a professional portfolio.

Charitable lead trust—Provides for payments to a 501(c)(3) organization for a stipulated period of time, free from federal gift and estate taxes. At the end of the trust term, the trust assets go to a designated individual.

Charitable remainder trust—Provides income to donor for life (or term of years) with the remainder of the trust going to a 501(c)(3) organization at death.

Constituency—The members of the "family" of an organization, such as faculty, alumni, staff, employees, users, parents, donors, and members.

Consultant (fundraising counsel)—A specialist in one or more areas of fundraising who is hired by an organization for the purpose of recommending solutions to problems and generally providing advice and guidance related to fundraising efforts.

Cultivation—The process of gradually developing the interest of an important prospective contributor through exposure to institutional activities, people, needs, and plans, to the point where the prospect might consider a major gift.

Development—A term used to define the total process of organizational fundraising, frequently inclusive of public relations and (in education) alumni affairs.

Development committee—A volunteer committee of the board of a nonprofit organization that is charged with the responsibility for oversight of fundraising and related activities.

Direct mail—Solicitation of funds by mail.

Donor recognition—The policy and practice of providing recognition to donors for their gifts, e.g., public expressions of appreciation directly to donors, published lists of contributors, and other appropriate ways such as gifts, mementos, naming of buildings, or other items.

Endowment fund—Funds invested by an organization to produce income for operations and other board-approved purposes.

Estate—The legal status or position of an owner with respect to property and other assets; total assets of a deceased person.

Evaluation (prospect rating)—A procedure for evaluating the giving potential of prospects by knowledgeable members of the campaign organization.

Face-to-face solicitation (personal solicitation)—Soliciting a prospective contributor at the prospect's home, office, or other location.

Fact sheet—A brief statement of an organization's purposes, programs, services, needs, plans, and other pertinent information, prepared for use by campaign volunteers

Fair market value (FMV)—A value generally defined as the amount that a willing purchaser would pay in the normal market.

Fiduciary—A person charged with the duty of a trust on behalf of a beneficiary, e.g., executors and trustees.

501(c)(3)—The section of the U.S. Internal Revenue Code that defines nonprofit, charitable, educational, religious, scientific, and like tax-exempt organizations. A 501(c)(3) organization is one that is gift supported and tax exempt. Gifts to 501(c)(3) organizations are generally tax deductible.

Gift-in-kind—A contribution of equipment, supplies, or other property in lieu of money. The donor may place a monetary value on in-kind gifts for tax purposes.

Giving clubs (donor clubs, recognition clubs)—Categories of donors who are grouped and recognized by the organization on the basis of similar gift level.

Goal—The amount of money to be achieved by a fundraising campaign.

Grant—Generally an allocation from a foundation, corporation, or government agency.

Independent sector (third sector)—A term used to describe all nonprofit organizations, as distinct from government entities and corporations that are formed to make a profit.

Indicia—A mailing permit that appears in the upper right corner of an envelope, which otherwise would be stamped or metered. A nonprofit permit allows the organization to use the lower, nonprofit mailing rate.

Inter vivos trust—A trust made during the grantor's lifetime.

Intestate—Not having made legal will as of time of death.

I.R.S. Form 990—A report annually submitted by almost all tax-exempt organizations to the Internal Revenue Service, which includes financial information on income sources, expenditures, and activities.

Kickoff—A formal public launching of a campaign, usually at a special event, to which major prospects are invited and where major funds commitments are announced.

Leadership—Chairpersons of a campaign who provide the drive and enthusiasm essential to motivating volunteers.

Letter of intent—A letter that states the prospect's intention to make a gift or legacy.

Long range development plan—That aspect of development concerned with future goals.

Mail campaign—A campaign, usually on a broad basis, conducted by mail, frequently with several mailings over a specific period.

Marketing—Bringing an organization's product to the marketplace.

Matching gift—A gift by a corporation matching a gift made by one of the corporation's employees.

Memorial gift—A gift to an organization commemorating either the donor or someone else. Memorial gifts are usually made in memory of a deceased person, while gifts "in honor of" are made to honor a living person or persons.

Mission statement—A concise description of the purpose of an organization.

Named gift opportunity—Name-bearing recognition of a gift for a specific purpose, normally available to donors in a campaign, publicized in advance as an incentive for giving.

Organization chart—A chart depicting the complete structure for a campaign, by committees, starting with the governing body of an organization or institution and extending down through all operating committees.

Philanthropy—Literally, "love of humankind." According to one dictionary, "the spirit of active good will toward one's fellow persons, especially as shown in efforts to promote their welfare. "Generally, the practice and philosophy of supporting, through financial and other contributions, programs, and campaigns conducted by charitable organizations.

Phonathon—A fundraising effort in which volunteers solicit gifts or pledges by telephone.

Planned giving—The integration of sound personal, financial, and estate planning concepts with the individual donor's plans for lifetime or testamentary giving.

Planning study—An objective survey of an organization's fundraising potential that measures the strength of its case and the availability of leadership, workers, and prospective donors. A written report includes the study findings, recommendations, and (when feasible) a campaign plan, timetable, and budget. Fundraising counsel usually conducts the study.

Pledge—A signed and dated commitment to make a gift over a specified period, generally three or more years, payable according to terms set by the donor; the total value of such a commitment.

Pledge card—A printed form used by solicitors in seeking what might or might not be a legally binding, must is usually a morally binding commitment from a prospect.

Press kit—Informational material relating to an organization and its fundraising plans, packaged for distribution to the media.

Professional ethics—Standards of conduct and methods of doing business, as determined by organizations of fundraisers, to which members agree to adhere and which provide assurances of professionalism.

Proposal—A written request or application for a gift or grant that includes why the project or program is needed, who will carry it out, and how much it will cost.

Prospect—Any logical source of potential support, whether it be individual, corporate, foundation, organization, or government (at all levels).

Prospect research—The ongoing search for new and pertinent information on prospects and contributors; identification of new individual, foundation, and corporate prospects.

Public relations—The practice of developing the reciprocal understanding and good will of an organization with opinion leaders and the general public.

Public service announcement (PSA)—A broadcast by radio or television that is contributed by the station as a public service.

Quid pro quo—Something for something; a mutual consideration; securing an advantage or receiving a concession in return for a similar favor. In fundraising, a good quid pro quo exchange is generally not a tax-deductible donation.

Restricted gift—A gift for a specified purpose clearly stated by the donor, such as for research purposes.

RFP (request for proposal)—A request sent by government or a foundation to organizations that might be interested in applying for a grant from the agency or foundation.

Screening—(see evaluation)

Solicitation—The process of asking for a contribution.

Special event—A public ceremony such as a dedication or ground-breaking ceremony, or an event specially contrived to focus attention on an institution during a fundraising campaign and thus aid the cultivation process; or a special event to raise funds or awareness of the organization.

Stewardship—The proper utilization of contributions received by an organization.

Strategic plan—A program incorporating a strategy for achieving organizational goals and objectives within a specific timeframe and with substantive support in the form of methods, priorities, and resources.

Support services—Technical aspects of a development program that deal with such areas as prospect research, mailings, gift processing, list preparation, computer, and clerical support.

Telethon—A fundraising campaign broadcast over television for the purpose of having viewers call in to make pledges to a charity. (A radiothon is similar to a telethon, broadcast over a radio station.)

Testamentary trust—A trust contained wholly within a will of a deceased person; effective only after death.

Trust—A fiduciary relationship with respect to property, subjecting the person by whom the title to property is held to equitable duties to deal with the property for the benefit of another.

UBIT-Unrelated Busines Income Tax—Income tax based on income not related to the mission and purpose of a nonprofit organization.

Vision—The hope and plans for the future of an organization; where the organization wants to be.

Volunteer—Any individual working on a temporary basis without compensation on behalf of a nonprofit organization.

Will—Normally a legally-executed written instrument by which a person makes disposition of property, to take effect after the person's death.

Year-end giving—The practice among many charitable organizations of seeking gifts, usually via mail campaigns, in the last two months of a calendar year, on the premise that prospects will take advantage of an opportunity for a last-minute tax deduction.

Appendix B

AFP Code of Ethical Principles and Standards

ETHICAL PRINCIPLES
Adopted 1964; amended Sept. 2007

The Association of Fundraising Professionals (AFP) exists to foster the development and growth of fundraising professionals and the profession, to promote high ethical behavior in the fundraising profession and to preserve and enhance philanthropy and volunteerism.

Members of AFP are motivated by an inner drive to improve the quality of life through the causes they serve. They serve the ideal of philanthropy, are committed to the preservation and enhancement of volunteerism; and hold stewardship of these concepts as the overriding direction of their professional life. They recognize their responsibility to ensure that needed resources are vigorously and ethically sought and that the intent of the donor is honestly fulfilled.

To these ends, AFP members, both individual and business, embrace certain values that they strive to uphold in performing their responsibilities for generating philanthropic support. AFP business members strive to promote and protect the work and mission of their client organizations.

AFP members both individual and business aspire to:

◆ practice their profession with integrity, honesty, truthfulness and adherence to the absolute obligation to safeguard the public trust

◆ act according to the highest goals and visions of their organizations, professions, clients and consciences

◆ put philanthropic mission above personal gain

◆ inspire others through their own sense of dedication and high purpose

◆ improve their professional knowledge and skills, so that their performance will better serve others

◆ demonstrate concern for the interests and well-being of individuals affected by their actions

◆ value the privacy, freedom of choice and interests of all those affected by their actions

◆ foster cultural diversity and pluralistic values and treat all people with dignity and respect

◆ affirm, through personal giving, a commitment to philanthropy and its role in society

◆ adhere to the spirit as well as the letter of all applicable laws and regulations

◆ advocate within their organizations adherence to all applicable laws and regulations

◆ avoid even the appearance of any criminal offense or professional misconduct

◆ bring credit to the fundraising profession by their public demeanor

◆ encourage colleagues to embrace and practice these ethical principles and standards

◆ be aware of the codes of ethics promulgated by other professional organizations that serve philanthropy

ETHICAL STANDARDS

Furthermore, while striving to act according to the above values, AFP members, both individual and business, agree to abide (and to ensure, to the best of their ability, that all members of their staff abide) by the AFP standards. Violation of the standards might subject the member to disciplinary sanctions, including expulsion, as provided in the AFP Ethics Enforcement Procedures.

Member Obligations

1. Members shall not engage in activities that harm the members' organizations, clients or profession.

2. Members shall not engage in activities that conflict with their fiduciary, ethical and legal obligations to their organizations, clients or profession.

3. Members shall effectively disclose all potential and actual conflicts of interest; such disclosure does not preclude or imply ethical impropriety.

4. Members shall not exploit any relationship with a donor, prospect, volunteer, client or employee for the benefit of the members or the members' organizations.

5. Members shall comply with all applicable local, state, provincial and federal civil and criminal laws.

6. Members recognize their individual boundaries of competence and are forthcoming and truthful about their professional experience and qualifications and will represent their achievements accurately and without exaggeration.

7. Members shall present and supply products and/or services honestly and without misrepresentation and will clearly identify the details of those products, such as availability of the products and/or services and other factors that might affect the suitability of the products and/or services for donors, clients or nonprofit organizations.

8. Members shall establish the nature and purpose of any contractual relationship at the outset and will be responsive and available to organizations and their employing organizations before, during and after any sale of materials and/or services. Members will comply with all fair and reasonable obligations created by the contract.

9. Members shall refrain from knowingly infringing the intellectual property rights of other parties at all times. Members shall address and rectify any inadvertent infringement that might occur.

10. Members shall protect the confidentiality of all privileged information relating to the provider/client relationships.

11. Members shall refrain from any activity designed to disparage competitors untruthfully.

Solicitation and Use of Philanthropic Funds

12. Members shall take care to ensure that all solicitation and communication materials are accurate and correctly reflect their organizations' mission and use of solicited funds.

13. Members shall take care to ensure that donors receive informed, accurate and ethical advice about the value and tax implications of contributions.

14. Members shall take care to ensure that contributions are used in accordance with donors' intentions.

15. Members shall take care to ensure proper stewardship of all revenue sources, including timely reports on the use and management of such funds.

16. Members shall obtain explicit consent by donors before altering the conditions of financial transactions.

Presentation of Information

17. Members shall not disclose privileged or confidential information to unauthorized parties.

18. Members shall adhere to the principle that all donor and prospect information created by, or on behalf of, an organization or a client is the property of that organization or client and shall not be transferred or utilized except on behalf of that organization or client.

19. Members shall give donors and clients the opportunity to have their names removed from lists that are sold to, rented to or exchanged with other organizations.

20. Members shall, when stating fundraising results, use accurate and consistent accounting methods that conform to the appropriate guidelines adopted by the American Institute of Certified Public Accountants (AICPA)* for the type of organization involved. (*In countries outside of the United States, comparable authority should be utilized.)

Compensation and Contracts

21. Members shall not accept compensation or enter into a contract that is based on a percentage of contributions; nor shall members accept finder's fees or contingent fees. Business members must refrain from receiving compensation from third parties derived from products or services for a client without disclosing that third-party compensation to the client (for example, volume rebates from vendors to business members).

22. Members may accept performance-based compensation, such as bonuses, provided such bonuses are in accord with prevailing practices within the members' own organizations and are not based on a percentage of contributions.

23. Members shall neither offer nor accept payments or special considerations for the purpose of influencing the selection of products or services.

24. Members shall not pay finder's fees, commissions or percentage compensation based on contributions, and shall take care to discourage their organizations from making such payments.

25. Any member receiving funds on behalf of a donor or client must meet the legal requirements for the disbursement of those funds. Any interest or income earned on the funds should be fully disclosed.

Appendix

A Donor Bill of Rights

Philanthropy is based on voluntary action for the common good. It is a tradition of giving and sharing that is primary to the quality of life. To assure that philanthropy merits the respect and trust of the general public, and that donors and prospective donors can have full confidence in the nonprofit organizations and causes they are asked to support, we declare that all donors have these rights:

I. To be informed of the organization's mission, the way the organization intends to use donated resources and of its capacity to use donations effectively for their intended purposes.

II. To be informed of the identity of those serving on the organization's governing board, and to expect the board to exercise prudent judgment in its stewardship responsibilities.

III. To have access to the organization's most recent financial statements.

IV. To be assured their gifts will be used for the purposes for which they were given.

V. To receive appropriate acknowledgment and recognition.

VI. To be assured that information about their donations is handled with respect and with confidentiality to the extent provided by law.

VII. To expect all relationships with individuals representing organization of interest to the donor will be professional in nature.

VIII. To be informed whether those seeking donations are volunteers, employees of the organization or hired solicitors.

IX. To have the opportunity for their names to be deleted from mailing lists that an organizations may intend to share.

X. To feel free to ask questions when making a donation and to receive prompt, truthful and forthright answers.

Developed by American Association of Fundraising Counsel (AAFRC), Association of Fundraising Professionals (AFP), Association for Healthcare Philanthropy (AHP), and Council of Advancement and Support of Education (CASE).

Endorsed by: Independent Sector, National Catholic Development Council (NCDC), National Committee on Planned Giving (NCPG), National Council for Resource Development (NCRD), and United Way of America.

Appendix D

Assessing Your Organization's Philanthropic Profile

✎ Does your organization have a development office?

✎ Do you have experienced professionals staffing your development office?

✎ Does your development budget include money for professional development (membership in professional organizations, conferences and workshops, books and periodicals, etc.) for the development staff?

✎ Has your organization allocated a budget for a donor software system to manage fundraising activities?

✎ Do all your staff members understand the importance of the development function? Does your organization's staff support the development office's efforts?

✎ Does your organization seek to hire development professionals that are certified (CFRE or ACFRE, FAHP, GPC, etc.) or assist current staff in obtaining credentials?

- Does the chief development officer attend board meetings?

- Is the board committed to development (do members give and get money for the organization)?

- Is there a development committee on your board, and does a development officer staff this committee?

- Is there clerical support for your chief development officer?

- Does your development staff act and look professional?

- Is the development office in a prominent location and does it have a professional appearance?

- Does your organization support the Donor Bill of Rights? (See **Appendix C.**)

- Is your organization aware of and supportive of the AFP Code of Ethical Principles and Standards? (See **Appendix B.**)

- Does your organization understand the importance of donor-centered fundraising?

- Does your organization understand that it takes time to establish a development program, and that building relationships with donors is the key role of the development office?

- Is your organization committed to work with consultants when it is appropriate to do so, and not expect staff to manage major efforts such as a capital campaign?

- Is your CEO involved in fundraising?

- Do you invite volunteers to be involved in your fundraising program?

Appendix E

Sample Board and Board Member Job Descriptions

Purpose

To act as a voting member of the board with full authority and responsibility to develop policies for the operation of the organization; to monitor the organization's financial health, programs, and overall performance; and to provide the chief executive officer with the resources to meet the needs of those persons the organization serves.

The full board's responsibilities

- Establish policy
- Hire and evaluate the executive director
- Secure adequate funding for the organization
- Monitor finances
- Create and update a long range plan for the organization

- Select and support the organization's board officers

- Adopt key operating policies

- Approve contracts as appropriate

Individual board members' duties:

- Attend board meetings regularly

- Become knowledgeable about the organization

- Come to board meetings well prepared and well-informed about issues on the agenda

- Contribute to meetings by expressing your point of view

- Consider other points of view, make constructive suggestions, and help the board make decisions that benefit those persons the organization serves

- Serve on at least one committee

- Represent the organization to individuals, the public, and other organizations in a positive and professional manner

- Support the organization through attendance at special events and activities and through meaningful financial contributions

- Board members are expected to make XYZ one of their top three charitable priorities

- Assume board leadership roles when asked

- Keep the executive director informed about any concerns the community may have

- Maintain confidentiality of board discussion

Rationale

Board members set corporate policies and goals and delegate authority to the executive director to implement them in the day to day management of the organization. Individual members of the board, however, have no authority to act independently of the full board. When they do, it can seriously damage the organization's ability to carry out its mission, board team spirit, and the organization's image in the community. Board members who abuse their position this way may be disciplined or censured.

Board members are also trustees of their organization who approve an annual budget that ensures it can meet its financial needs. In addition, board members monitor the overall financial health of their organization by reviewing annual reports of an auditor recommended by the executive director. The executive director retains responsibility for the day-to-day operational expenditures.

Individual board members should attend all board meetings and actively participate in them and serve on committees or as board officers. Finally, board members have the responsibility to know and fulfill their proper role as board members and to act in the best interest of those persons the organization serves.

Appendix F

Potential Donors for our Organization

Your Name:_____

Category	Name & Address	Potential Major Donor Y or N	Potential Board Member or Fund-raising Volunteer
My accountant			
My car dealer			
My banker(s)			
My attorney			
Members of my professional association			
My insurance agent			

Category	Name & Address	Potential Major Donor Y or N	Potential Board Member or Fundraising Volunteer
My doctor(s)			
My dentist(s)			
Members of a service club to which I belong			
Neighbors			
Relatives			
Clients/customers of mine			
Politicians I know			
People with whom I worship			
People with whom I work			
People with whom I went to school			
Parents of children with whom my children go to school			
My realtor			
People with whom I do business			

Category	Name & Address	Potential Major Donor Y or N	Potential Board Member or Fund-raising Volunteer
People with whom I play sports			
People I know who support other charities			
People who have asked me to support their favorite charity			
People I know who volunteer for other nonprofit organizations			
Others			

Appendix

Board Organization Chart

(Starts next page.)

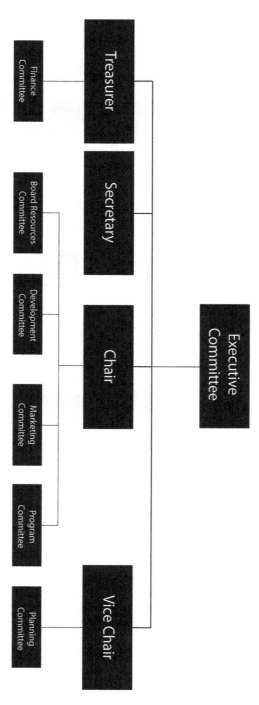

Appendix

Development Committee Organization Chart

(Starts next page.)

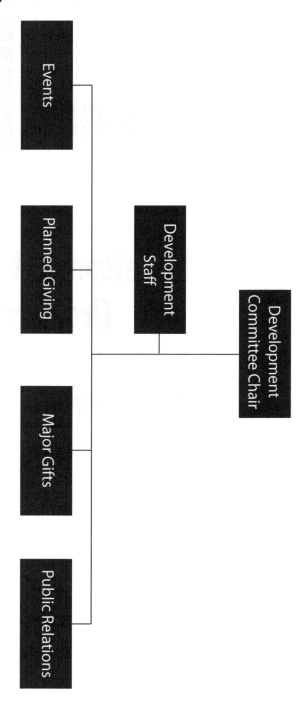

Appendix

Development Committee Position Description

◆ Work with appropriate staff to develop a long-range and a short-range development plan.

◆ Plan and oversee all fundraising activities of the organization.

◆ Contribute financially to the organization, and assure full board participation in all campaigns and projects.

◆ Educate the full board on the theory and techniques of development programs.

◆ Encourage the participation of all board members in fundraising activities and programs.

◆ Attend all fundraising events, and encourage board member attendance.

◆ Work with or assume the duties of a public relations committee.

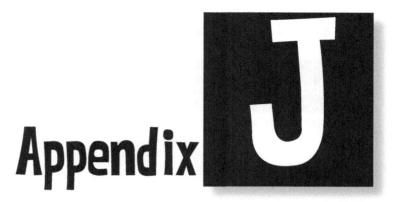

Appendix J

Volunteer Recruitment Packets

Before approaching the prospective volunteer, you need to develop volunteer recruitment packets for each volunteer function. Here are some items that should be in the packet.

Board Recruitment Packet	Development Committee Recruitment Packet	Fundraising Volunteer Recruitment Packet
Bylaws of the organization		
Board member position description*	Development committee member position description*	Volunteer position description*
List of board meeting dates with times and locations	List of development committee meeting dates with times and locations	List of committee meeting dates with times and locations
List of current board members	List of current development committee members and list of current board members	List of other volunteers involved in this committee or project and list of current board members

Board Recruitment Packet	Development Committee Recruitment Packet	Fundraising Volunteer Recruitment Packet
Your organization's case for support	Your organization's case for support	Your organization's case for support
Your development plan	Your development plan	
		Timeline of project or campaign on which you are asking the volunteer to work
Organization budget for current fiscal year		
Any other information about your organization that might be helpful to the prospective board member	Any other information about your organization that might be helpful to the prospective development committee member	Any other information about your organization that might be helpful to the prospective volunteer

Position descriptions should include term limits, general roles and responsibilities, and the level of time and financial commitment expected of the volunteer.

Appendix K

Sample Job Description for Director of Development

Reports to: Executive Director

Qualifications: Bachelor's degree or CFRE (Certified Fund Raising Executive) credential and at least five years successful fundraising experience. Membership in the Association of Fundraising Professionals or other professional association encouraged and will be paid by employer.

Responsibilities: All fundraising activities including:

◆ Work with the executive director and board of directors to ensure the financial stability of XYZ through the development and implementation of a full range of development programs.

◆ Develop and manage yearly development budget.

◆ Develop a comprehensive, board-approved development plan including timelines, goals, strategies and committee job descriptions.

◆ Assemble, research and update past and prospective donor linkage.

◆ Oversee yearly annual fund, phonathon and fundraising events.

- Train and guide the development committee in how to make the ask.

- Coordinate and attend face-to-face ask meetings.

- Produce personalized ask letters, brochures and invitations.

- Solicit corporate sponsorships.

- Solicit foundation support.

- Implement fundraising capability on agency web site.

- Oversee maintenance of donor tracking system and timely production of bulk mailings, thank-you letters and development progress reports.

- Network with philanthropic community through appropriate organizations.

- Promote public awareness of XYZ through the preparation and distribution of press releases, website, brochures and other appropriate communications methods, including public speaking.

Appendix

Sample Organization Charts

Chief Development Officer reports directly to the Executive Director/CEO

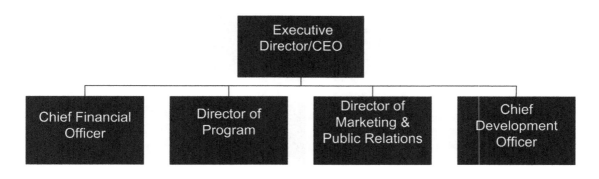

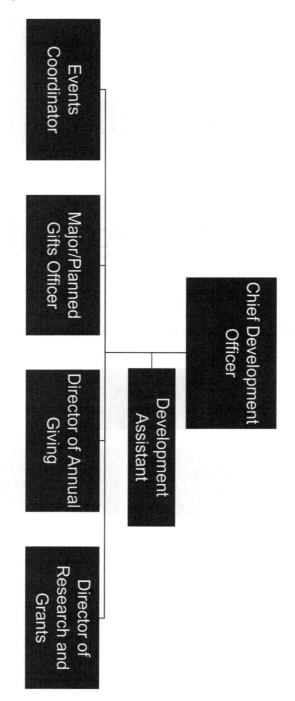

Typical Small Development Office Organization Chart

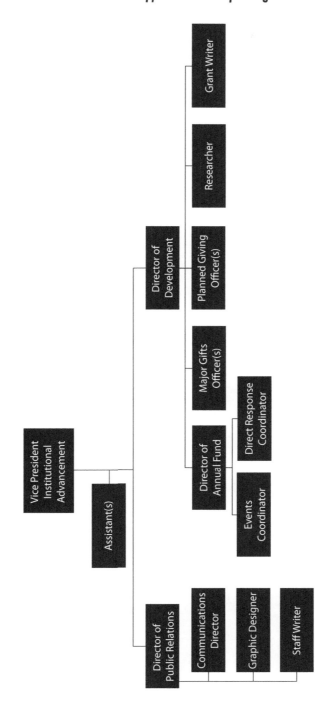

Typical Large Development Office Organization Chart

Appendix

Foundation Prospects

(Starts next page.)

Foundation Prospects for XYZ as of MM/DD/YYYY					
Organization Address Phone Email/Website	Contact	Trustees	Interest	Deadline	Guidelines

Appendix N

Prospect Worksheets

XYZ Organization
Foundation Research Form

Name:
_____

Address:
_____

Telephone: Fax:
_____

Email: Website:
_____

Management/Directors:
_____

Areas of Interest:
_____

Limitations:
_____

Deadlines:

History:

Assets:

Total Grants:

Sample Grants to
other Organizations:

Researcher:

Date:

Sources:

Use additional sheets as needed

XYZ Organization
Corporate Research Form

Name:
_____

Address:
_____

Contact Person:
_____

Management/Directors:
_____

History of Company:
_____

Financial Information Sales:
_____

Net Income:
_____

Employees:

_____

Network:
_____

Gifts to other Organizations:
_____

Researcher:

Date:

_____

Sources:

_____

Use additional sheets as needed

XYZ Organization
Individual Research Form

Name: _____ I.D. # _____

Address: _____

Telephone: _____ Fax: _____

Business: _____ Title _____

Address: _____

Telephone: _____ Fax: _____

Educational History

(Husband) _____ (Wife) _____

(Husband) _____ (Wife) _____

(Husband) _____ (Wife) _____

(Husband) _____ (Wife) _____

Personal Information

Spouse: _____

Children: _____

Community Activities: _____

Awards:

Corporate Affiliations:

Other Memberships:

Career History:

Financial Information

Salary (or Estimated):

Bonus or Additional Compensation:

Stock Holdings:

Dividends:

Retirement Income:

Property:

Inheritance:

Personal Foundation:

Giving Information:

Suggested Potential Contacts:

Comments:

Researcher:

Date:

Sources:

Use additional sheets as needed

Appendix

Tasks by Timeline

(Starts next page.)

Date	Responsible	Cost	Action Step	Objective	Goal
2/14/12	President Elect	N/A	3.5.1 Invite old and new board members to participate in retreat	Obj. 3.5 Schedule a mini-board retreat in March, 2012 to review the strategic plan, inviting new members to participate	Goal 3: The AFP XYZ Chapter will engage in ongoing strategic planning.
2/14/12 and ongoing	President Elect	N/A	Step 3.1 Update on any changes to other goals (objectives/action steps) at each board meeting beginning in February, 2012	Obj. 3.1 Establish a standing agenda item for strategic planning at every board meeting, ensuring time for continuing strategic plan discussion and refinement beginning in Jan, 2012	Goal 3: The AFP XYZ Chapter will engage in ongoing strategic planning.
2/14/12 and ongoing	President Elect	N/A	3.1.1 Dedicate time (@15 minutes) every board meeting to the review of one goal's objectives, action steps, and accomplishments beginning in January, 2012	Obj. 3.1 Establish a standing agenda item for strategic planning at every board meeting, ensuring time for continuing strategic plan discussion and refinement beginning in Jan, 2012	Goal 3: The AFP XYZ Chapter will engage in ongoing strategic planning.
2/14/12	Membership Committee	N/A	1.3.1 Create a list of membership minute topics and schedule	Obj. 1.3 Present a "membership minute" at each chapter meeting starting in January, 2012	Goal 1: The AFP XYZ Chapter will recruit, engage and retain members.
2/14/12	Board	N/A	1.1.4 Identify list of volunteers the chapter wants to recruit	Obj. 1.1 Provide a website page that lists volunteer opportunities for members to be involved in the chapter by March 31, 2012	Goal 1: The AFP XYZ Chapter will recruit, engage and retain members.

Appendix P

Tasks by Responsibility

Board Task Detail

Ref. # Tasks	Responsible	Timeline	
		Start Date	End Date
2013			
1.3 Develop Policies & Procedures for Development Office	Development Director/Board		
2.2.2 Recruit chairperson for Development Committee	Exec Director/Development Director/Board		01/15/2013
2.1.3 Recruit Board members	Exec Director/Board		01/15/2013

Consultant Task Detail

Ref. # Tasks	Responsible	Timeline Start Date	End Date
		2013	
2.2 Develop case statement for annual giving which includes annual fund goal	Director/Consultant		
3.3 Develop appropriate materials to be used in constituency appeals	Development Director/ Consultant		Development
2.1.1 Develop Board organization chart	Consultant		11/15/2013
2.2.2 Develop position descriptions for all Board members and committees	Exec Director/ Consultant		12/15/2013
2.2.1 Develop position descriptions for Development Committee	Consultant		12/15/2013
3.1.1 Review current case for support document	Development Director/ Consultant		12/15/2013
3.2.1 Develop levels of giving and giving opportunities	Development Director/ Consultant		12/15/2013

Development Committee Chair Task Detail

Ref. # Tasks	Responsible	Timeline Start Date	End Date
		2013	
4.2 Develop a subcommittee to work on each constituency appeal	Development Director/ DC Chair		02/28/2013
4.2.1 Enlist the help of Board, past Advisory Board members to identify volunteers and approaches	Development Director/ DC Chair		03/03/2013

| 2.2.3 Recruit Development Committee members | Development Director/ DC Chair | 03/15/2013 |
| 2.2.4 Have Development Committee affirm plan and enlist Board's help to implement plan | DC Chair | 04/15/2013 |

Development Committee Task Detail

			Timeline	
Ref. #	Tasks	Responsible	Start Date	End Date
		2013		
4.4.1	Enlist volunteers for each constituency	Development Director/ Dev. Comm.		05/30/2013
6.2	Develop a Planned Giving prospect list	Development Director. Dev. Comm.		08/30/2013
6.4	Develop relationships with professionals to help in Planned Giving Program	Development Director/ Dev. Comm.		10/31/2013
4.4.4	Make major gift solicitation visits	Dev. Comm.		11/01/2013
6.5	Conduct a Planned Giving Seminar	Development Director/ Dev. Comm.		11/30/2013
6.7	Follow up with Planned Giving prospects	Development Director/ Dev. Comm.	01/01/2013	

Development Assistant Task Detail

Ref. # Tasks	Responsible	Timeline Start Date	End Date
	2013		
1.1.1 Purchase a donor database designed for fundraising	Dev Assistant/ Development Director		12/15/2013

Executive Director Task Detail

Ref. # Tasks	Responsible	Timeline Start Date	End Date
	2013		
1.2 Develop Adequate Staffing Structure for Development Office	Exec Director/ Development Director		
2.1.2 Develop position descriptions for all Board members and committees	Exec Director/ Consultant		12/15/2013

Development Director Task Detail

Ref. # Tasks	Responsible	Timeline Start Date	End Date
	2013		
1.2 Develop Adequate Staffing Structure for Development Office	Exec Director/ Development Director		
1.3 Develop Policies & Procedures for Development Office	Development Director/ Board		

3.2 Develop case statement for annual giving which includes annual fund goal	Development Director/ Consultant	
4.3 Develop appropriate materials to be used in constituency appeals	Development Director/ Consultant	
3.1.1 Review current case for support document	Development Director/ Consultant	12/15/2013
3.2.1 Develop levels of giving and giving opportunities	Development Director/ Consultant	12/15/2013
1.1.1 Purchase a donor database designed for fundraising	Dev Assistant/ Development Director	12/15/2013

Appendix Q

Development Budget

Item	Current Year Budget	Current Year Actual	Next Year Budget
Equipment			
Computer Hardware			
Software			
Photocopier			
Postage Machine			
Folder			
Phone System			
Fax			

Item	Current Year Budget	Current Year Actual	Next Year Budget
Cell Phones			
Furniture			
Publication/Mailing			
Annual Report			
Brochures			
Stationery			
Postage			
Library Expenses			
Newspapers			
Journals			
Books			
Directories			
Membership Dues			

Item	Current Year Budget	Current Year Actual	Next Year Budget
Chamber of Commerce			
AFP			
Other Professional Organizations			
Events			
Meetings			
Recognition			
Special Events			
Professional Development			
Conferences			
Training			
Salaries & Benefits			
Travel Expenses			

Appendix

Capital Campaign Organization Chart

(Starts next page.)

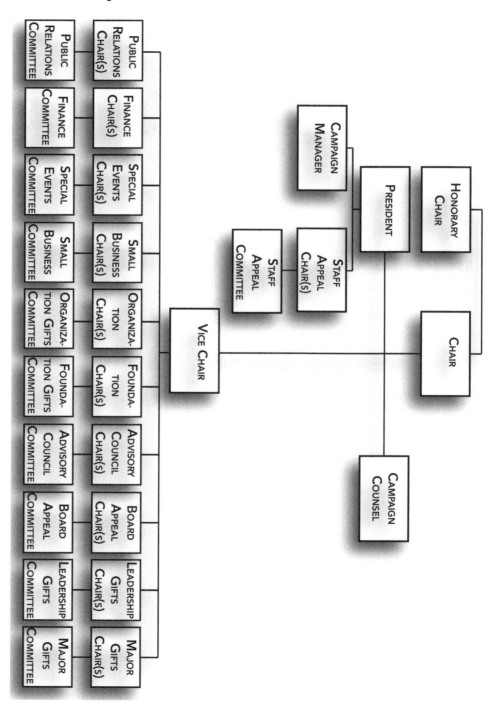

Appendix S

Campaign Chair and Cabinet Member Job Descriptions

ABC Organization
"Campaign Theme"

CAMPAIGN CABINET

The Campaign Cabinet is responsible for guiding all aspects of the campaign. The Campaign Cabinet should be comprised of community leaders—board members, staff, donors and others who are recognized community leaders. An outline of key leadership positions as well as a general position description for all Campaign Cabinet members follows.

Members of the Capital Campaign Cabinet will provide leadership and direction for the campaign. Members will be recruited from ABC's constituents and will have the following responsibilities, in addition to the responsibilities outlined in the position description of the position filled on the Campaign Cabinet:

- ◆ Serve as chair, co-chair or member of one of the Campaign Cabinet subcommittees.

- ◆ Recruit others to serve on various committees, as needed.

- ◆ Make a meaningful gift to the campaign.

- ◆ Identify and solicit possible leadership and major donors to the campaign.

- ◆ Attend campaign events and functions.
- ◆ Attend monthly meetings of the Campaign Cabinet.
- ◆ Promote the campaign in the community.

CAMPAIGN CHAIR

The Campaign Chair is the acknowledged and recognized leader of the Capital Campaign who personally subscribes to and supports the financial goals of the campaign, as well as encourages and stimulates the capabilities and generosity of others. A Campaign Cabinet will assist enlistment of committee leadership. All leadership will be accountable to the Campaign Chair for the performance of their responsibilities.

- ◆ Be the official spokesperson for the campaign.
- ◆ Chair the Campaign Cabinet meetings.
- ◆ Provide leadership to the various committee kick-off meetings.
- ◆ Provide leadership and assistance, as needed in soliciting leadership, major, business, foundation and individual gifts.
- ◆ Work with Campaign Counsel and Campaign Manager to bring the campaign to a successful conclusion on schedule.

The Campaign Chair is the representative of the organization's campaign and reflects its values, ideals and objectives. The Chair brings status, inspiration and motivation to the campaign.

Appendix

Board of Directors Self-Evaluation

The following self-evaluation should be used by all board members to get an impression, or indication of how well the board is generally doing in performing its role and conducting its responsibilities.

	Considerations	5 Very good	4 Good	3 Ave	2 Fair	1 Poor
1	Board has full and common understanding of the roles and responsibilities of a board of directors.					
2	Board members understand the organization's missions and its programs.					
3	The structural pattern of the board, officers, committees, are clear regarding individual and group roles and responsibilities.					
4	Board has clear goals and actions resulting from relevant and realistic strategic planning.					

	Considerations	5 Very good	4 Good	3 Ave	2 Fair	1 Poor
5	Board attends to policy-related decisions which effectively guide operational activities.					
6	Board receives regular reports on and understands finances/budgets, products/program performance, and other important matter.					
7	Board helps set fundraising goals and is actively involved in fundraising.					
8	Board effectively represents the organization to the community.					
9	Board meeting facilitates focus and progress on important organizational matters.					
10	Board regularly monitors and evaluates progress on important organizational matters.					
11	Board has approved comprehensive volunteer and personnel policies.					
12	Each member of the board feels involved and interested in the board's work.					
13	All necessary skills, stakeholders, and diversity are represented on the board.					

Please list the three to five points on which you believe the board should focus its attention in the next year. Be as specific as possible:

Appendix

Board of Directors Evaluation Grid

(Starts next page.)

Individual Board Member Performance Evaluation

Select only one answer**

(Each category=10 points maximum)

Category		Points 1-10	Name			Segment Totals
Attendance	Attended 75-100% of meetings in 12 months	10				
	Attended 50-74% of meetings in 12 months	7				
	Attended 25-49% of meetings in 12 months	4				
	Attended less than 25% of meetings	1				
Committee Participation	Actively participate on at least 1 Board Committee	10				
Support Generation	Directly raised more than $10,000	10				
	Directly raised more than $5,000	8				
	Directly raised more than $1,000	6				
	Directly raised more than $500	4				
	Directly raised less than $500	2				
	Directly raised less than $0	0				
External Ambassador	Served as Ambassador (speeches, participation in events, fundraising)	10				
Understanding	Is informed on agency business & direction	10				
Personal Support	Actively took part in organization's events	10				
Skills	Brings needed technical skills to board	10				
Name	Name adds credibility to organization	10				
Leadership	Served as officer, committee chair, or major assignment	10				
Commitment	Is committed; enthusiastic; recruits members	10				
Demeanor	Is productive and focused	10				
100-110	Excellent					
80-99	Good					
60-79	Consider Replacing					
0-59	Definitely Replace					

This Column of scores serves as an indication of Board performance

Individual Board Member Performance Evaluation Matrix

Category	Criteria												Totals
Age	Over 60												
	45-59												
	25-44												
	Under 25												
Sex	Male												
	Female												
Diversity	Asian												
	African American												
	Hispanic												
	Native American												
	Caucasian												
	Other												
People who are Physically and/or Mentally Challenged													
	Non-Profit												
	Government												
	Business												
	Professional												
	Clergy												
	Education												
	Private Corporation												
	Foundation												
Expertise	Administration												
	Budget/Finance												
	Business												
	Legal												
	Marketing/Advertising												
	Public Relations												
	Fundraising												
	Planning												
	Program Services												
	Communication Contacts												
	Technology												

Recommendations for Board Recruitment

Appendix

Board Fundraising Assessment Form

1. What percentage of the board makes a meaningful financial commitment to the organization on an annual basis?

_____100 percent (10)   _____40 percent (4)

_____90 percent (9)   _____30 percent (3)

_____80 percent (8)   _____20 percent (2)

_____70 percent (7)   _____10 percent (1)

_____60 percent (6)   _____0 percent (0)

_____50 percent (5)

POINTS_____

2. What percentage of the board has made a planned gift to the organization?

_____100 percent (10)   _____40 percent (4)

_____90 percent (9)   _____30 percent (3)

_____80 percent (8)   _____20 percent (2)

_____70 percent (7)   _____10 percent (1)

_____60 percent (6)   _____0 percent (0)

_____50 percent (5)

POINTS_____

3. What percentage of the board made a contribution to the last capital campaign run by the organization (where applicable)?

_____100 percent (10)   _____40 percent (4)

_____90 percent (9)   _____30 percent (3)

_____80 percent (8)   _____20 percent (2)

_____70 percent (7)   _____10 percent (1)

_____60 percent (6)   _____0 percent (0)

_____50 percent (5)

POINTS_____

4. What percentage of the board attends events held by the organization?

_____100 percent (10)   _____40 percent (4)

_____90 percent (9)   _____30 percent (3)

_____80 percent (8)   _____20 percent (2)

_____70 percent (7)   _____10 percent (1)

_____60 percent (6)   _____0 percent (0)

_____50 percent (5)

POINTS_____

5. The board helps develop our long range and annual development (fundraising) plan?

_____Yes, all are involved (10)

_____Some are involved (5)

_____None Are involved (0)

POINTS_____

6. The board is involved in recruiting volunteer fundraisers?

_____Yes, all are involved (10)

_____Some are involved (5)

_____None Are involved (0)

POINTS_____

7. The board helps identify potential donors to the organization?

_____Yes, all are involved (10)

_____Some are involved (5)

_____None Are involved (0)

POINTS_____

8. The board plans and attends cultivation events regularly?

_____Yes, all are involved (10)

_____Some are involved (5)

_____None Are involved (0)

POINTS_____

9. The board has an adequate number of people with affluence and influence in the community?

_____All (10)

_____Some (5)

_____None (0)

POINTS_____

10. The board understands that each member has a sphere of influence that can be helpful to the organization, and members are willing to promote the organization within their own sphere of influence?

_____Yes, all are involved (10)

_____Some are involved (5)

_____None Are involved (0)

POINTS_____

TOTAL POINTS: _____

Appendix W

Board Meeting Evaluation

What	O.K.	Needs Improvement	Suggestions for Improvement
1. The agenda was clear, supported by the necessary documents, and circulated prior to meeting.			
2. All board members were prepared to discuss materials sent in advance.			
3. Reports were clear and contained needed information.			
4. We avoided getting into administrative/management details.			
5. A diversity of opinions were expressed and issues were dealt with in a respectful manner.			

What	O.K.	Needs Improve-ment	Suggestions for Improvement
6. The chair guided the meeting effectively and members participated responsibly.			
7. Next steps were identified and responsibility assigned.			
8. All board members were present.			
9. The meeting began and ended on time.			
10. The meeting room was conductive to work.			
11. We enjoyed being together.			

Appendix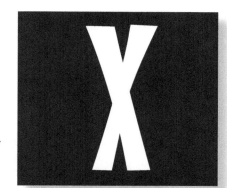

Special Events Evaluation

Name of Organization

Event

Purpose of Event: Fundraising ❑   If yes, anticipated net proceeds $_____

                    Friend Raising ❑   If yes, anticipated number people_____

                    Other ❑

Strengths of this Event: _____
                                    _____

Weaknesses of this Event: _____
                                    _____

Ideas to Make this Event   _____
Better
                                    _____

Appendix Y

Special Event Analysis

(Starts next page.)

Special Event Budget Planner

Target Net Income (your $$$ Goal)	Plus	Estimated Expenses (see sheet #2)	Equals	Total Income (Revenues) Required	Divided by	Cost per ticket	Equals	Number of tickets to be sold
	+		=		÷		=	

Income	Qty.	Price	Total Income Goal	1st Progress Report	2nd Progress Report	3rd Progress Report	Final Results	% + or -Budget
Activity Area								
Regular Tickets								
Patron Tickets								
Advertisements								
Raffle								
Auction								
In-kind Donations*								
Sponsorship								

*(Include only those items that offset expense budget items)

Expenses (D = Donated or in-kind)	Qty.	Design	Printing	Distribution Cost	Other	Total Est. Expense	Final Cost	% + or -Budget
Activity Area								
Invitations								
Program								
Tickets								
Facility Rental								
Catering								
Entertainment								
Photography								
Advertising								
Printing Ad Books								
Liability Insurance								
Decorations								
Posters								
Mailing Lists								
Transportation								

Special Event Activity Analysis

Fundraising Activity	Date	Estimated Cost	Estimated Income	Est. Profit $000s	Staff Hours Req'd	Vol. Hours Req'd	New Names Acq'd	Taps Large Donors	Builds Awareness	Risk Factor	Bonds Donors	Total	Ranking
				<25=5	<100=5	200+ =5	10+ =5	High=5	Low=5	High=5	High=5		
				25-100=3	100-200=3	100-199=3	5-9=3	Med=3	Med=3	Med=3	Med=3		
				100>=1	200>=1	0-99=1	1-5=1	Low=1	High=1	Low=1	Low=1		

Appendix Z

XYZ Organization Moves Management Intake Form

Name_____

Title_____

Company or Organization_____

Address_____

Phone_____   Fax_____

Email_____   Website:_____

Type of Prospect: ❑ Individual ❑ Corporation ❑ Foundation ❑ Organization

❑ Board   ❑ Staff   ❑ Leadership   ❑ Major
❑ Other_____

❑ Volunteer Prospect ❑ Volunteer   ❑ Committee_____

❑ Solicitor_____

❑ Recruiter_____

❑ Ask Amount $_____

❑ History with XYZ_____

❑ Source_____

❑ Area of interest_____

Next Step:

    ❑ Assigned for cultivation to   Date _____

    ❑ Ask to serve on committee   Date_____

    ❑ Invite to cultivation event   Date_____

    ❑ Invited to cultivation event   Date_____

    ❑ Attended cultivation event   Date_____

    ❑ Agreed to serve on committee   Date_____

    ❑ Proposal/ask letter prepared   Date_____

    ❑ Ask for gift   Date_____

    ❑ Solicited—pending response   Date_____

    ❑ Declined   Date_____

    ❑ Solicit later   Date_____

    ❑ Follow-up information to be sent Date_____

    ❑ Follow-up information sent   Date_____

    ❑ Acknowledgement letter sent   Date_____

    ❑ Pledge reminder sent   Date_____

    ❑ Recognition gift sent   Date_____

    ❑ Future involvement suggested   Date_____

Confidential Contact Report

CONTACT SUMMARY: Information obtained should be as comprehensive as possible, e.g., indications of political or religious preference, remarks about family, hobbies, community interests, state of health, quality of reception, personality traits, degree of familiarity with organization, attitudes, etc. (Please write clearly)

Contact Name: _____ Date of Contact: _____

Volunteer and/or Staff Member: _____

Type of Call:	❑ Personal Visit	❑ Telephone	❑ Letter

Business Address:	Home Address:
Email:	Email:
Telephone: ( )	Telephone: ( )

Date of Next Action Step:

Next Step:

❑ Send Literature   ❑ In-Person Visit   ❑ Solicit

❑ Send Letter   ❑ No Further Action   ❑ Post-Solicit

❑ Phone Call   ❑ Cultivate   ❑ Re-solicit

❑ Other

REQUEST AMOUNT:

Suggested:_____

Actually Requested:

_____

PRIORITY:

RECOMMENDATION AFTER CALL

❑ Close within 30 days

❑ Close within 90 days

❑ Close within 180 days

❑ Close within 1 year

STEP: RECOMMEND AFTER CALL:

❑ Possible Prospect/ Needs Research

❑ Capability Determined/ Research Done

❑ Cultivation/Solicitor Assignment Made

❑ Solicited/No Decision

❑ Solicited/Favorable

❑ Solicited/Decline

LEVEL OF INTEREST:

❑ High

❑ Moderate

❑ Low

❑ Uncertain

CAPABILITY:

❑ $1 million plus

❑ $500, 000 - $999,999

❑ $250,000 - $499,999

❑ $100,000 - $249,000

❑ $50,000 - $99,000

❑ $25,000 - $49,999

❑ $5,000 - $24,999

Interest/Project

Appendix BB

XYZ Organization Development Plan Needs Assessment

1. Past Year Goal $_____ Past Year Raised $_____

2. Current Year Goal $ _____

3. Total Number Constituents in Database _____

4. Staff Available to Work on Development Plan:

   Name _____ Title _____FT _____
   PT _____

   Name _____ Title _____FT _____
   PT _____

   Name _____ Title _____FT _____
   PT _____

   Name _____ Title _____FT _____
   PT _____

   Name _____ Title _____FT _____
   PT _____

5. Volunteers Available to Work on Development Plan:

Name _____ Title _____ Hours per
wk. _____

Name _____ Title _____ Hours per
wk. _____

Name _____ Title _____ Hours per
wk. _____

Name _____ Title _____ Hours per
wk. _____

Name _____ Title _____ Hours per
wk. _____

Appendix CC

Development Planning Worksheet

_____Organization

Overall Fundraising Goal $ _____ for Fiscal Year _____

Membership	Last Yr Total	Goal Year 1	Goal Year 2	Goal Year 3
Member Count	#	#	#	#
Total Dollars Raised	$	$	$	$

Resources Available:

_____

Issues to Overcome:

_____

Strategies:

_____

Target Date: _____   Coordinator Assigned: _____

Committee:

_____

409 Fundraising for the GENIUS ···

Event*	Last Yr Total	Goal Year 1	Goal Year 2	Goal Year 3
Attendee Count	#	#	#	#
Total Dollars Raised	$	$	$	$

Resources Available:

_____

Issues to Overcome:

_____

Strategies:

_____

Target Date: Coordinator Assigned:

_____

Committee:

_____

Repeat "Event" for additional events for the year.

Foundation Grants	Last Yr Total	Goal Year 1	Goal Year 2	Goal Year 3
Number Grants Awarded	#	#	#	#
Total Dollars Raised	$	$	$	$

Resources Available:

_____

Issues to Overcome:

_____

Strategies:

_____

Target Date: Coordinator Assigned:

_____

Committee:

_____

Corporate Appeal	Last Yr Total	Goal Year 1	Goal Year 2	Goal Year 3
Number Gifts Received	#	#	#	#
Total Dollars Raised	$	$	$	$

Resources Available:

_____

Issues to Overcome:

_____

Strategies:

_____

Target Date: Coordinator Assigned:

_____

Committee:

_____

Major/Planned Gifts	Last Yr Total	Goal Year 1	Goal Year 2	Goal Year 3
Number Gifts Received	#	#	#	#
Total Dollars Raised	$	$	$	$

Resources Available:

_____

Issues to Overcome:

_____

Strategies:

_____

Target Date: Coordinator Assigned:

_____

Committee:

_____

Phone Appeal	Last Yr Total	Goal Year 1	Goal Year 2	Goal Year 3
Number Gifts Received	#	#	#	#
Total Dollars Raised	$	$	$	$

Resources Available:

_____

Issues to Overcome:

_____

Strategies:

_____

Target Date: Coordinator Assigned:

_____

Committee:

_____

Mail Appeal	Last Yr Total	Goal Year 1	Goal Year 2	Goal Year 3
Number Gifts Received	#	#	#	#
Total Dollars Raised	$	$	$	$

Resources Available:

_____

Issues to Overcome:

_____

Strategies:

_____

Target Date: Coordinator Assigned:

_____

Committee:

_____

Appendix

Plan of Action

Organization Name:_____

Address: _____

Staff Name: _____

Mission: _____

Vision:_____

3-Month Goals for Development Office:

_____

_____

_____

Specific Objectives:

_____

_____

_____

Strategies to reach these Objectives:

Date to Complete:_____

_____

_____

_____

_____

_____

_____

1-Year Goals for Development Office:

_____

_____

_____

Specific Objectives:

_____

_____

_____

Strategies to reach these Objectives:

Date to Complete:_____

_____

_____

_____

_____

_____

_____

3-Year Goals for Development Office:

_____

_____

_____

Specific Objectives:

_____

_____

Strategies to reach these Objectives:

Date to Complete:_____

_____

_____

_____

_____

_____

Appendix  EE

Suggested Reading

Allison, Michael and Jude Kaye. 1997. *Strategic Planning for Nonprofit Organizations.* New York: John Wiley & Sons.

Connors, Tracey Daniel, ed. 1993. *The Nonprofit Management Handbook.* New York: John Wiley & Sons.

Eisenstein, Amy. 2011. *50 Asks in 50 Weeks: A Guide to Better Fundraising for Your Small Development Shop.* Rancho Santa Margarita: CharityChannel Press.

Grace, Kay Sprinkel. 1997. *Beyond Fundraising.* New York: John Wiley & Sons.

Greenfield, James M. *Fund Raising,* 2nd edition. 1999. New York: John Wiley & Sons.

Hancks, Meredith. 2011. *Getting Started in Prospect Research: What You Need to Know to Find Who You Need to Find.* Rancho Santa Margarita: CharityChannel Press.

Hopkins, Bruce. 2008. *Law of Fundraising.* New York: John Wiley & Sons.

Houle, Cyril. 1989. *Governing Boards.* San Francisco: Jossey-Bass.

Lysakowski, Linda. 2011. *Capital Campaigns: Everything You NEED to Know.* Rancho Santa Margarita: CharityChannel Press.

Lysakowski, Linda. 2011. *Fundraising as a Career: What, Are you Crazy?* Rancho Santa Margarita: CharityChannel Press.

Lysakowski, Linda. 2012. *Raise More Money from Your Business Community.* Rancho Santa Margarita: CharityChannel Press.

Lysakowski, Linda. 2005. *Recruiting and Training Fundraising Volunteers.* New York: John Wiley & Sons.

Lysakowski, Linda. 2007. *The Development Plan.* New York: John Wiley & Sons.

Lysakowski, Linda and Norman Olshansky, eds. 2011. *You and Your Nonprofit: Practical Advice and Tips from the CharityChannel Professional Community.* Rancho Santa Margarita: CharityChannel Press.

McLeish, Barry J. 1995. *Successful Marketing Strategies for Nonprofit Organizations.* New York: Wiley & Sons.

Nichols, Judith. 1991. *Targeted Fundraising.* Los Angeles: Bonus Books.

Oppelt, Joanne. 2011. *Confessions of a Successful Grants Writer: A Complete Guide to Discovering and Obtaining Funding.* Rancho Santa Margarita: CharityChannel Press.

Stroman, M. Kent. 2011. *Asking about Asking: Mastering the Art of Conversational Fundraising.* Rancho Santa Margarita: CharityChannel Press.

Sturtevant, William. 1997. *The Artful Journey.* Chicago: Bonus Books.

Woodward, Jeannette. 2006. *Managing Technology.* New York: John Wiley & Sons.

Index

DEC 0 5 2012

Only copy in Midyork System

CZ 11/12/12

9 780984 158010